# RETURN FROM DUNKIRK

# DUNKIRK

## RAILWAYS TO THE RESCUE

## Operation Dynamo (1940)

*by*
*Peter Tatlow*

# THE OAKWOOD PRESS

© Oakwood Press & Peter Tatlow 2010

British Library Cataloguing in Publication Data
A Record for this book is available from the British Library
ISBN 978 0 85361 697 9

Typeset by Oakwood Graphics.
Repro by PKmediaworks, Cranborne, Dorset.
Printed by Cambrian Printers, Aberystwyth, Ceredigion.

# Note on the Author

Peter Tatlow is well-known for his contribution to railway research for nearly 50 years. Starting with a journey to the Isle of Bute in September 1940 to escape the Blitz, an interest in railways has been his main pastime since he can remember. Some of his earliest memories are of journeys undertaken during World War II. At the time of leaving school in 1954, national service was in line for every male so he volunteered to sign on as a regular in the Royal Engineers. He trained in field engineering and as a surveyor topographical, after which he was posted to the Joint Air Photo Intelligence Unit of the Headquarters of Allied Forces Central Europe at Fontainebleau, France. On release from military service three years later, he joined the Chief Civil Engineer's Department of the Southern Region of British Railways and left over 10 years later having qualified as a chartered civil engineer. He then worked on the design and construction of bridges, both in United Kingdom and overseas and is now retired from full-time employment.

His interest in railways and modelling has led to his writing numerous articles in the prototype and model railway press and in specialist journals on a wide range of subjects including locomotives, coaches, wagons, travelling cranes, bridges, train ferries and civil engineering activities. His books include: *A Pictorial Record of LNER Wagons* (OPC 1976), *A History of Highland Locomotives* (OPC 1979), *Highland Railway Miscellany* (OPC 1985). He compiled *Historic Carriage Drawings, Volume 3 – Non-Passenger Coaching Stock* (Pendragon 2000), and wrote *Harrow & Wealdstone Accident, 50 years on, Clearing up the aftermath* (Oakwood Press, 2002), *St John's Lewisham, 50 years on, Restoring the traffic* (Oakwood Press, 2007), and is currently revisiting the subject of his first work with *An Illustrated History of LNER Wagons* in four volumes, the first three of which were published by Wild Swan in 2005, 2007 and 2009.

*Front cover:* A troop train of LNER stock taking British troops away from the Kent coast following their evacuation from Dunkirk in May/June 1940 is stopped short of Factory Junction, probably to change engines. Beside is Wandsworth Road station on the South London line from where a young woman reaches out to offer drinks to thirsty soldiers leaning out of the windows. *Author's Collection*

Published by The Oakwood Press (Usk), P.O. Box 13, Usk, Mon., NP15 1YS.
E-mail: sales@oakwoodpress.co.uk
Website: www.oakwoodpress.co.uk

# Contents

Allied troops massed on the beach at Dunkirk awaiting evacuation.    *Author's Collection*

# Introduction

Following Germany's invasion of the neutral countries: Holland, Belgium and Luxembourg on 10th May, 1940, much has been written about the British Expeditionary Force (BEF) rushing in across Belgium to meet the invader; the German break through of the French lines in the Ardennes; the fighting retreat to Dunkirk and subsequent evacuation across the English Channel of the BEF, together with French and Belgian soldiers, in late May/early June 1940. Nonetheless, whilst in no way wishing to belittle these magnificent achievements, little appears to have been published on how the arrival of over a third of a million men, deposited in what they stood up in on a small corner of south-east England, mainly in Kent, within a period of 10 days, was dealt with. This work will consider the dispersal of these troops, following their disembarkation from 'Operation Dynamo' and the subsequent evacuations from the rest of France.

My personal interest stems from my father's involvement. He joined the East Surrey Regiment, was commissioned as a 2nd lieutenant and was called up to the colours shortly before the outbreak of World War II on 3rd September, 1939, three days before my third birthday. In due course his unit was sent to France and, like so many, found itself retreating from Belgium as the BEF was caught by Germany's pincer movement. Withdrawing relatively late in the action, he arrived at Dunkirk by the evening of 1st June and embarked early the next day on the destroyer HMS *Venomous*. Having disembarked at Dover on the morning of 2nd June, he was taken by train to Aldershot from where my mother's father collected him in time to join my younger brother's first birthday party on the same day at Cobham in Surrey. But there was much more to this vast movement of men and their rehabilitation, which it may be contended was the greatest logistical operation ever carried out at such short notice.

Adjacent to Wandsworth Road station trains were sometimes stopped to enable locomotives to be changed. This provided an opportunity for members of the public on the eastbound platform of the South London line to reach across to soldiers leaning out of the window to receive sustenance. *Courtesy British Red Cross*

# Notes

The statistics quoted are included to provide an indication of the size and the proportions of troops landed etc., and thereby enable the reader to gain a feeling for the magnitude of the task undertaken. It is recognised that, perhaps not surprisingly in the circumstances, there is a small discrepancy between the figures collected by the Admiralty and the War Office and those from the latter have been quoted here. Bearing mind that these figures were collected by officers, either as troops left the vessels or as trains departed, working under great pressure and under orders not to delay either disembarkation or dispatch of the trains, this may be excused. Whilst every individual is important and we may set great store by them now, at the time their purpose would have been to forewarn the reception camps of the order of numbers to be expected to arrive by train within a few hours.

Likewise there are discrepancies in the actual number of special trains operated on given days and from each departure point. These probably depend on the source, the date one considers was the start of the evacuation or the specific dates of Operation Dynamo and whether it includes hospital trains or not. As above the significance is the magnitude rather than the finite number, now almost impossible to establish beyond dispute.

To improve the presentation of long linear arrangements, some railway station layouts have been drawn with their lateral dimension at a scale twice that of the longitudinal one. As a consequence some distortion occurs, i.e. unless parallel with one of the main axes, rectangular features appear as parallelograms, circles as ellipses and the points of the compass are no longer at right angles.

Our fighting forces have long used the 24 hour clock to express time and such has been employed here in the military context. The railways on the other hand at this period still used 'am' and 'pm' and this has been adopted in the civilian context.

Once arrived at Dover, these French Poilu, the equivalent term to the British Tommy, were afforded a brief rest to enable them to write a card or smoke a cigarette, before being taken by train to such places as Southampton, Bournemouth, Weymouth or Plymouth, where under-used seaside holiday accommodation provided billets. *Pendragon Collection*

# Chronology

**1919**

18th June    Treaty of Versailles signed concluding World War I.

**1923**

1st January    Independent railway companies grouped into four, viz: London, Midland & Scottish Railway (LMS), London & North Eastern Railway (LNER), Great Western Railway (GWR) and Southern Railway (SR).

January    Germany unable to pay reparations.

**1926**

3rd-13th May    General Strike.

**1929**

24th-29th October    Wall Street stock market crash followed by a decade of the Great Depression.

**1930**

14th September    Nazi party win election in Germany.

**1933**

30th January    Hitler becomes Chancellor of Germany.

5th March    Nazi party win further election.

**1935**

3rd October    Italy invade Abyssinia (Ethiopia).

**1936**

7th March    German armed forces re-enter the Rhineland.

July    Germany and Italy lend military support to General Franco in Spanish Civil War.

**1938**

11th/12th March    Nazis enter Austria.

28th August    Emergency Powers (Defence Act) enacted.

Late Sep./early Oct.    Munich crisis.

**1939**

15th March    German forces march into Czechoslovakia.

1st April    Spanish Civil War ceases.

27th April    Parliament passed the Military Training Act, introducing conscription from 3rd June.

16th May    Women's Voluntary Service (WVS) set up.

23rd August    Germany and Russia sign non-aggression pact.

**1939**

| | |
|---|---|
| 24th August | Parliament recalled to implement the Emergency Powers (Defence) Act 1939. Army reservists called up. Civil Defence placed on alert. |
| 25th August | Britain and France provide guarantees to Poland. |
| 31st August | Royal Navy mobilized. |
| 1st September | Germany invades Poland. General mobilization in UK. Railway Executive Committee formally appointed. |
| 3rd September | United Kingdom declares war on Germany at 11.15 am - French Ultimatum expires 5.00 pm. |
| 30th November | Russia invades Finland. |

**1940**

| | |
|---|---|
| 8th January | First food rationing introduced. |
| 9th April | Germany invades Denmark and Norway. |
| 19th April | British and French invade central Norway. |
| 10th May | Germany invades Netherlands, Belgium and Luxembourg. Prime Minister Neville Chamberlain resigns and Winston Churchill takes up office. |
| 14th May | In evening General Winkelman of Dutch Army announces surrender on Hilversum Radio. |
| 15th May | Germans break through French lines at Sedan. |
| 19th May | First formal meetings to consider evacuation of British troops from NE France. |
| 21st May | German forces reach Channel coast cutting off the Allied forces from their bases. |
| 22nd May | The Emergency Powers (Defence) Act 1940 passed. |
| 25th May | Boulogne captured. |
| 26th May | Formal commencement of Operation Dynamo, the evacuation of Dunkirk. National day of prayer. |
| 27th May | Calais fell. |
| 28th May | King of the Belgians announces surrender of armed forces at 4.00 am. |
| 30th May | Phase 2 of reception of troops commenced with the reassembly of individual units. |
| 31st May | Churchill instructs that at Dunkirk French and British troops were to be embarked in equal numbers. Mayors of south coast towns approached to accommodate French troops. |
| 2nd June | Evacuation of 48,000 children from south-east England. |
| 4th June | Operation Dynamo naval operations concluded. |

*1940*

| | |
|---|---|
| 8th June | Allied forces, with King Haarkon, evacuate Norway (Narvik). Phase 3 of reception of British troops initiated with re-equipping of units and re-assembling of fighting divisions. |
| 12th June | Surrender of elements of 51st Division and French troops at St Valery-en-Caux. |
| 14th June | Operation Aerial initiated. German forces enter Paris. |
| 16th June | French Government resigns. |
| 16th-19th June | Large scale movement of troops to Northern Ireland. |
| 17th June | Sinking of HMT *Lancastria* with loss of thousands of troops. |
| 22nd June | French Government concludes an armistice with Germany. |
| 25th June | French Government declares that evacuation of Allied troops must cease. |
| 3rd July | French naval units in British waters and at Alexandria (Egypt) taken over by Royal Navy, while French fleet at Mers el Kebir (Oran) attacked by Royal Navy. |
| 9th July | Commencement of Battle of Britain (RAF vs Luftwaffe). |
| 14th August | Allied troops still escaping from French Mediterranean ports. |
| 14th September | Hitler postpones Operation Sea Lion (invasion of England). |
| 12th October | Operation Sea Lion called off until spring. |
| 31st October | Battle of Britain concluded. |

*1941*

| | |
|---|---|
| 22nd June | Germany invades Russia. |

*1942*

| | |
|---|---|
| 13th February | Hitler cancels invasion of Britain, Operation Sea Lion. |

*1944*

| | |
|---|---|
| 6th June | Operation Overlord, the western Allies' invasion of France commenced (commonly called D Day). |

*1945*

| | |
|---|---|
| 8th May | Germany surrenders unconditionally. |
| 2nd September | Japan surrenders. |

*1948*

| | |
|---|---|
| 1st January | Railways nationalized. Railway Executive Committee stood down. |

2nd lieutenant Alan Tatlow of the East Surrey Regiment in uniform, Sam Browne and sword soon after being commissioned.

*The Gainsborough Press/Author's Collection*

# Prologue

My father, Alan, like a lot of others of his generation, as the political climate in Europe declined so rapidly during the late 1930s and as appeasement of dictators appeared to fail, felt he ought to do something. With no more experience than as an 18-year-old having ridden 'shot-gun' on a London bus during the General Strike as a temporary special constable, he volunteered for the Territorial Army on 17th April, 1939. This included an agreement to serve outside the United Kingdom in the event of a national emergency upon embodiment of the Territorial Army within the Regular Army by Act of Parliament. At the age of 31 he worked in London as an architect and we were living at Cobham at the time, so he joined the rapidly expanding 6th Battalion of the East Surrey Regiment based at Kingston-on-Thames.

On 7th June, 1939 he applied for a commission. Apparently on the strength of his having obtained his Certificate A in March 1926 while a cadet in the Junior Division of the Officer Training Corps at his school, Radley College, and as a special case on account of his age, this was approved and he was commissioned a 2nd lieutenant No. 93465 on 26th July, 1939. By the time of the annual camp at Otterpool, Lympne near Hythe in Kent from 30th July to 13th August, 1939, numbers were sufficient to form two battalions, the first sixth and second sixth. These were mobilized on 1st September, 1939, two days before the outbreak of World War II. Around November the 1/6th moved to Lyme Regis for intensive training prior to posting overseas. In December Russia, our eventual ally, had invaded Finland and in the New Year rumours circulated in the batallion that they were going there to expel them! During this period men under 20 years of age were transferred to the second battalion and replaced by reservists and militia in preparation for going overseas.

During October he attended a two week junior leader's training course at Layswood, Groombridge. As a chartered and registered architect, his Commanding Officer recognised an ideal candidate to act as billeting officer. On 27th December, 1939, he applied to be transferred to the Royal Engineers, where he felt that his services would be of more value to the Country. Following an interview on 17th January, 1940, his application was recommended to the War Office on 21st March, who responded with an urgent postal telegram on 25th April, regretting that his transfer could not be approved. No wonder, he was by then already in France and about to join battle.

For during the interval, on 2nd April, 1940 his unit left Lyme Regis and three days later sailed from Southampton on board MV *Ulster Prince* to Cherbourg France, where they entrained for Conlie, in the base area south of Le Mans. Then five days later they moved eastwards to an assembly area near Grandvilliers, Seine et Marne from where they marched some 100 miles in five days, through Amiens to Bailleul on the Belgian border. Here, under a new Commanding Officer Lieut-Colonel C.D. 'Nipper' Armstrong MC, they joined the 44th Division before on 4th May moving up to Wattrelos near Roubaix. On 14th May, as part of the 10th Brigade now in the 4th Division of III Corps, they followed other units by motor transport into Belgium through Oudenarde to Alost and marched to Vilvorde north of Brussels, taking up position alongside the 1st East Surrey Battalion to confront the Germans, as refugees streamed through.

By 17th May, following the collapse of the line in front of the French further south, they brought up the rear as the 10th Brigade withdrew, blowing up a bridge as the Germans appeared on the scene. After a brief halt in Brussels, the battalion marched back a distance of 50 miles to Avelghem on the Escaut Canal. The roads were again thronged with numbed and aimless refugees, which did not enhance their speedy journey. I recall my father, who as a young man had worked for more than two years on farms in Sussex and Canada, saying that, in order to clear the road and the carter failing to obey his command to move to one side, he grabbed the reins of the horse and physically forced it into a ditch beside the road. The battalion took up position in the morning of 19th May to defend a bridge at Rugge, with a stream of more refugees crossing as well as the division's armoured cars and light tanks. The next morning an air battle took place overhead, while under cover of an artillery barrage, the two forward companies were withdrawn across the canal late in the day after which the Royal Engineers demolished the bridge with explosives.

The Battalion having taken its first casualties was relieved that night and held in reserve to the north of Avelghem. In the early morning of 22nd May it was in action properly for the first time, when they were ordered back into the line and to relieve the Duke of Cornwall's Light Infantry while under shell fire. After an exchange of patrols and on the receiving end of artillery directed by a light aircraft, a heavy mortar barrage portended an attack. During this the CO protected the company's HQ with a Bren gun to such effect that the enemy retired until after dark. My father recounted how a fellow officer had warned those around of the activities of a sniper only a short while later for this officer to step into the line of fire with depressing consequences. By then after little rest in the previous two days, however, the battalion was ordered to withdraw yet again under covering fire from a platoon of tracked universal (Bren gun) carriers, as the deteriorating situation further south dictated. They marched back exhausted to the BEF's old position along the Belgium/French border near Neuville between Halluin and Tourcoing.

On 23rd May, improving on the scant French trenches on the frontier and sending out patrols, the battalion waited for three days during which they were approached by enemy cycle patrols, sometimes dressed as civilians, and taking casualties due to artillery fire. On the evening of 27th May the battalion were relieved by a Guards' battalion and moved westwards again, marching 10 miles to woods near Voormezeele, a village thought to be occupied by the enemy. The next evening, tired as they were, the troops resumed their retreat by marching throughout the night towards Dunkirk along roads crowded with confused troops and refugees. West of Poperinghe, two hours rest and a cross-country march for a short way led to very welcome waiting motor transport to take them to Furnes, near the Channel coast. Here, where the fields and ditches were already full of abandoned trucks, their transport was to be immobilized, by smashing the engines or deliberately seizing them up and slashing the tyres, before making for Dunkirk. Likewise the artillery's guns were being destroyed and the Quartermaster's stores dumped enabling the troops to replace any defective clothing. My father recounted to me of the driver, who not so long before had been on a charge for some minor misdemeanour in connection with his vehicle, fairly laying into it for all the trouble it had caused him!

Their trials were not to be over that quickly though, as, following the capitulation of much of the Belgian Army, the Germans were attempting to break into the Dunkirk perimeter in the extreme east by massing south of Nieuport to cross the canal. The Battalion was rushed by truck under shell fire to Nieuport and marched to an area between there and Oost-Dunkirke, arriving early in the evening of 29th May, where under sniper fire they took up defensive positions, as the enemy crossed the canal bridge just south of the town. Here the Battalion under bombardment of all kinds, but well dug in, fought valiantly to keep the Germans out for 52 hectic hours and thus enable other units of the BEF to embark for England. In the confusion finding food was difficult, rest impossible and casualties mounted as the Germans brought up more guns on the second day.

Matters were not eased when the Battalion was ordered to extend their line to take over part of an adjacent unit's sector that evening, but which had to be implemented earlier than planned due to the losses being suffered by this unit. One of the battalion's companies, already reduced in numbers, was sent to take over a brickworks, and despite this being a rather easy target attacks on the flanks were driven off. The British Forces in the area held on to all their positions overnight until assailed early in the morning by a determined attack along the whole perimeter, particularly on the 1/6th Surrey's front. Nonetheless, apart from one platoon overrun, the Battalion still clung on. The Germans made better progress on the left, however, exposing its flank. To remedy this potential break through, their sister battalion 1st East Surrey's were sent in alongside to restore the position. While the two colonels were assessing the situation, some Germans were spotted in an orchard advancing towards B Company, but were repulsed by the two COs operating a Bren gun. The two battalions fought side by side for the rest of the day and were fed in the evening on Oxo and tinned fish. At 22.00 hours the 1/6th were given the order to withdraw and arrived on the beach at La Panne at 05.30 hours just as the German aircraft were attacking, but these were driven off by concentrated rifle fire.

By this time, due to increasing enemy air attack which the RAF was unable to smother leading to a serious loss of shipping and continual interruption of embarkation off the beaches and in Dunkirk, daylight evacuation had been abandoned. At 12.58 hours on 1st June my father's report records that his platoon was sheltering in a ditch south of a road near a crossroads. A sharp lookout had been kept but no enemy were sighted. Contact had been established with adjacent units and breakfast and hot tea taken. Heavy shelling had been experienced about 08.00 hours, but no casualties. The morale of his men was good. By this stage of the evacuation little was taking place off the beaches and embarkation was mainly from the East Mole in Dunkirk under the cover of darkness. Reassembled as a unit following the aerial attack the Battalion made for some buildings on the sea front to rest and feed on some Bovril and hard Belgian Army biscuits. Still under the command of its own officers, each man was expected to be fully equipped and have with him his rifle, or other personal weapon. During the afternoon it became plain that they must make for crowded Dunkirk. They marched as a unit the 12 miles to the town, now with numerous uncontrollable fires, before joining the long solid queue of men slowing moving up the mole at dusk.

Private Hester Fairlie standing beside a Harrods motor van converted for use as an ambulance.
*Hester Hopkins Collection*

2nd lieutenant Hester Fairlie, driver to Brigadier R. Richards, standing beside his car.
*Hester Hopkins Collection*

Destroyer HMS *Venomous* of the Modified 'W' class launched on Clydebank in December
1918.                                                                *Author's Collection*

By 02.00 hours on a dark night word of mouth passed down the queue that the
last two ships to sail that night, a destroyer and paddle steamer, were already
moored alongside and due to depart in an hour, so it would be touch and go
whether the battalion made it aboard. The Colonel allocated half to the destroyer
and the rest to the paddle steamer. Due to impending dawn and hence daylight
in which German artillery could fire on the vessels as they left, and shortly before
the last of the men were about to board the Captain of the vessel gave the order
to cast off. So the Colonel pushed the last on and jumped himself.

Dad was among the 630 embarked on the destroyer HMS *Venomous*, D75 of the
16th Flotilla, under the command of Lt Cdr J.E.H. McBeath RN and attached to
Dover Command, which sailed at 03.45 hours arriving at Dover at 05.30 on the
morning of 2nd June. From here he was promptly taken by train to Aldershot, the
home of the British Army, and from there on to Tweseldown, where all weapons
and ammunition had to be handed in. Living at Cobham in Surrey, not more than
17 miles away and realising that it was my younger brother's birthday, he
telephoned home to advise my mother of his safe return. Fortuitously her father
was visiting and motored across to bring him back for a few hours. Upon arrival
my mother noticed a small round hole in his battledress and thought he had been
shot, but it was no more than a cigarette burn!

Like my father, my mother's sister, Hester Fairlie considered what she could
contribute to the war, which seemed to be becoming increasingly inevitable. She
decided in 1937 at the age of 20, partly to encourage the boys to enlist in the
Territorial Army, to join the Air Raid Precaution (ARP). She then got to hear
about the First Aid Nursing Yeomanry (FANY) and having been awarded her
certificate in First Aid and able to drive motor cars, she transferred to them at
the Duke of York's barracks near Hyde Park in London on 9th December, 1938.

My aunt's unit became the 5th (London) Motor Company of the Women's
Transport Service, now under military discipline, based at Hounslow. Initially
they were equipped with redundant 16-year-old Harrods delivery vans without
self-starters, crash gear boxes and brakes on only two wheels. So decrepit were
they that one van had to be cannibalized to provide spare parts for the
remainder. During the crucial time of the evacuation of Dunkirk and by then
equipped with better vehicles, private Fairlie was, as an ambulance driver
stationed near Ipswich, waiting at Harwich for the return of our troops with
eyes glued and ears pinned back for any sight or word of my father.

The western end of Dover Harbour with Prince of Wales Pier on the left, Admiralty Pier in the distance upon which is Dover Marine railway station with several cross-Channel packets moored alongside. In front between it and the Commercial Harbour is the then new train ferry terminal and dock.

*Skyfotos/Author's Collection*

# Chapter One

# The Transport Infrastructure
# of Southern England

The transport infrastructure of southern England was, for its day, fully developed. Over the previous century the railways had largely taken over from coastal shipping and inland from horse-drawn road vehicles for journeys of any length. Coastal shipping, nonetheless, still fulfilled a useful role in conveying excursionists and goods to the harbours and estuaries along the north Kent and the South Coast. Only since the end of World War I did motor transport begin to make any significant impact upon its rivals. This could provide an alternative to trains in the form of private cars for members of the upper and some middle classes, together with taxis, while buses and coaches could offer very competitive fares, if a little slower. The conveyance of goods by motor lorry was developing, but as yet its organization was, in contrast to the bus and coaching larger well-organized businesses, fragmented.

## Ports and Harbours

The south-east corner of England, with its history of communications with the Continent, is well equipped with ports and harbours to handle either the cross-Channel or coastal traffic, as well as providing a home for fishing boats.

Overlooked by the castle from where Operation Dynamo was commanded, Dover Harbour is the last remaining of the Cinque Ports of Kent and Sussex to continue as a large scale commercial port. Changes in the shore line or the silting up of river estuaries had largely rendered the others ineffectual particularly for the larger vessels by then in use. Situated at the point of the shortest crossing to the Continent, it has long been an important embarkation point, until now the Port of Dover has grown into one of Europe's largest passenger ports. It is owned and operated by the Dover Harbour Board, a statutory corporation, since it was formed by Royal Charter in 1606 by James I.

At the beginning of the 19th century, it was proposed that a haven of refuge for the Fleet should be constructed in Dover Bay and in 1847 the Government commenced the construction of the Admiralty Pier, which was envisaged as its Western Arm. The development of the harbour took a step further in 1897, when work started on the Eastern Arm, the Southern Breakwater and the extension to the Admiralty Pier all of which was completed in 1909. The gradual development of the port throughout the centuries has produced a vast artificial harbour. At the time of the evacuation Dover was the base for a flotilla of destroyers.

Through much of recorded history the military importance of Dover has warranted fortifications appropriate to the day. Dover Castle was built on the site of an Iron Age fort and incorporated a Roman lighthouse and Saxon church. It has been repeatedly rebuilt, developed and equipped with the artillery of the day. By the time of World War II it had become the headquarters of Vice-

Steam from a train drifts across Folkestone harbour as it crosses a viaduct over the inner harbour and ascends the 1 in 30 gradient up to Folkestone Junction during the 1950s. Leading is an ex-SECR 0-6-0 tank engine of the 'R1' class with more than likely two or three others pushing at the rear. In the far distance a cross-Channel packet boat, thought to be SS *Canterbury*, is moored alongside the breakwater beyond the Harbour station.                    *R.K. Blencowe Collection*

A view looking at Ramsgate town across the harbour during the 1930s.
                    *A.W.V. Mace, courtesy Mile Post 92½ Picture Library*

Admiral Ramsey and from the underground tunnels, cut into the chalk cliff beneath the Castle, Operation Dynamo was directed.

On the hills above the other end of the harbour, The Western Heights is a series of fortifications that together formed the largest Napoleonic fortification in Britain. Structures include the Citadel, the Drop Redoubt, the Detached Bastion and the North Entrance as well as many other important features designed to work together to fight off a French invasion by Napoleon. In 1860 Fort Burgoyne was built just north of the castle. Early in the 20th century, gun batteries were installed on the central breakwater and in the Western Heights to defend the harbour from seaborne attack.

Until the 19th century Folkestone remained a small fishing community whose seafront was continually battered by storms and encroaching shingle, making the landing of boats difficult. As a result of an Act of Parliament in 1807 a pier and harbour was built until by 1820 a harbour area of 14 acres had been created. Following the owning company's bankruptcy in 1842 it was acquired by the South Eastern Railway (SER), which had yet to reach Dover. Dredging the harbour and the construction of a rail route down to it commenced almost immediately and the town soon became the SER's principal packet station for the Continental traffic to Boulogne. Although partially eclipsed by Dover, once the line was extended through, Folkestone continued to function as a commercial cross-Channel port.

Newhaven stands at the mouth of the River Ouse, which breaks through the South Downs south of Lewes. It was of little maritime importance until the opening of the railway line to Lewes in 1847. The London, Brighton & South Coast Railway (LBSCR) constructed its own wharf and facilities on the east side of the river, and opened the Newhaven Harbour railway station. From July 1852, the LBSCR inaugurated a steamer service with Dieppe, France, and this subsequently resulted in improvements to the harbour under the auspices of the Harbour Board funded by the railway. In World War I the port and harbour facilities, rail sidings and warehousing were greatly enlarged to cope with military traffic. During the first year of World War II it was again used to convey men and materials to support the BEF. It was the principal receiving port for hospital ships and only vessels of this type appear to have landed troops at Newhaven during Operation Dynamo.

At the north-east tip of Kent, Margate, Ramsgate and Broadstairs have been traditional holiday sea-side destinations for Londoners drawn to its sandy beaches. So popular were the steam boat excursions that in 1841 there were six different companies competing for the Margate passenger traffic. Even with the advent of the railway in 1846 the steamboats continued in service, running to Margate Pier. Between 1890 and 1939 about 30 pleasure boats operated from the beach. Margate is also noted for the building of Thanet wherries, where before World War I great numbers were turned out.

Round the North Foreland, Ramsgate, another holiday destination, is a member of the ancient confederation of Cinque Ports. The construction of its harbour began in 1749 and was completed in about 1850 and has the unique distinction of being the only Royal Harbour in the United Kingdom.

Deal pier, which might have been useful for disembarking troops, had regrettably been put out of action after being hit by a ship earlier in the year.

Likewise, Richborough Port, which had been developed and extensively used during the previous conflict, had sadly fallen into disrepair.

Sheerness is a town located in the Thames Estuary at the mouth of the River Medway on the north-west corner of the Isle of Sheppey in north Kent. It began as a fort built in the 16th century to protect the River Medway from naval invasion. In 1665, plans were first laid for a Royal Navy dockyard where warships might be provisioned and repaired. After the raid on the Medway in 1667, the older fortification was strengthened; and two years later the Royal Navy dockyard in the town was established, where warships were stocked and repaired. Beginning with the construction of a pier and a promenade in the 19th century, Sheerness acquired the added attractions of a seaside resort.

North of the Thames estuary strategically located in the south-east quadrant of the British Isles, Harwich is on the southern side of the River Stour. Its role as a packet station for the carriage of passengers and mail to the Netherlands dates back at least to the 17th century. By 1872, shipping trade had increased so that more capacity was required and the Great Eastern Railway obtained permission to reclaim land at Ray Farm, a mile upstream of Harwich town, where it built a new quay, known as Parkeston Quay, with its own railway station, and a hotel. In 1939 the Admiralty requisitioned Parkeston Quay from the (now) LNER for naval purposes, naming it HMS *Badger*. At the time of the evacuation Harwich was the base for the 2nd and 5th destroyer flotillas.

*Development of the railways in south-eastern England*

In 1940 the vast majority of troops were landed in east Kent, between Ramsgate and Folkestone, although small numbers came ashore as far away as Harwich and Newhaven. Once landed, they were transported inland as soon as practical, almost exclusively by train, although, unless the nearest railway station was close to hand, such as at Dover Marine, Folkestone and Newhaven, commandeered buses and coaches were employed to convey troops to the nearest railway station and likewise possibly at the station of arrival to camp. The extent to which buses may have been used to move troops all the way to their destinations remains unclear. At the time, the railways of almost all of Southern England were in the hands of the Southern Railway. This had been constituted in 1923 from three previous companies; starting in the west of the combined territory with the London & South Western Railway (LSWR); the London, Brighton & South Coast Railway; and lastly the South Eastern & Chatham Railway (SECR) in the east, although there had been some penetrations into neighbouring constituent companies' territories.

The railway geography of the south-east of England is governed by the presence of the barrier created by North Downs running east-west 15 to 20 miles south of London, with the Thames Marshes to the north and the Weald to the south. By the end of the 19th century the network serving the Channel ports consisted of lines belonging to either the former South Eastern Railway or, the London, Chatham & Dover Railway (LC&DR). These two had for much of the latter half of that century been arch rivals. Towards the end of this period, however, they recognized that endless competition was futile and buried the hatchet. Whilst continuing to maintain their independent legal status, from 1st January, 1899 they entered into an agreement for a working union under a Joint Management Committee composed of Directors of both companies and one set of senior officers. From then on it was known as the South Eastern & Chatham Railway and, following the above mentioned Grouping of the railways in 1923, constituted the London (East) and Eastern Divisions of the Southern Railway.

Referring to the map included as *Figure 1*, it will be seen that first on the scene was the London & Greenwich Railway, which opened in stages between 1836 and 1838, the first in London. From May 1844, the London, Deptford and Dover Railway started operations from a terminus near to London Bridge from where it then shared its route to Redhill with, what was soon to be known as, the London, Brighton and South Coast Railway to penetrate the North Downs. From Redhill, on what was to become the South Eastern Railway's original main line to the Channel ports, it turned almost due east to run parallel with the North Downs through Tonbridge, Ashford, Folkestone and finally through a series of tunnels penetrating the North Downs again to terminate at Dover. The first rail connection with London was thereby established by the South Eastern Railway on 7th February, 1844, when it opened from Folkestone the final section of its main line to Dover Town Station. In 1862 the SER opened an extension from the Town Station to connect with rails laid by the Admiralty on the Admiralty Pier. This allowed trains to be run onto the pier alongside the steamers, which had been docking there since 1851.

In taking over the Reading, Guildford & Reigate Railway company, the SER also directed its attention westwards from Redhill along the southern flank of the North Downs past Reigate, through the gap at Guildford, to North Camp serving the home of the Army and on to Reading with a connection to the Great Western Railway. To complete the development of the SER to the Metropolis, passenger train services were continued from Bricklayers Arms first to London Bridge. This was subsequently extended, to Charing Cross in the West End of London from 11th January, 1864 for local trains and from 1st May the same year for main line trains, and later to Cannon Street in the City of London from 1st September, 1866.

To bypass the SER's original 'dog leg' route via the LBSCR's line from London Bridge to Redhill, the construction of a direct route to the Kent coast from St John's, Lewisham, via Chislehurst and Sevenoaks, to Tonbridge was undertaken and opened in stages until complete throughout on 1st May, 1868, becoming known as the New Main Line.

Before that, however, Dover benefited from a second rail link with London via Canterbury, Faversham and Chatham when on 22nd July, 1861 the LC&DR opened a temporary terminus at Dover Priory station. Between the Priory Station and the harbour, however, it was necessary to drive a 685-yard tunnel under the Western Heights and this was completed a few months later and the Harbour station was opened on 1st November the same year. Arrangements then followed in 1862 to build a junction with the Admiralty Pier line and from 30th August, 1864 boat trains of both companies were able to use the pier. On 15th June, 1881 a jointly-owned direct link between the SER Town and LC&DR

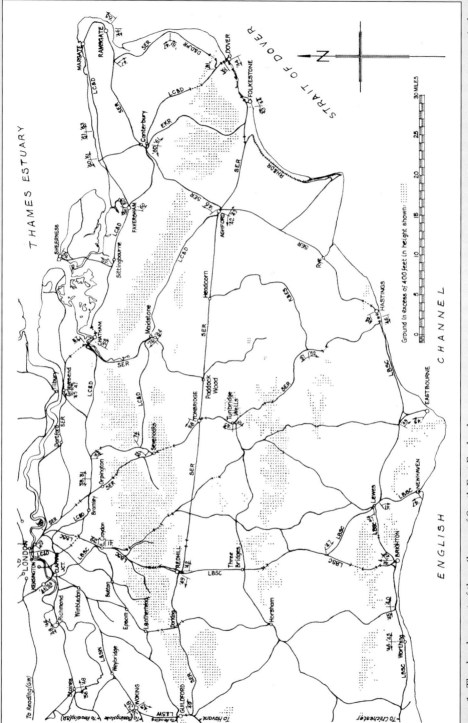

*Figure 1:* The development of the railways of South East England.

Harbour stations was opened to permit through running between Canterbury and Ramsgate to Folkestone etc.

Soon after the setting up of the joint venture between the SER and LC&DR in 1899, the new management of the Joint Committee initiated steps to rationalize and enhance the operational potential of their combined network. Several connections between the two systems were installed to improve flexibility in operation. The most obvious of those impinging on the events that took place were the improvements at Dover. Here the two rival companies had a station in the vicinity of the harbour, each with rail access to the narrow Admiralty Pier against which by the early 1860s the packet vessels moored, as far as passengers were concerned, in a rather exposed location. From 1909 chalk recovered from East Cliff was used to fill an area to the east of Admiralty Pier to create land upon which to construct a fine new terminal station to serve both lines. This was known as Dover Marine and, although not yet quite complete, was opened in December 1914 for use by the military during World War I. It only offered facilities to civilian traffic to the Continent from January 1920 and a full service from February 1922. This allowed the closing of the Town and Harbour stations, leaving Priory station on the former LC&DR line to serve the inhabitants of the town.

Out on the Kent coast, Margate and Ramsgate had been served by both companies with separate unconnected competing stations in each town. Under the auspices of the SR, for the beginning of the 1926 season (2nd July), the two lines were joined by the construction of a loop and a new station, with locomotive and carriage servicing facilities, at the back of Ramsgate. This created the Thanet Loop with through running and permitted the closure of three terminal stations (see Figure 2). The site and buildings of the L&CDR's old Harbour station, situated beneath the cliffs on the eastern side of the harbour, was taken over as an entertainment complex and will feature again in our story.

The Southern Railway continued improvements in the Dover area by opening up the Archcliffe tunnel on the line to Folkestone thereby affording space for the building of a combined new locomotive depot on the site of the old Town station. This then permitted the closure of the engine shed at Priory station and the reconstruction of that station, which formally reopened in May 1932. This was followed by the installation of a wet dock between the Admiralty and Princes piers and associated facilities to accommodate one of three train ferry vessels acquired in 1935. After much difficulty in construction this was brought into use on 12th October, 1936 with the inauguration of the overnight *Night Ferry* service of through Wagon Lits sleeping cars from London Victoria to Gare du Nord in Paris, via Dover and Dunkirk.

The construction of the line from Folkestone to Dover had been fraught with geological difficulties as it passes through the various strata making up the elevated ground of the North Downs where it meets the sea. Over the years there had been several cliff falls and earth movements which disrupted rail traffic in some cases to such an extent that consideration had been given to the building of a diversion inland, but at some cost due to the long tunnels necessary. During World War I a major earth slip of 65 million tons occurred on 19th December, 1915 at Warren Halt which resulted in a train being derailed.

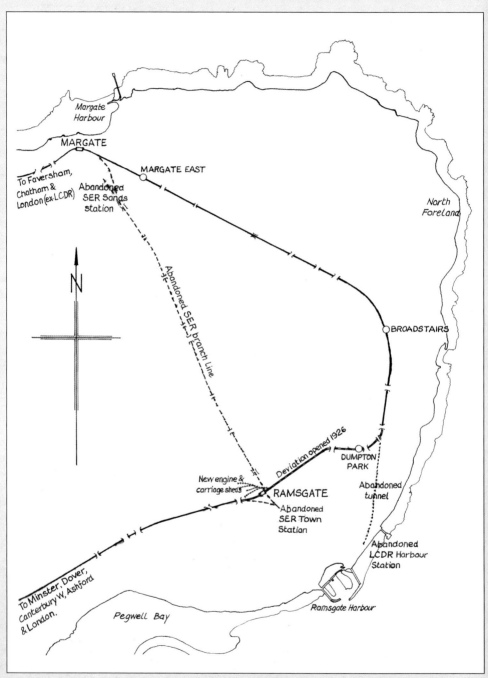

*Figure 2:* The rationalization of railways in the Margate and Ramsgate area.  Author

Despite the importance of Dover as a port through which troops were passing on their way to the Western Front, resources could not be spared during the conflict, so the line remained closed until reinstated by the SECR on 11th August, 1919.

Likewise, soon after the outbreak of World War II, following abnormally heavy rainfall the previous month, another smaller but nonetheless disruptive chalk cliff fall took place at Folkestone Warren near Shakespeare Cliff at 5.00pm on 28th November, 1939. About 80 yards of track were covered to a depth of up to 20 ft by a 20,000 ton rock fall, some lumps of chalk weighing up to 10 tons, as a consequence of which the Folkestone to Dover main line was blocked. Perhaps fortunately in view of subsequent events the line was cleared and initially reopened on 7th January, 1940 with a speed restriction. A thaw following severe frost, however, led to the detachment of rock fragments from the cliff and for the line to have to be temporarily closed again from 5th to 8th February, 1940, after which traffic was only permitted to run during daylight hours. A further two falls on 24th February, one of 10,000 tons from the 450 ft high cliff which swept the permanent way into the sea and 100,000 tons a little back from the track led to the line being shut once again until 10th March under speed restriction. Unfettered running was resumed on 21st April. During the closures through passenger and freight services were rerouted via the Chatham line, while local passengers were conveyed by buses of the East Kent Road Car Co. Ltd between Folkestone Junction and Dover Priory.

## Motor Bus and Coach Companies

The East Kent Road Car Company Ltd was one of those bus companies, whose buses were requisitioned by the military authorities during Operation Dynamo to provide transport to convey troops from their point of landing, in most cases, to the nearest railway station. The company had been formed in August 1916 to operate bus and coach services in Kent, initially based on Canterbury. This was created by an amalgamation of Canterbury & District; Deal & District Motor Services; Folkestone & District; Ramsgate Motor Coaches; and Watcher & Co. of Herne Bay. In the 1930s the tramways of Dover and Thanet were also taken over and the trams replaced with motor buses in 1937.

Another company was the Maidstone & District Motor Services Ltd (M&D), the origins of which can be traced back to 1908. In 1910, the undertaking was purchased by W.F. French, the company being registered as Maidstone & District Motor Services Ltd in March 1911. From 1914, new routes were introduced from Maidstone to Ashford, Faversham, Hastings, Sevenoaks and Tenterden as well as between Chatham and Faversham.

Tillings acquired an interest in the company in 1921 while Maidstone & District became a public company in 1922. In 1929 it acquired the Chatham & District Traction Company, however retaining the Chatham & District fleet-name and the operation remained separate until 1955, vehicles remaining in a green, brown and cream livery. The advent of the Road Traffic Act 1930 saw the demise of a number of independents, many of which were acquired by M&D.

Maidstone & District Motor Services Ltd's Tilling-Stevens type B9A single-deck bus No. 415, registration No. KO 107 supplied new in April 1927. In May 1934 its Harrington body had been replaced by Eastern Counties, in which condition the vehicle lasted until withdrawal in 1940.                                    *Author's Collection*

In 1933 the formation of the London Passenger Transport Board (LPTB) required M&D to hand over much of its operations in the Dartford and Gravesend areas. This led the company to look westwards for other opportunities, such as Autocar Services acquired in 1928, again trading as a separate company until the purchase of its rival, Redcar in 1935. The same year also saw the purchase of Hastings Tramways Company, which brought trolleybuses into the M&D fleet. Although the Hastings Tramway fleet-name was retained the vehicles were repainted into the company's green and cream livery.

At the home of the British Army, the Aldershot & District was inaugurated in July 1912 when the British Automobile Traction Company Limited (a subsidiary of British Electric Traction Company) bought the pioneering Aldershot & Farnborough Motor Omnibus Company Ltd, whose five buses had operated services between those two towns since 1906. The initial livery was dark green and white, later cream, with the upper deck of double-deckers being a lighter green. The looped fleet-name was introduced in 1923. In common with many other rural bus companies, it also carried parcels on its buses.

Further west the Bournemouth & District Motor Services Ltd was incorporated in 1916. A change of name to Hants & Dorset in 1920 reflected the wider aspirations of its owners. From that year Hants & Dorset grew rapidly, until 1929 when it became jointly owned by the two emerging transport groups of the time, British Associated Transport and Tilling. Within a few years the network of Hants & Dorset bus services was largely complete, by when it operated buses in Bournemouth, Poole, Southampton, Lymington, Fareham and Winchester and replaced the trams operated by Poole Corporation, in 1934.

# Chapter Two

# The Deteriorating Political Situation in Europe

The harsh terms of the Treaty of Versailles, signed on 28th June, 1919 at the conclusion of negotiations at the end of World War I, or Great War as it was termed at the time, left the vanquished Germany with insuperable financial prospects. With huge reparations of £6,000 million to be made to the Allies, it found itself unable to pay leading, in January 1923, to France under its Premier Raymond Pointaré sending its army into the Ruhr to extract its due. The result was that the German mark crashed inducing rampant inflation and civil unrest.

Despite various processes of reconciliation during the mid-twenties and the easing of Germany's debt, any improvement in her economy was brought to an abrupt halt by the onset of the world-wide Great Depression of 1929. Economic stagnation and extremely high unemployment in Germany ensued leading to the advance of political parties with extreme policies. Opposed to communism was the Nazi Party, led by Adolf Hitler, which gained power in the elections of 14th September, 1930, followed by his becoming Chancellor on 30th January, 1933.

Unpredictable, reclusive and ruthless in dealing with opposition parties within the Government he acted quickly as his public support began to wane. By blaming the Communists for the fire bombing of the Reichstag, he was able, despite foreign adverse opinion, to win enough votes at the election on 5th March to subsequently obtain dictatorial powers and place Germany, in contravention of its treaty obligations, on the road to re-armament with a view to World domination. He then repeatedly challenged the neighbouring powers, introducing conscription; reorganizing German industry; instigating censorship; and disabling the trade unions. He terrorized the Jews, communists and socialists, setting up concentration camps for their internment.

Buoyed up by the democracies' feeble efforts to restrain Italy's invasion of Abyssinia, in 1936 his armed forces re-entered the Rhineland, de-militarized following World War I. Hitler and Mussolini of Italy then lent military support to General Franco during the Spanish Civil War from July 1936 to April 1939, thereby gaining useful experience for their armed services. In the spring of 1938, despite his pledge to honour its independence, he engineered the entry of the Nazis into Austria on 11th/12th March. Loath to enter again into war after the horrors of World War I, the democracies huffed and puffed on the touch line, in response to which Hitler uttered the infamous and oft repeated remark that, 'He had no further territorial claims in Europe'.

Cynically in April he then put Czechoslovakia under pressure by stirring up the German inhabitants of the Sudetenland to demand autonomy. Increasing propaganda denouncing the government in Prague led to the conclusion that armed incursion was imminent. Diplomacy intervened on 24th May to postpone the impending invasion for a while, but by 2nd September full cession was demanded backed up by a threat to take it by force. With France and Russia bound by treaty to protect Czechoslovakia and by implication Great Britain due to her alliance with France, Britain's Prime Minister Neville Chamberlain embarked on an early example of 'shuttle diplomacy' between heads of state. On 15th September in full view of the media he flew to Munich to meet face to face with Adolf Hitler at the Berchtesgaden in an attempt to avert a catastrophic war. At a subsequent meeting of the two at Godesberg on 23rd September Hitler increased his demands and war began to look inevitable. However, as a result of Chamberlain inviting Mussolini to act as a mediator, a four-power conference was arranged for 29th September at Munich, with M. Daladier, the French Premier as the fourth member, but without the Czechs. At the expense of considerable loss of land to the unrepresented and powerless Czechs, to the benefit of not just the Germans, but the Poles, Hungarians and Carpathian Russians as well, war was averted, for the moment. Despite this on 15th March, 1939, Hitler marched his forces into Czechoslovakia without warning or any justification to place Bohemia and Moravia under 'protection'. A week later he likewise added to the Reich the port of Memel in Lithuania, abutting East Prussia. Whilst other nations objected strongly, France and Britain overlooking their guarantee to the Czechs, declined to come to their rescue. One consequence was, however, that on 27th April the decision was taken that conscription would be introduced in United Kingdom.

With the fall of Czechoslovakia on 29th March, 1939 Britain and France offered guarantees to Poland, while on 18th April Russia proposed a tri-partite agreement to form an eastern front, but this was not taken up by the western powers until too late. Then in the summer Hitler continued his bullying tactics on Poland to return the Danzig corridor ceded to them at the conclusion of World War I. On 23rd August Hitler and Stalin in Soviet Russia signed a non-aggression pact, leading Britain, two days later, and France to ratify their guarantees to Poland. Banking that there was little France and Britain could do in support of their guarantees in the short term, Germany, without specifying any demands, sought the attendance of an emissary from the Polish Government with unlimited power to sign any agreement that should be demanded of him. Upon their refusal the Germans issued an ultimatum to the Polish ambassador in Berlin and, before he had had time to transmit the contents to his government in Warsaw, Hitler announced that it had been rejected and promptly marched his troops across the frontier on 1st September, 1939.

Recognising that they were bound by their guarantees, both France and United Kingdom issued notes to Germany insisting on its immediate withdrawal and seeking an assurance by 11.00 am on Sunday 3rd September, 1939 that this would be implemented. As this was not received, the Prime Minister, Neville Chamberlain made his now well-known broadcast announcing that Britain was at war with Nazi Germany.

# Chapter Three

# Preparations for War

*Rearmament*

As a consequence of the horrors of World War I, and later the economic melt down of the Depression, Great Britain along with other countries signed up to a number of disarmament treaties. Gradually this process resulted in the nation's Army, Navy and Air Force contracting until by the early 1930s we were no longer in a position and unprepared adequately to defend ourselves and our then still considerable Empire against a determined aggressor.

By the early 1930s, however, the possible danger signs were detectable and the perceptive, most notably Winston Churchill, were beginning to voice their concerns that the prospects of another war in Europe was sadly becoming obvious and the need to rebuild our armed forces was becoming increasingly urgent. On 23rd March, 1932 Ramsey MacDonald's Government abandoned the assumption that war was unlikely within 10 years. Rearmament was initiated in 1934 and after a slow start, preparations were well under way when the Munich Crisis galvanized everybody involved into realising how serious the situation was. However, the Germans were well ahead in the game and their munitions industry was already coming on stream.

In the belief that Britain's main contribution would be in the field of the sea and air, by April 1938 priority was given to our naval and air forces, rather than the army which was seen as largely for defensive purposes. There had been a failure to appreciate that on land the use of tanks, motorized units and aircraft had largely eclipsed static trench warfare of the previous war. Only at the end of March the following year did the British Government recognize that it would have to contribute a significant military input to the alliance in Europe. As a consequence it doubled the establishment of the Territorial Army and the following month decided on the introduction of conscription. Naturally when six months later war broke out, preparations were still inadequate, with the training and equipping of these additional forces far from complete.

In September 1935 Stanley Baldwin, the Prime Minister, published a circular entitled Air Raid Precautions, inviting local authorities to make plans for the protection of their people in event of a war. Some towns responded by arranging the building of public air raid shelters. These shelters were built of brick with roofs of reinforced concrete. However, other local authorities ignored the circular and in April 1937 the government decided to create an Air Raid Wardens' Service and during the next year recruited around 200,000 volunteers.

As Hitler was making speeches that suggested he was going to send the German Army into Czechoslovakia, the British Government now began to fear a war with Nazi Germany was ultimately inevitable. On 28th August Parliament passed the Emergency Powers (Defence Act), which empowered the government to take measures to secure public safety, the defence of the realm and the maintenance of the public order. Over the next five days around 100 new measures were taken.

This included the calling-up of all military reservists and mobilizing Air Raid Precautions (ARP) volunteers. About half a million people enrolled in the ARP and others enlisted in the Territorial Army or the RAF Volunteer Reserve.

For their part the French had built the Maginot Line. This was a line of concrete and steel defences that stretched between Luxembourg and Switzerland along France's border with Germany, built between 1930 and 1935. It had three interdependent fortified belts with anti-tank emplacements and pillboxes standing in front of bombproof artillery casements. Named after Andre Maginot, the French war minister, it cost 7,000 million francs to build and was claimed at the time to provide an impregnable defence against the German Army.

Amongst the numerous preparations made in Britain, it was decided that Supplementary Reserve units of the Royal Engineers should be raised and trained, movement control duties within the Quartermaster-Master-General's Directorate of Movements were included. These tended, however, to concentrate on the requirements in the field of battle, rather than at home. Short introductory courses were held for certain officers destined for employment in war on movement duties, including Railway Traffic Officers (RTOs) and Embarkation Staff Officers (ESOs) at home, but excluded members of the newly formed Army Officers Emergency Reserve from which large numbers of Movement Officers were subsequently drawn. With the outbreak of war, a Movement Control organization was hurriedly set up in each Command with a small staff.

On the eve of war RTOs were sent to the main line stations in big towns and cities to smooth the journeys of the troops being mobilized and the urgently needed stores being delivered. Gradually they gained the respect of the railwaymen with whom they had contact and were useful to the members of the forces in ironing out difficulties, particularly in the event of delays. For this purpose they gathered round them a small staff, who were found accommodation and billets. So on 24th May, 1940 when they were told to hold themselves in readiness to proceed anywhere at a moment's notice for an indefinite period, they were fully prepared to play their part in Operation Dynamo.

At Ramsgate the site and buildings of the former Harbour railway station had been acquired by the Town Corporation and was leased to Thanet Amusements Ltd who built their Pleasureland Amusement Park, including a scenic railway within part of the existing tunnel giving access to the station, but closed at the outbreak of war. It was then taken over as a naval base, known as HMS *Fervent*, with the headquarters of the Naval Officer in Command, together with the officers' mess based in the Royal Temple Yacht Club. This operated Contraband Control Base Number 1, with motor torpedo boats and motor gun boats carrying out operations against enemy naval forces in the Channel and North Sea.

With the gathering of storm clouds in 1938, the town's borough engineer and surveyor R.D. Brimmell proposed tunnelling galleries out of the chalk to create shelters. After repeated refusal by the Home Office for authority, until the spring of 1939, when, following Germany's incursion into Czechoslovakia, they relented and construction was put in hand. By the outbreak of war, work was nearing completion on what was to become one of the most extensive networks of deep air-raid shelters anywhere in the country, which included seating, lighting and chemical toilets. By the outbreak of war, the Navy had shore establishments entitled HMS *Fervent* and HMS *Robertson* and Ramsgate Harbour played a key role in Dunkirk as well as much else.

On 27th April, 1939, Parliament passed the Military Training Act. This act introduced conscription for men aged 20 and 21 who were now required to undertake six months' military training.

With the international situation rapidly declining, Parliament was recalled in order to pass the Emergency Powers (Defence) Act 1939 just prior to the outbreak of World War II and provided the Prime Minister with powers from 24th August, 1939. This legislation enabled the British Government to put in place emergency measures to prosecute the war. It contained clauses giving wide powers to create Defence Regulations which regulated almost every aspect of everyday life in the country. The Defence Regulations were Orders in Council and could amend any primary or secondary legislation within the limits of the enabling Acts to allow the effective prosecution of the war. Subsequently on 22nd May the Emergency Powers (Defence) Act 1940 was passed in the aftermath of the German attack on France in 1940, granting the government even more authority to control persons and property for the duration of the war. This Act included provision under the Defence Regulations for orders to be made in respect of such matters as conscription into industry and internment of people suspected of being Nazi sympathizers. Since the emergency conditions created during the war persisted after the conflict, the last of the Defence Regulations, mainly those on food rationing, were not abolished until the early 1950s.

## The Railways

Ever since 1871, the Government had had under the Regulation of the Forces Act the powers to direct the affairs of the railways in the event of war. The General Managers of the railways had been in touch with the Ministry of Transport as early as 1937 about the problems that were bound to arise if war broke out. Rather than recourse to the 1871 Act, The Minister intimated in September 1938 that control of the railways would be taken under a Defence of the Realm Act to be enacted in the event of the country being in danger of enemy aggression. On 24th September that year in anticipation the Minister appointed the Railway Executive Committee (REC) as an advisory body. This was made up of the General Managers of the four railway companies, plus the London Transport Board, who in turn set up 16 consultative sub-committees to explore the implications of the various facets on the railways. With the implementing of the Defence of the Realm Act, on 1st September, 1939, the REC formally became the Minister's agents for the purpose of implementing his directions and the sub-committees were placed on a more formal footing.

During the spring and summer of 1939 the REC's offices were created in Down Street, a disused deep level tube station on the Piccadilly line of London Underground. Meeting rooms, offices, mess rooms, sleeping accommodation

Offices of the Railway Executive in a disused Underground Railway station at Down Street.
*Courtesy Subterranea Britannia*

The Southern Railway's buried control room at Deepdene, from where the overall direction of the SR's operations was coordinated.      *Courtesy Subterranea Britannia*

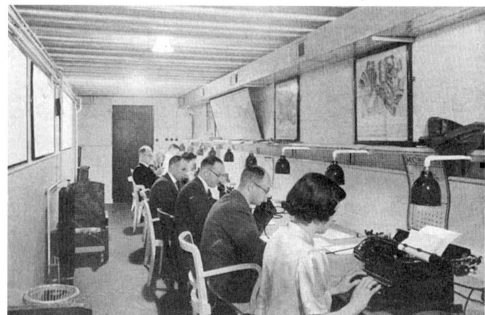

and necessary welfare facilities were installed; possession being taken on the day war broke out.

As part of their preparations, the railway companies assessed the implications of the likely effects of aerial bombardment on their networks and organizations. One of the conclusions reached was that the railway's headquarters offices and staff should be dispersed from London. The Southern Railway went to Deepdene House, a former hotel on the edge of Dorking; the LMS to The Grove on the outskirts of Watford; the LNER to The Hoo, a country mansion at Hitchin; and Great Western to Beenham Grange, near Aldermaston station together with other properties at Reading, Thatcham, Brimpton and Chosley.

The grounds of Deepdene House were on a Greensand ridge containing a network of existing natural caves. The Southern Railway took advantage of these to create an underground control centre from which to administer the railway during the times of attack on London and elsewhere. Because of the natural protection afforded by the location of the caves in the hillside they were eminently suitable for development as a bunker within which to accommodate both the headquarters' telephone exchange and system-wide traffic control. The latter was in communication with its underground divisional controls at Orpington, Redhill, Woking, Southampton and Exeter. The bunker was constructed within the caves which were enlarged to accommodate the staff on duty during an emergency. The underground control centre consisted of a series of tunnels driven into the steep hillside to the rear of the house. There were three entrances plus a fourth emergency exit. A 60-ft vertical shaft at the rear of the complex provided an air inlet and the emergency exit. The lawn between the caves and the house was the site of a 99 ft-tall mast upon which were mounted aerials for the emergency radio.

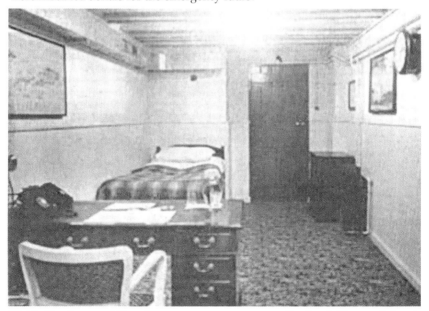

Night officer's room at Deepdene.                    *Courtesy Subterranea Britannia*

The network of tunnels included a control room; switchboard; battery room; main distribution frame/maintenance person's room; meeting room; a bedroom for the night officer; and an air plant and toilet facilities. The tunnels were well ventilated and the temperature was regulated by radiators in each room. The switchboard was a three-positioned installation with connections to Post Office and railway telephone lines, with direct lines to the various divisional traffic and engineering officers, together with extensions serving the headquarters staff located in the House. It was manned 24 hours a day. The night staff of the Operating Motive Power Chief Mechanical Engineer; and Chief Electrical Engineer's Departments also worked in the tunnels, which accommodated a total of 30 staff. The accommodation included a meeting room suitable for any conferences which might have to be held under emergency conditions. Among the features of the control centre here were diagrams of all important junctions on the Southern Railway, giving staff immediate access to all information necessary to enable them to make emergency or alternative arrangements for any diversion of traffic necessitated by damage caused by enemy action. Each of the rooms was fitted with a radio receiver for the reception, under emergency conditions, of any important Government announcements which might have been broadcast.

During its peacetime existence the SR had avoided over centralization in its operational matters and prior to the war had not had a control organization. Instead it relied on the men on the ground, especially signalmen, arguing that they were better able to judge the best solution to a local problem. Under the provisions of Air Raid Precautions, however, train supervisory offices had been set up in 1938. These were located as follows:

**Southern Railway Operating Divisions & Train Supervision Offices (TSO)**

| Division | Location of TSO | Area covered |
|---|---|---|
| London (East) | Orpington | Former SECR lines |
| London (Central) | Redhill | Former LBSC lines |
| London (West) | Woking | LSWR lines to Portsmouth via Haslemere, Hayling Island and the Isle of Wight |
| South West | Southampton West | All lines west of Worting Jn and Southampton Docks to Dorchester and Weymouth with Fareham lines between Southampton and Portsmouth and as far as Salisbury |
| Western | Exeter | West of England main line and branches west of Salisbury |

They were mostly accommodated in purpose-built underground bunkers, which would have resisted all but a direct hit, to protect the staff and enable their work to continue through air raids. The rooms containing the control function were provided with gas tight doors and extractor fans that exhausted air to the exterior, but there was no provision for the supply of uncontaminated fresh air. At Redhill the only time this was tried, as an exercise, it was quickly concluded that it was preferable to work with a gas mask on. Each control had an ARP warden appointed.

In the ordinary course of events, the staff were organized into teams who dealt with either freight or passenger traffics. The controllers would take executive decisions as to which trains were to have priority, how to allocate scarce resources and so on. For this purpose they were equipped with dedicated 'Control' telephone lines to every signal cabin in their division and to other strategic locations such as: other control offices; main motive power depots; electrical control offices, etc. Within each train supervisory office, panels were set up on the wall beneath which there was a concentrator panel containing telephones, many of the omnibus type and intercom connections. In front of these sat a number of individuals each responsible for a section of the line and overseen by a supervisor. For all this, perhaps in contrast to the LMS, considerable responsibility nonetheless still rested with the district operating inspectors out on the line.

Orpington's underground control was on the down (east) side, behind the former engine shed, by then used for the storage of carriages. Redhill's, also below ground, was beside the fork of the junction and south of the goods shed. In addition there were permanent sub-controls at East Croydon, situated in the basement of the station buildings facing George Street, and at Brighton, with the idea that in the event of a failure in communications, or Redhill being knocked out, these could continue to regulate trains in their locality. At Woking the offices of the Traffic Department and District Engineer (London West) had been relocated into hurriedly constructed wooden huts on the down side at the London end on the site of an old rifle range, known as 'Furnival's folly' after the district engineer responsible for supervising its construction. The control was placed underground and to disguise it, wooden single-storey buildings were placed on top containing the canteen and the toilets, the elevated level of both affording sufficient gradient to the drains to reach the public sewer system.

Other railway companies dispersed their control points to locations less likely to suffer from aerial attack. In this way the LNER's Southern Area superintendent set up his Western Control at Gerrards Cross, whilst his Eastern Control went to Shenfield. Their Train and Traffic Control District operational offices for King's Cross, Doncaster, Lincoln, Leeds, Manchester and Nottingham relocated respectively to Knebworth, Bawtry, Blankley, Driglington, Godley and East Leake. Each was specially constructed of reinforced concrete with steel doors and steel shutters to cover the windows capable of being battened down during an air raid. To clear the stuffy atmosphere that soon arose, it was necessary to temporarily suspend operations and turn the lights out prior to opening the shutters for a short spell. Innovative solutions were found at York and Edinburgh: at the first an excavation was made beneath the city walls, while at the latter use was made of a disused tunnel adjacent to Waverley station. Norwich District Control found refuge in a rampart near Thorpe station and Cambridge in a semi-basement. These controls were operated 24 hours a day and staff worked alternate 12 hour shifts with a day off once every three weeks.

In pre-war days there had been occasional movements of large numbers of troops e.g. manoeuvres, the trooping season (connected with troopship sailings), but of course these were all well planned in advance. Another important feature of special railway operations were the tattoos, spreading tentacles of trains from the West of England, South Wales and as far north as Blackpool. As war broke army units were mobilized from a variety of counties and depots and it would have been a considerable logistical problem getting the men to their appropriate depot. Again all of these would have been planned sufficiently far in advance for either the printed weekly, or daily stencilled special traffic notices (STNs) to be issued for private circulation amongst railway staff. These advised them of the detailed arrangements, including the timing of the trains; empty stock; shunting movements; and light engine workings, together with platform allocations; head boards to be carried, to identify the trains; signal boxes to be opened for extended hours; and any adjustments to other timetabled train workings. The Southern Railway and other railways ran so many special trains that its experienced staff were familiar with similar previous such workings and would have a framework to hand. For instance, its working timetables would include possible paths for such trains on busy main lines, known as Q or conditional paths, which could be adopted in whole or part as required.

As well as the skill necessary to efficiently drive a steam locomotive, the driver has to be familiar with the line along which it is intended the train should work. He needed to know the location of every signal and all speed restrictions at junctions and severe curves, the gradient profile and the layout of stations and goods yards along the way. Once he thought he was sufficiently au fait with a route, he would sign for the road, thus allowing him to be rostered for this line. The work of locomotive sheds would often include the occasional duty along less obvious routes to enable crews to keep their hand in thus affording flexibility when allocating duties for special workings and diverted trains, and would prove invaluable in the operation about to be undertaken.

Unlike the other three main line railway companies, the Southern's income principally derived from passenger traffic. It had a great tradition and huge experience of running special trains, often at relatively short notice, coping with enormous crowds for such things as extra trains at busy times of holidays; special trains for sporting events of soccer and rugby football, University Boat Race, and particularly horse racing; army tattoos; hop-pickers and theatrical specials; Sunday school outings; boarding school pupils to and from school; boat trains and ocean liner specials, whose timings might vary due to the tide, etc. Spare sets of coaching stock, usually cascaded from front line duties, were kept in sidings scattered around the system available for use at short notice. Furthermore, if they, along with the other companies, did but know it, in September 1939 they had to a large extent already had a full-scale rehearsal in the form of the evacuation of school children, expectant mothers and those with young children from the city and town centres likely to be bombed to reception areas in the country. Although this had been carefully pre-planned, it had involved central and local government, the railway companies and the WVS coping with not just their transport, but their collection, feeding during the journey and upon arrival placing in homes or other accommodation.

Most telephones on the railways were of the omnibus type, whereby a number of instruments were all connected to a single line. Instead of a discrete number, each instrument had a code which when rung would alert that extension to answer, or a special code so that all extensions could be contacted at the same time. In addition, each signal box had a line to its neighbouring boxes. As part of the ARP, arrangements were made for a system of passing messages down the line from one box to another in the event of the trunk lines being severed.

As an economy measure the Southern Railway had closed the small 4-lever signal box at Westcott between Dorking Town and Gomshall on 13th March, 1935. In the down direction this 4½ mile section of line, however, contained a gradient of over three miles in length and at an inclination of 1 in 96, which the Westcott box had conveniently split roughly into two equal halves. So to reinstate line capacity for anticipated wartime traffic, the SR effectively put back Westcott box by providing an intermediate block section (IBS) on the down (uphill, westbound) line. This comprised a semaphore IBS home signal, near where Westcott box had been, and a distant signal 800 yards in the rear. Both were electrically operated from the box in rear, Dorking Town. As some track circuiting would also have been necessary, the work incurred the relatively high cost of £1,000, although no extra manpower. This small scheme was commissioned on 6th February, 1940, just in time to be of use to the Operation Dynamo trains about to use the line extensively.

Improved connection between Southern and Great Western railways at Reading and Staines was contemplated in early 1940. The intention was to afford an alternative route for freight traffic between the GN and GE Sections of the LNER to and from the SR's SE Section in the event of the original peace time routes through London, via the Metropolitan Widened Lines, East London Line, West London Line or North & South Western Joint Railway being obstructed. Instead they could be routed via Cambridge, Sandy, Bedford, Bletchley, Oxford, Reading, Guildford, Redhill and Tonbridge. The facility at Reading did not, however, become available until a year after the Dunkirk evacuation and instead the old steeply-graded connection immediately to the east of Reading (GWR) station had to be used.

*Ambulance Trains*

As in the previous conflict, the railways were called upon to provide ambulance, or hospital trains for wounded and sick troops. These fell into two categories. Overseas ambulance trains were for conveying military service patients from the casualty clearing stations to base hospital or for shipment home and were coded OAT. Home ambulance trains, coded HAT were used to transfer patients landed from hospital ships at south coast ports to military hospitals and then to hospitals which were local to the patients' home. The accommodation for lying patients on stretchers in the ward cars was arranged in six tiers of three beds on each side with the middle beds being capable of being folded up to allow sitting cases to be seated on the bottom bed. Although the relevant REC sub-committee had held discussions with the War Office as early as 1937, leading to drawings being prepared by the LMS, instructions for the provision of eight ambulance trains for use at home and four, for overseas, were not issued until 2nd September, 1939. The trains were built to a standard design with coaches converted for use as wards, office and accommodation, medical, and kitchens for the staff and patients. The wards were capable of taking both stretchered and sitting patients. Those trains for use at home initially consisted of nine gangway-connected coaches, later increased to 11, while the trains for overseas were made up of 16 coaches each. All 136 coaches were taken from existing LMS 57 ft-long stock and converted and equipped. This was put in hand at very short notice and the work shared between the workshops of all four railway companies. The task was undertaken at: Derby and Wolverton on the LMS; Doncaster and York on the LNER; Swindon on the Great Western; and Eastleigh and Lancing on the Southern. Each company concentrated on one type of vehicle, after which these were brought together, probably either at the Longmoor Military Railway in north-east Hampshire or Cambridge. Two home trains and four overseas trains were completed and handed over to the military authorities in less than three weeks. Of those coaches worked on at Swindon 12 were for overseas and six for home use, and were completed by mid-October 1939. At the first formal meeting of the Ambulance Train Committee in October 1939, further requisitions were made for trains. By March 1940 twelve trains for use at home and 13 for overseas were available, another 344 LMS vehicles being commandeered. Nine of the trains already across the Channel, amounting to 144 vehicles, were lost with the fall of France in 1940.

Over 80 vehicles were derived from LMS wooden-panelled Period I brake corridor third class coaches to diagram 1696 and in excess of 60 from corridor thirds to diagram 1695. Later others were also taken from similar period third open and corridor composite coaches to diagrams 1692 and 1694 respectively. The interiors of the coaches were stripped out and fitted out as personnel cars with living compartments for the medical staff of officers, nursing sisters, orderlies and other supporting personnel and ward coaches for lying as well as sitting patients, with separate accommodation for mental and other special categories of patient. To protect patients and staff from glass splinters in the event of a nearby bomb explosion or artillery attack, the window glazing was covered by mesh fabric.

All were re-painted in khaki on the body sides and ends and the windows painted black so that full lighting could be employed inside during the blackout. When built those equipped to carry casualties in addition had white roofs with a central large red cross, together with a small white panels and red cross on each side. Whilst photographs appear to confirm that the roofs were initially white, by December 1940 written evidence suggests this may have been changed to grey. This was all in accordance with the Geneva Convention, which provided protection for all designated and marked medical staff and equipment which were being used solely for military purposes. The equivalent casualty evacuation trains for civilians where not identified by red cross emblems.

The complete trains, including a locomotive, were normally stood at suitable stabling points up and down the country, from where they could be summoned at short notice to collect casualties as required by arrangement with the railways, in Britain through the Railway Executive. The sidings needed to be long enough for the entire train and its engine, located near to a locomotive depot and wagon/carriage repair works, as well as the route for which the train would be used. There had to be road access for restocking of train supplies, drinking water available, provision for heating in cold weather and toilets for train staff. These trains were treated as ordinary passenger trains being given a clear run as far as possible. They accommodated between 150 (home) and 250

A 16-coach hospital train No. 8 for use overseas photographed in September 1939 soon after having been converted from LMS 57 ft-long Period 1 coaching stock. Coach No. 816 is an ex-LMS brake corridor third altered for use as a brake and stores van as the 16th vehicle in train No 8. *Author's Collection*

(overseas) patients together with the Medical Officer and his staff of nurses and orderlies. The cleaning of the interior of the trains was the responsibility of the ambulance train personnel, while that of the exterior, together with maintenance was undertaken by the railway companies' staff.

On 26th March, H.E.O. Wheeler, superintendent of operation on the Southern Railway at Deepdene, issued Special Notice AMB. No. 1, *Working of ambulance trains*. This gave all the necessary instructions for the operation of such trains and pre-planned as much as possible, so that when the need arose the train could be dispatched with the minimum of delay. At that time, this shows HATs Nos. 59 to 62 were based on Newhaven and Nos. 55 to 58 and 63 to 66 on Southampton Docks. The train formation was given as:

    1 staff and brake car
    1 personnel car
    1 kitchen car
    1 administrative car
    2 ward cars
    1 sitting cases car
    1 ward car
    2 open thirds
    1 ward and brake car

In addition the Ministry of Health had organized the assembly of 23 casualty evacuation trains, so as to be able to transport civilian casualties as a result of bombing for treatment at hospitals located in safer areas of the country. Each train consisted of 10 gangwayed bogie passenger brake vans with a brake corridor bogie coach at each end. Within each van provision was made for carrying 36 stretchers by means of brackets on each side in tiers of three, while

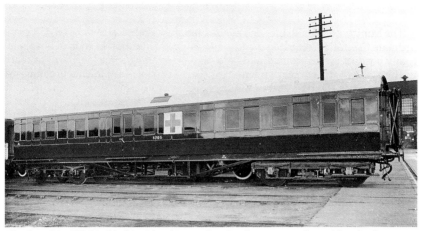

Ward car No. 5705 in khaki with white roof and red cross, together with a further cross on a panel on the sides is the fifth vehicle in train No. 57. The absence of lugs projecting below the solebar over the bogies confirms that this was a train for use at home and, when not in use, at times was stationed at Bellahouston, Glasgow.          *Author's Collection*

the coaches were for the conveyance of the accompanying doctors, nurses etc, together with medical stores, hot and cold water. These were coded CET followed by an individual number and this was painted on the ends of each passenger coach. As bombing in a serious way had yet to be launched against the country, CET Nos. 8 and 10 were allocated to the War Office and stationed at Romsey at the time of Dunkirk.

As it was uncertain at what times, day or night, the hospital trains might be expected to leave either Newhaven Harbour or Southampton Docks for a variety of destinations on the SR and other companies' lines, running times were listed to numerous places all over the country from Aberdeen or Invergordon in the North to Pembroke Dock and Ely. The de-training stations anticipated amounted to 53 from Newhaven and 51 from Southampton. For these 23 and 20 respectively intended routes and running times were tabulated to destinations on the SR or to hand-over points to other companies, a similar number of schedules being available for the returning empty trains. Details included the places at which change-over engines or assisting engines/double-heading was required, together with water stops, engines to turn, or calls if required to pick up a conductor for enginemen unfamiliar with the route. Various restrictions were noted and the maximum speed of the train stated as 45 mph.

The stations from which the train was to start were instructed to arrange for the line over which the train was to run; to advise by telephone the next signal box, together with their respective divisional control office, and the message from thereon passed through the signal boxes to the destination station or transfer junction with another railway. Station masters were obliged to advise the staff of other departments as necessary and arrange for signal boxes to be opened as required.

*Medical Facilities*

The Ministry of Health established the Emergency Medical Service (EMS) to co-ordinate the utilization of hospitals, clinic and bed allocation in civilian hospitals. Many hospitals were brought into the scheme, relocating some long term patients to the north of the country so that beds were available for patients brought out from the cities. During early 1939 they were in the process of extending and supplementing the number of beds in a number of civilian hospitals to provide facilities for the large number of civilian casualties that were expected as a result of aerial bombardment, as well as members of the armed forces. These hospitals were then designated Emergency Medical Services, or EMS hospitals.

During the previous conflict between 1914 and 1918, to be able to work more effectively it had been found expedient for the British Red Cross Society and the Order of St John of Jerusalem to work together as the one War Organization of the two bodies. The Joint War Committee of this organization was still in being to fulfil its responsibilities to disabled servicemen and women from the war, when the deteriorating political situation in Europe suggested its work might have to resume. A sub-committee was set up and this recommended that the two bodies should yet again work together. The necessary arrangements were put in hand and contacts re-established with the three services during the summer of 1939, a formal agreement being signed on 2nd September, 1939. With the outbreak of World War II, the War Office initially only requested the Joint War Organization to provide auxiliary homes and hospitals for officers. However, by June 1940 the War Office approached the Organization for further assistance by providing 20,000 beds in homes and hospitals for other ranks. Again, many privately-owned properties were used to house patients, which helped to create an atmosphere more conducive to recovery than might have been found in a more formal institution.

Voluntary Aid Detachments (VADs), staffed by members of both parent bodies, were available to supplement the medical services of the armed forces on general mobilization as part of Territorial Army in any part of the World. These fell into two groups: mobile – those between the ages of 21 and 40 (later 19 to 45) who were willing to be sent to wherever required, and immobile – those between 18 and 65 whose availability was limited to places within reach of their home. Although the majority of members were necessarily women, eligible men being called up for military service, both sexes could enlist as VADs. Members undertook a variety of work from cleaning, cooking and elementary nursing, to driving, porterage and mechanical repairs. Their role was essentially a supportive one, assisting trained nursing staff and helping to keep hospitals and ambulance services operating. As those engaged in the care of the sick and wounded, under the terms of the Geneva Convention, they were to be regarded as neutral and required to wear a Red Cross brass badge on their left arm. Amongst the many activities in which they were involved was the care of servicemen both at home and overseas. The staffing of hospital trains was by a combination of Royal Army Medical Corps (RAMC) personnel and VADs and the provision of these during both wars would not have been possible without the use of volunteer labour to carry out the non-medical care tasks.

When the wounded needed to travel, it was arranged for escorts to accompany the patient on public transport or for the provision of motor ambulances and drivers. In the spring of 1939, the Army Council realised that it would not need the immobile members in Service hospitals in Britain, as a consequence of which most were released to join the Civil Nursing Reserve and thereby provide staff for the EMS hospitals. In supporting the medical staff these worthies were from the VAD, Friends Ambulance, conscientious objectors and other non-fighting troops. As the war progressed the Red Cross homes and hospitals themselves started to become more specialized. Certain homes were selected for servicemen of particular nationalities, in order that their needs be more specifically catered for, while some hospitals allocated cases on the basis of the nature of the service. Separate homes were also established to deal with the needs of liberated prisoners of war as they convalesced.

A percentage of the hospitals were reserved for the treatment of specific disabilities. Physiotherapy played an important role in the recovery of many of the patients and selected homes were able to organize physical training and remedial exercise classes under the supervision of an Army Physical Training Instructor.

During the Crimean War (1853-1856) the Government initiated steps to construct the first military hospital to be built in the United Kingdom. A site was found at Netley Abbey and Queen Victoria gave her blessing to the proposal and allowed it to be called the Royal Victoria Hospital, taking a continuing interest in it during the rest of her life. Its purpose was to train army nurses and doctors and to treat military patients to ensure their swift return to duty. Netley was chosen as the site because it was near to Southampton where hospital ships from around the British Empire could safely dock and disembark patients. Whilst the buildings overlooked Southampton Water, it was the administrative staff that benefited rather than the patients whose outlook was onto a courtyard.

The railway from Southampton as far as Netley village was opened by the London & South Western Railway on 5th March, 1866. Although most of the patients being admitted into the hospital in fact arrived by tender from ships moored in Southampton Water, discharged patients did travel by train. The line on from Netley to Fareham, however, was not opened until 2nd September, 1889, thereby creating a through route between Southampton and Portsmouth. In January 1900, during the Boer War in South Africa, the War Department asked the LSWR to construct a short branch line from Netley station to a terminal directly behind the main building of the hospital, a distance of 48 chains. The covered platform, some 200 feet long, was sufficient for four coaches. During both World Wars, the branch line from Netley to the Royal Victoria Hospital experienced considerable traffic. Heavy trains of ambulance coaches, carrying hundreds of casualties, carefully descended the steep bank from Netley station with a locomotive at each end both with the continuous brake pipe coupled up throughout. Wet rails combined with the steep gradient frequently made progress difficult, and the return journey from the Hospital to the main line could take as long as 45 minutes.

Members of the Queen Alexandra's Imperial Military Nursing Service, the QAIMNS(R), and the TANS (Territorial Army Nursing Service) reported to Netley Hospital when in 1939 they were called up. Likewise the muster point for

No. 4 British General Hospital was also at Royal Victoria Military Hospital Netley and their destination was soon to be La Baule in France. In 1939 No. 11 General Hospital formed at Netley and was deployed to Le Havre. During the Dunkirk evacuation all No. 4's equipment, except one typewriter, was destroyed, whilst No. 11 General Hospital was evacuated from Cherbourg to England.

### Other Bodies

The First Aid Nursing Yeomanry (Princess Royal's Volunteer Corps), or FANY(PRVC), is a British independent all-female unit affiliated to, but not part of, the Territorial Army. It was formed as the First Aid Nursing Yeomanry in 1907 as a first aid link between the field hospitals and the front lines, and was given the title yeomanry as all its members were originally mounted on horseback. During World War I, FANYs ran field hospitals, graduated to motor ambulances and set up soup kitchens and canteens for the troops, often under highly dangerous conditions. In September 1938, the Corps, having changed its title to Women's Transport Service (FANY), was called upon to form the nucleus of the Motor Driver Companies of the Auxiliary Territorial Service (ATS), most joining the ATS for this purpose.

Male nurses and members of the FANYs demonstrate the loading of stretchers onto motor ambulances.                                                          *Hester Hopkins Collection*

As war began to look imminent, in 1938 the Home Secretary Sir Samuel Hoare conceived the idea of a women's voluntary organization, in a way parallel to the Air Raid Wardens, to provide assistance in the community in the event of air attacks. The Women's Voluntary Service therefore was set up on 16th May, 1938, with The Dowager Marchioness Lady Reading, as chairman and the Queen and Queen Mary as joint patrons. It was called at first WVS for Air Raid Precautions, but in 1939 this was changed to WVS for Civil Defence. By then it had 165,000 members made up of women, such as the old, the young, and those with dependents, who were therefore prevented from enlisting in the services or undertaking other essential war work. They took on a wide range of roles including managing the evacuation of children and young mothers from large towns and cities at risk of being bombed; staffing hostels and hospitals, sick bays and communal feeding centres; undertaking welfare work for the troops; providing food and clothing for over 22,000 refugees; organizing rest centres for those made homeless by bomb damage as a result of air raids. They also staffed Incident Inquiry Points set up in the vicinity of incidents, at which people could enquire about those who might have been killed or injured, following a raid. In 1945 'for Civil Defence' was dropped from its name; in 1966 'Royal' was added by the Queen to create the WRVS.

Unlike the multitude of mostly small motor lorry transport firms of the period, bus and coach companies tended to be much larger organizations, which made it considerably easier for the Services to identify and deal with bus companies when arranging to requisition motor transport. As a consequence they were better placed to adjust their work schedules and rotas to release the necessary vehicles. Further they were well used to supplying motor transport in connection with the regular Army's manoeuvres, the summer camps of the Reserve units and increasing number of Territorial units brought into being during the late 1930s.

Once war started and conscription was introduced, it meant that fewer men were available to serve as bus crews, service engineers and administrators. A start had been made to introduce women as bus conductors to enable the younger men to be released for war service. Nonetheless, maintenance of the vehicles remained difficult; the requisitioning of vehicles to replace destroyed vehicles in London or for conversion to military ambulances caused shortages locally. Many companies' vehicles were soon in continuous demand for the transport of troops.

Like the railways, the Tilling Group, with 23 bus and road transport companies, foresaw the need to relocate the company's national headquarters out of London. They therefore purchased Bovingdon Grange near Hemel Hempstead in Hertfordshire for the purpose, transferring there on 1st September, 1939. They had already in the previous May set up an agreement between member companies whereby, in the event of one or more being short of vehicles due to loss, it could hire some from other member companies at a moment's notice to enable it to continue essential services.

Likewise major cities were likely targets for bombing and the Hampshire branch of the British Red Cross took the precaution of relocating its headquarters in the City of Southampton to Hurn Court near Christchurch. This proved a wise move, as the property in 63 London Road was destroyed.

Within a month of the outbreak of war, the East Kent Bus Co. and Maidstone & District Motor Services had provided a number of buses for use as ambulances by the Emergency Medical Services. The windows were blacked out, the roofs painted grey and arrangements were made to be able to load up to four stretcher cases through the rear doors. When converted these ambulances were intended solely for use by the civilian population in the event of air raids and were not available to the military. However, during the evacuation of troops from Dunkirk, there seems to have been a change of heart.

*Rationing*

At the beginning of the war, the United Kingdom imported 55 million tons of foodstuffs per year (70 per cent), including more than 50 per cent of its meat, 70 per cent of its cheese and sugar, nearly 80 per cent of fruits and about 90 per cent of cereals and fats. As one of the principal strategies of Germany was to attack shipping bound for the UK, Ration Books were issued by the Ministry of Food in October 1939. Although the start of rationing had been proposed from November 1939, it was postponed until Monday 8th January, 1940. The ration books contained points that could be used against the purchase of specific foods per week or month. Each person registered with their local shops, and the shopkeeper was provided with enough food for his registered customers. In this way each person was enabled to buy a specific mount of basic foods.

On 8th January, 1940, bacon, butter and sugar were rationed, soon to be followed by meat, tea, jam, biscuits, breakfast cereals, cheese, eggs, milk and canned fruit. Typical examples allowed to each person were:

| | |
|---|---|
| Meat | between 1 and 2 shillings a head a week (i.e. no weight specified) |
| Bacon | 4 to 8 oz. (113-227 gm) a week |
| Tea | 2-4 oz. (57-113 gm) a week, |
| Cheese | 1 to 8 oz. (28-227 gm) a week |
| Sugar | 8 oz. (227 gm) a week. |

Special provision was made for pregnant mothers and children under five years of age by way of enhanced milk rations and the availability of orange juice, while schoolchildren up to the age of 18 received half a pint a day. As the war progressed, most kinds of food came to be rationed, as were clothing and petrol. Some of the few foods not rationed were fish, rabbits and potatoes.

Five East Kent single-decker Leyland Tiger TS7 buses with bodywork provided by Park Royal in 1935. Twenty-five were converted for use as ambulances, some of which await the call of duty at Ashford depot.                              *The M&D and East Kent Bus Club Collection*

The Maidstone & District also contributed buses for conversion into ambulances in October 1939. Here No. 166 was an ex-A. Timpson & Sons Ltd AEC Reliance supplied in June 1929 for its Hastings operations and acquired by the Maidstone company on 3rd March, 1934. The new owners had Harrington fit a new body two years later, after which it lasted until 1948. Here, it and its neighbour have blacked-out windows, hooded head lights, the edges to the mudguards highlighted in white paint and Ambulance displayed on its destination scroll.                              *Author's Collection*

# Chapter Four

# Military Events in France and Flanders

Following the declaration of war by Britain and France, the first units of the British Expeditionary Force were soon sent across the English Channel to Northern France under the command of General The Viscount John Vereker Gort VC. To avoid the risk of attack from the Luftwaffe, although resulting in a longer sea passage and subsequent land journey, ports in the west were chosen, such as Cherbourg, even Brest and St Nazaire on the Atlantic coast of France. Through these ports British forces were gradually strengthened by a steady stream of reinforcements, while little else occurred in Western Europe until on 9th April, 1940 Germany seized Denmark and made an assault on Norway. This, then, was quickly followed by the invasion of the neutral countries of Netherlands, Belgium and the Grand Duchy of Luxembourg early on the morning of Friday 10th May, 1940. Both military incursions on land and aerial bombardment of important towns were made. On the same day, following mounting criticism of the conduct of the war, Neville Chamberlain resigned and a coalition Government was set up under Winston Churchill's premiership. In view of the critical military situation in Europe, the Government announced at 1.00 pm that the Whitsun bank holiday (the following Monday) was cancelled to enable the people to remain at work and avoid holiday travel. Sadly Chamberlain subsequently died in November that year.

Whilst previously constrained by Belgium's neutrality, the French 1st Army and BEF were now in a position to advance rapidly to a prepared plan to occupy as much of Belgium as they could in the face of the German onslaught and to support the Belgian Army by taking up positions along the line of the rivers Dyle and Meuse. On 11th May, having captured two bridges across the Albert Canal the previous day, the invaders crossed the supposedly impassable Albert Canal in force and entered Liege. Two days later the Germans crossed the Ijssel and Maas rivers to outflank the Dutch fortifications. This led to Queen Wilhelmina and the rest of the Dutch royal family, Government and much bullion having to sail for England. By 14th May the out-numbered Dutch army had been surrounded and over-powered. During the evening General Henri G. Winkelman, the Commander in Chief announced the surrender of Holland on Hilversum radio - stating that further resistance would lead only to the complete destruction of the country, a formal surrender being concluded at 11.00 am the next day.

In its preplanning for the anticipated invasion, the French military hierarchy had realised that the heavily fortified Maginot Line from the Swiss border to the Luxembourg border was likely to cause the main thrust to be made further north. They and others therefore assumed that this would come across the Belgian Plain, but discarded the possibility of it being through the Ardennes because it was assumed to be impassable to modern military vehicles. They therefore placed their weakest least experienced troops to defend this sector. To shorten the line of defence from the end of the Maginot Line northwards to the sea, it was considered necessary to advance the French and British armies from

The Belgian civilian population wave at British gunners passing through in a Light Dragon tractor hauling a quick-firing 18 or 25-pounder field gun.      *Author's Collection*

the French border with Belgium as far as possible to meet the Germans attack. Protective of their neutrality, the Belgians would not permit this to take place prior to such an attack. Nonetheless, once this took place, French and British forces rushed through Belgium to take up positions alongside the Belgian Army on the line of the rivers Dyle and Meuse by 12th May.

The German's initial attacks of the Netherlands and northern Belgium lulled the leaders into believing they had correctly anticipated the enemy's move, only by 14th May for it to become clear that the German's main armoured thrust was to occur against the River Meuse, resulting in the the French Army's collapse at Sedan. Finding its way without undue difficulty through the discounted and lightly defended Ardennes region, the German armoured forces were able to advance rapidly to capture Amiens by 20th May. With no Allied strategic reserves behind the lines to resist, the Germans quickly took Arras two days later. On the night of 16th/17th May the Belgian Government left Brussels for Ostend and the capital Brussels fell into enemy hands on 17th May, although Antwerp was not occupied until 18th May.

*Surrounding of BEF and French 1st Army*

British reinforcements had continued to be sent to France, such as by ferry to Dunkirk, up to 13th May, 1940. As a consequence of the German advance, however, all ports in North East France were closed on 17th May, 1940, followed by the withdrawal of the Le Havre and Southampton service on 20th.

While on Sunday 19th May communications with Abbeville across the River Somme by road and rail were still passable, it seemed more than possible that the German armoured forces in the area would soon break through and reach the coast. In this event the BEF and elements of the French Army would be cut off from their supply bases and causing large reserves to be unable to join battle, while the remnants of the Belgian Army would be equally isolated. With only four days' battle supplies within reach and even if they moved south, many would still be cut off. At 11.30 hours, therefore, in accordance with Lord Gort's instruction his Chief of General Staff, Lt Gen. H.R. Pownall discussed the worsening situation over the telephone with Major-General R.H. Dewing, Director of Military Operations and Plans at the War Office in London, suggesting that the possibility of evacuation had to be considered and the necessary plans prepared. A second call at lunch time was followed by a summoning of the War Cabinet to meet at 4.30 pm. They decided to dispatch General Sir Edmund Ironside, Chief of the Imperial General Staff, to France the next day with a view to persuading Gort instead to move the BEF south towards Amiens and re-establish lines of communications with the rest of France.

By that Sunday evening enemy troops had arrived on the outskirts of the City of Amiens which was about to be besieged. Likewise difficulties in communications rendered it impractical for the RAF component of the British presence, under Air Vice-Marshal C.H.B. Blount, to continue and orders were therefore given for the majority to be withdrawn to England. They then set up headquarters at Hawkinge in Kent.

Upon receipt of General Pownall's message, a conference was called at the War Office, at which Vice Admiral B.H. Ramsey at Dover was represented. At this the temporary maintenance of the BEF through the limited number of ports in the north-east of France still remaining in Allied hands, i.e. Dunkirk, Calais and Boulogne, was discussed, presumably until such time as the previous lines of communication could be re-established. The full implication of the military situation was only slowing dawning and the possibility of evacuating very large forces was merely discussed in passing. Nonetheless, it was agreed that, as the man on the spot, control of such either operation should be delegated to Vice-Admiral Dover. Also from this time the men were put on half-rations, while troops in the lines of communications in support of the fighting units, somewhat disparagingly termed 'useless mouths', less those working in the docks were sent back across the Channel. For instance, the Royal Engineers 153 Railway Operating Company based at Romescamps in France drove to Boulogne and crossed to Dover aboard TSS *Canterbury* on 21st May, ending up at Oxney Camp at Bordon. In a week's time, in advance of the formal commencement of Operation Dynamo on 26th May, these accounted for 21,410 British, together with 4,992 casualties, and 1,534 Allied troops, as follows:

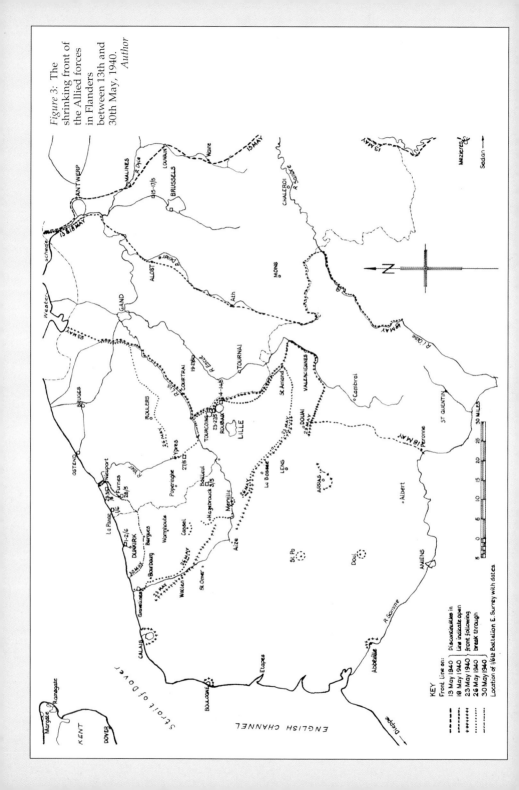

*Figure 3*: The shrinking front of the Allied forces in Flanders between 13th and 30th May, 1940. *Author*

KEY

Front Line on:

13 May 1940
18 May 1940
23 May 1940
26 May 1940
30 May 1940

Discontinuities in Line indicate open front following break through

Location of 1/6th Battalion E. Surrey with dates

**Daily Landings of Troops Pre-Dynamo**

| Period | Port | Fit | Personnel Casualties | Allies | Totals |
|---|---|---|---|---|---|
| 20 May | Dover | 2,089 | | 1 | |
| | Southampton | | 196 | | 2,286 |
| 21 May | Dover | 2,593 | | | |
| | Southampton | | 175 | | 2,768 |
| 22 May | Dover | 3,818 | 344 | 187 | |
| | Folkestone | 6 | | | |
| | Southampton | | 50 | | 4,405 |
| 23 May | Dover | 3,498 | 189 | *1,117 | |
| | Folkestone | | | 5 | 4,809 |
| 24 May | Dover | 29 | 200 | | |
| | Folkestone | 292 | | | |
| | Newhaven | | 851 | | |
| | Southampton | 1,233 | 467 | | 3,072 |
| 25 May | Dover | 6,272 | | | |
| | Newhaven | | 1,489 | | 3,073 |
| 26 May | Dover | 1,580 | 95 | 224 | |
| | Newhaven | | 936 | | 2,835 |
| Totals | | 21,410 | 4,992 | 1,534 | 27,936 |

* Including some refugees.

By the next day, 20th May, the breach at Arras had deepened and widened and it became clear that the German armoured forces were aiming for the Somme Valley and the Channel ports. At Dover the possibility of a large-scale evacuation led to a meeting of naval staffs with liaison officers from the War Office Movement Control and Ministry of Shipping to consider the maritime aspects of mounting such an operation and protection from the air that such would require. Another meeting took place a day later at the War Office to consider arrangements, once the troops had arrived.

In France, however, plans had been made at high level for the French in the south and units of the 1st French Army and the BEF in the north to counter attack, but neither had the reserves to be able to mount the vigorous operation required. With the railway line cut at Abbeville on 21st May, the BEF could now no longer be supplied through ports south of the Somme, as they had largely been thus far, and the bulk of reserves in the rearward areas were now unable to provide replacements and supplies to the front. With such a crisis impending and having considered various alternatives, Gort concluded that the withdrawal of the BEF from the Continent was the only viable option. The Germans reached the Channel at Boulogne on 22nd May, although it was another three days before all resistance there was subdued during which time 4,368 persons were evacuated.

*Rescue from Dunkirk*

In the following days the military situation continued to deteriorate further, and some units were moved to the north to prevent encirclement. By 22nd May, not only had the counter-attack on Arras ground to a halt, but Boulogne and Calais had ceased to function, leaving a quarter of a million men of the BEF cut off from the necessary 2,000 tons of ammunition and supplies a day essential for ongoing activities, other than through Dunkirk. A day later the water supply to Dunkirk had failed, followed by the fall of Calais on 26th May.

Fortunately on 24th May the German Panzers and motorized divisions that had reached the coast paused to rest and carry out maintenance on the orders of General von Rundstedt confirmed by Hitler. These valuable armoured forces were required for the push further south into France added to which the by then flooded fields behind Dunkirk were hardly ideal country for tanks. This respite enabled the Allied forces to put in place units to defend their Western flank and thereby extend the window during which to evacuate their troops.

A German attack on the Belgian Army's front, however, late in the afternoon of 25th May soon left a gap north of the BEF. As Commander in Chief of the Belgium armed forces, the King of the Belgians had, to the dismay of the British, ordered a surrender at 4.00 am on 28th May. This was subsequently repudiated by the Belgium Prime Minister as an action contrary to the Constitution and considered he was no longer fit to reign. Not all units, however, obeyed and, perhaps as a result of the dropping of leaflets indicating that there was a better chance, some 45,000 continued to fight on with the Allies. The Belgian Military Attaché informed the War Office that a hundred Belgian officers had refused to capitulate and had by 30th May arrived at La Panne seeking to be evacuated to the United Kingdom. The Belgian Mission, in London's, request that an order be given for this was granted on the same basis as the policy laid down for other Allied forces. On 31st May the French struck the King's name off the roll of the Legion of Honour.

Although Anthony Eden, the British War Secretary, had authorized an evacuation of the BEF at 04.10 hours on 26th May, this information does not appear to have been transmitted to the French Government in unambiguous terms, and it was not until three days later that the French 1st Army received orders to follow. Operation Dynamo is believed to have been named after the room within the underground headquarters at Dover, containing electrical plant used in the last war and known as the 'Dynamo Room', reputedly because Prime Minister Winston Churchill and Vice-Admiral Bertram Ramsey could converse there without being overheard.

As well as troops evacuated from Flanders, in the earlier stages a certain number of civilian refugees had managed to find their way across the Channel to England. Unlike troops, who could account for their status, civilians disembarking in United Kingdom might be potential enemy spies or fifth columnists. This necessitated the implementation of a thorough Customs and Immigration examination, after which some were cared for in the Town Hall at Dover. It was, however, soon decided that civilian arrivals should be directed to Folkestone where proper procedures were put in place to ascertain their bona fides.

By 28th May the dock basins of Dunkirk had been rendered unusable by enemy action. Instead some food, water and ammunition were landed on the beaches east

The BEF in 1940 was reasonably well equipped with modern motor transport. The hurried evacuation of huge numbers of troops nonetheless precluded the inclusion of all heavy plant, resulting in the loss of vast amounts of artillery, equipment and supplies which necessarily had to be left behind. Here abandoned military and civilian vehicles are seen on the sea front at Dunkirk. The subsequent lack of these would have severely limited the British Army's ability to repel any invasion of the British Isles until replaced. *Eigenopname van Laarmans/Author's Collection*

of the town, while troops were lifted off in small boats and transferred to larger vessels anchored off shore. Nonetheless, despite the town appearing to be ablaze, it was also found possible to board men from the east pier at the entrance to the docks and this proved to be a much more effective means of embarkation. Whilst rescuing troops from the beaches and harbour moles proved in the extreme circumstances to be the only course feasible, it was clearly impossible to ship back any of the vast quantity of heavy equipment of the BEF. Instead, once units reached the final defensive perimeter, they were ordered to abandon and immobilize their vehicles and destroy their guns, before proceeding to the beaches.

Initially it had been considered that enemy action might have prevented more than 45,000 troops being rescued within the two days it was thought might be available. It was also realised that, if the situation was reached where further effective resistance was impossible consideration might have to be given to the surrender of a large part of the BEF. Fortunately things did not work out that way and evacuation continued, latterly mainly at night from the east mole until most of the British troops had been saved by 3rd June and many French taken to England up to the night of 4th/5th June.

Although not to the extent feared when the operation commenced and despite the numbers actually lifted, many allied troops still failed to make it back across the Channel. As well as those killed, the more seriously wounded and unable to walk were by the later stages of the operation of necessity left behind under the care of a limited number of medical staff to be taken prisoners of war. Likewise many individuals who through no fault of their own had become separated from their units found their way into German hands, together with the units, many of them French, which made up the final rearguard until forced to surrender. Conversely a few hundred German soldiers were captured and some returned to England.

British troops boarding a ship moored beside the East Mole at Dunkirk.

*Courtesy British Red Cross*

# Chapter Five

# Preparations for Dispersing the Troops

*Shipping Troops across the Channel*

As if the Royal Navy did not already have enough on its plate, it was now being asked to consider lifting large numbers of troops off the ever-decreasing enclave centred on the French Channel port of Dunkirk. As well as protecting the merchant ships conveying vital food and supplies to the British Isles, it had since April been involved in combined operations in Norway. In an attempt to cut off the supplies of Swedish iron ore to German industry, shipped out through the Norwegian northern port of Narvik, the British and French had landed troops there on 19th April, subsequent to the Germans invasion of the country in the south on 10th April. Initially the Allied forces met with some success, including the sinking of eight German destroyers which would have adverse implications for them when the time came to consider invading England. But by the end of May the Germans were gaining the upper hand and the decision was taken to evacuate 16,000 Allied troops from Narvik from 2nd June, an operation completed by 8th June.

On Sunday 19th May, once it was concluded that the possibility of evacuation of the BEF might be necessary, the Admiralty was asked for its advice and on the Monday morning a meeting was held with Admiral Ramsey, the Flag Officer Dover, in the dynamo room of his underground headquarters to make arrangements at extremely short notice for the evacuation of allied troops. For this purpose all the ships that could be spared – destroyers, minesweepers, cross-Channel ferries, coasters were quickly gathered. At the time of laying plans for Operation Dynamo, the number of troops to be evacuated and the rate of their arrival on shore were unknown, the whole movement was organized and executed as circumstances dictated.

The ports at which the landing of troops was envisaged were divided into two groups, viz:

> East Kent Group – Ramsgate, Margate, Dover and Folkestone.
> Sussex Group – Hastings, Eastbourne, Newhaven and Brighton.

Ports west of Brighton or in the Thames Estuary would only be used in an emergency. As it turned out, apart from Newhaven and further flung ports, such as Harwich and even Clacton, due to the fall of Boulogne and Calais in the intervening period, all arrived in the East Kent Group.

This meeting was attended by two representatives of the War Office Movement Directorate and it was decided to appoint an officer of the Directorate resident at Dover as soon as possible to act as liaison officer between the Vice-Admiral and the Director of Movements at the War Office,

*Accommodation*

Likewise, the War Office organized a conference on 19th May with representatives of all the Commands to discuss the arrangements that would have to be put in place to accommodate the returning troops. Although at the time events were moving very fast, the scale of the potential disaster staring them in the face now made it necessary to prepare plans for complete withdrawal from northern France. The problem facing the Quartermaster-General's Department was formidable and on a scale without precedent in the history of war. Arrangements had to be made at very short notice to receive, accommodate, clothe and pay an unknown number of the BEF and equally nebulous allied contingent, arriving under conditions of great disorganization.

In making their plans for receiving the returning troops, the following was foreseen:

It would only be possible to evacuate the personnel and all equipment not carried by hand would have to be abandoned.

The organization and formation of units might not be fully preserved and some bodies of men would arrive at random, separated from their officers and non-commissioned officers and without knowledge of the whereabouts of the rest of the unit.

The normal machinery for providing men with quarters, pay, clothing, blankets and above all food would have ceased to exist. No reliance could be placed on cooking equipment or on cooks and no transport of any kind would be available.

The number of men to be dealt with might run to a total of 300,000 and, in order to keep the railway journeys from the ports as short as possible, they should be quartered in the southern half of England.

No delay of any kind should be allowed at the ports, but the men must be put into waiting trains and each must draw out as soon as it was full.

The first thing the public would wish to know were the names of those who were safe and those who were missing.

Although the men would know to which unit they belonged, it could not be taken for granted that they knew which division this was part of, let alone which Corps.

Three phases were envisaged for the dispersal of landed personnel, as follows:

*Phase 1* – Troops were to be moved away from the coastal areas liable to be invaded as and when they arrived and sent directly to Reception Areas without any specific attempt to sort them out, but merely to rest and feed them at host units.

*Phase 2* – Divisional troops were to be reformed in Redistribution Areas into units in new divisional areas, re-equipped and if possible sent on leave, while corps and General Headquarters (GHQ) troops were to be assembled by arms, i.e. Royal Engineers (RE), Royal Artillery (RA), Royal Army Service Corps (RASC) etc, at Reorganization Areas. GHQ was to be reassembled in the London area.

*Phase 3* – Involved recreating the fighting formations of divisions and corps with the necessary non-divisional units, such as lines of communication units, in corps areas.

Locations were therefore selected in southern England, in which troops were already stationed to act as hosts, to receive the required number of 300,000 and where in effect each existing man took in a guest. These host units would be responsible for feeding and the comfort of their guests until the latter moved on to the second phase of the scheme. Each receiving unit was to be prepared to accept up to a maximum of 100 per cent of its own strength.

General instructions were issued verbally at a meeting on 22nd May in which, based on the existing strength in each command, preparations were to be made to receive the following numbers:

**Operation Dynamo - Proposed Accommodation of Evacuated Troops**

| Command | No of troops | Remarks |
|---------|--------------|---------|
| Aldershot | 60,000 | |
| Southern | 150,000 | Plus 3 Divisional & 1 Corps Troops area |
| Northern* | 40,000 | Plus 2 Divisional & 1 Corps Troops area |
| Western | 80,000 | Plus 2 Divisional & 1 Corps Troops area |

* South of a line from Derby to the Wash

In addition, one divisional area was to be prepared in Scotland for the second phase. At the time, it was thought that the French and Belgian troops could be evacuated from Dunkirk direct to French Channel ports further west in French shipping, so provision was only made for 5,000 French in the Wimborne area.

These instructions were formally issued on 28th May in the expectation that the plan might be simplified should fewer numbers arrive. In the event, however, most of these assumptions were borne out, only the inclusion of 100,000 French and Belgian and 18,000 Polish troops had been unforeseen.

## Inland Transportation of Troops

On hearing of the first intimation of impending evacuation, Major General M.G. Holmes, Director of Movements at the War Office, convened a meeting on the afternoon of Tuesday 21st May with senior officers of the Southern Railway. Messrs H.E.O. Wheeler, chief operating superintendent, and Percy Nunn, divisional superintendent of the South East Division, were summoned to a military conference at the Metropole Buildings in London. During this 2½ hour session the probable task for the railways was outlined and the technical arrangements necessary considered. They were warned to make provision for landing up to 300,000 troops at a rate of up to 30,000 a day, mainly at ports on the south coast. They were told that troops might soon be arriving at Margate, Ramsgate, Dover and Folkestone, together with, should the emergency worsen, also at Newhaven, Eastbourne and Brighton, although Dover would be used as the main disembarkation port for as long as possible. No indication could be given as to the time, date, or numbers to be expected, nor until they landed and already started on their journey, their ultimate destinations. Likewise, the start time/date and duration of the operation were equally uncertain. Emphasis was placed on having empty trains waiting, so that once landed the troops could be moved away from the coastal areas as soon as practical, with as few as possible passing through London, to remove them from the risk of attack from the air by strafing or bombing. Finally the purpose of the preparations in withdrawing from Northern France was to be kept as a secret from those who would have to fulfil the operation.

The next day representatives of the four main line railway companies, which as well as the previously mentioned SR men is thought to have included: LNER superintendent, LMS chief operating manager and GWR superintendent of line; G. Cole Deacon - Secretary Railway Executive Committee, R.H. Hill Railway Control Office of the Ministry of Transport, met with the War Office officials. Before proceedings began, the SR's superintendent persuaded the representatives of the military that, to obtain the other railway companies' full cooperation, it would be advisable to bring those present into their confidence. Although no further information was available on the expected arrivals, agreement was reached on the provision of the stock for the trains, the points at which those from the other companies would be handed over to the Southern. From here the SR would haul them to stabling points somewhere reasonably accessible to the expected points of disembarkation and from where they could easily be worked forward.

The only information available to the railways at the time upon which to base the plan was as follows:

a)    Troops would probably arrive disorganized and not in units or formations.
b)    Probable numbers to be conveyed by rail might amount to 300,000, with a possible maximum load in any one day of up to 30,000.
c)    Disembarkation might take place anywhere between Margate and Brighton although Dover would be used as the main port of disembarkation as long as possible.
d)    General arrangements for disembarkation would be under the control of Vice-Admiral, Dover.
e)    It was essential that trains should leave ports of disembarkation as soon as possible.
f)    It was impossible to specify destinations, but trains would be sent to a large number of points in the Southern half of England to conform with accommodation requirements.

It was agreed that a possible way of meeting this rather indeterminate problem was by a flexible plan on the following general lines:

a)    The rapid collection of coaching stock from all the railway companies and the formation of as many trains as possible of more or less standard composition.
b)    The selection of suitable regulating stations at which a reserve of empty trains should be held to be called forward to any of the possible disembarkation points as required.
c)    The selection of one or more regulating stations (Ashford and Redhill were suggested) to which all loaded trains should be directed in the first instance and at which they would receive subsequent route and destination instructions.
d)    The provision of 'halte-repas' en route at which trains would stop briefly to enable refreshments to be provided for the troops.

As well as the officer from the Directorate of Supplies & Transport lent for movement control to the Vice-Admiral's staff, one was also sent to Redhill. A Movement Control Office was set up in the Lord Warden Hotel, close by Dover Marine station on Admiralty Pier. Radio, or wireless as it was referred to in those days, signal communications was inaugurated by Lt Col Crump between Port V Dover, and the railway control office at Redhill, transmitting in cipher.

In anticipation of possible damage through enemy air action to the railways in the South-East of England vitally concerned in this plan, comprehensive arrangements were made to assist the Southern Railway in the repair and maintenance of these lines. Headquarters No. 4 Railway Construction & Maintenance Group (RCE4) together with 160 and 162 Railway Construction Companies, stationed at No. 1 RTC, Longmoor were allotted and equipped with a special scale of motor transport and tools. On 27th May, Group Headquarters moved to Dorking; Headquarters and two sections of 160 RC Coy to Redhill and two sections to Ashford, while 162 RC Coy remained in reserve at Longmoor. Detailed arrangements were made by RCE4 with George Ellson, the Chief Engineer of the Southern Railway for the organization and employment of these units. In the event no air attacks, however, were made on the railway, and their services were not actually required.

On Thursday 23rd May a further meeting of all the railway representatives was held to work out the details regarding the provision of rolling stock and as far as possible routes. Immediate arrangements for the provision of coaching stock and locomotive power were made with the other railway companies, as a consequence of which a common pool of 186 trains was created. The intention was that each train was to consist of 10 coaches so that they could be easily hauled by any suitable locomotive available, although it appears some were augmented to as many as 12 vehicles. Trains were to be made up to carry 500 personnel, and be of the corridor type where possible, were drawn from all four railway companies, amounting to nearly 2,000 vehicles, and these were distributed to locations close to the anticipated landing places. For their part, the SR earmarked 186 engines and crew. The GWR's contribution was handed over to the SR at Andover Junction and Salisbury; the LMS trains arrived via Kensington, Addison Road and the LNER's travelled by Banbury and Reading. Due to incompatibility of corridor connections and couplings on the rolling stock of different companies, trains are likely to have been kept in the sets as provided. Modern SR and LNER coaches were fitted with retractable side buffers and the more impact resistant automatic couplings with associated Pullman gangway connections, while those of the GWR and LMS relied on the older side buffers, screw couplings and British Standard corridor connections. Whilst the former arrangement was capable of being adapted to couple up to the latter, this was a time consuming process best avoided in the circumstances.

**Operation Dynamo - Special Trains Provided**

| Company | No. of special trains sets provided | No. of special trains operated |
|---------|------------------------------------|-------------------------------|
| GWR | 40 | 293 |
| LMS | 44 | unknown |
| LNER | 47 | 95 |
| SR | 55 | 620 |
| *Total* | *186* | |

Despite the extensive siding accommodation at Ashford and the fact that many of these were cleared of other traffic, it was not easy to find sufficient standing space close by to accommodate the waiting trains. It therefore became necessary to close the down line between Hothfield and Ashford (Kent) on the line from Maidstone (East) and this was used for the storage of the close-marshalled trains, while the up line was temporarily worked as a single line. From here, the trains could be drawn forward through Ashford and sent to Ramsgate and Margate via Canterbury (West); Folkestone and Dover via the main line; or Newhaven, Eastbourne and Brighton via the line through Rye and Hastings.

The divisional superintendent (Eastern) at Orpington set up temporary sub-control offices at Dover Marine; Tonbridge; Ashford; Faversham; Chatham; and Dartford, with traffic inspectors at Dover Marine and Priory; Folkestone Harbour and Central; Ramsgate; Margate; Ashford; Headcorn; Paddock Wood; and Faversham stations. On the Central Division temporary sub-controls were inaugurated at Haywards Heath; Chichester; and Shalford. Two liaison officers of the Divisional Office Movements Section, on alternative shifts, provided 24 hour contact with the military authorities at Dover Marine. On the SR, War Office representatives were stationed at their headquarters at Deepdene (Military Liaison Staff-Transportation); Dover (Military Liaison Officer); Redhill; Faversham; and Salisbury to dictate onward movements.

The uncertainty and random nature of the trains to be anticipated meant that in this case there was no time to prepare and issue the usual stencilled special traffic notices. Instead all the necessary arrangements were made by railway officials over the telephone. As well as advising the approximate timings and interim or final destination of the actual trains carrying troops, suitable engines and empty trains had to be located, engine crew and guard allocated and relieved as necessary.

It was foreseen that Redhill might become congested and plans were prepared to clear entirely the line from there to Reading of all non-military traffic and provide an alternative service for passengers by bus. Likewise to clear the old Brighton line through Redhill, a bus service was laid on between Earlswood to Coulsdon, where through traffic could use the Quarry line avoiding Redhill.

To avoid London, troop trains from Ramsgate and Margate were to be routed via Reading; those from Hastings, Eastbourne, Newhaven, Brighton or Southampton were to go to Salisbury via Chichester; and those from Dover and Folkestone via Redhill for distribution to Aldershot, Salisbury or Reading, from where trains were sometimes to be re-directed on to stations, such as Tidworth, Dorchester, Blandford, Oxford and Tetbury, nearby to other camps. Units were to be kept together where possible. Any stragglers finding their way to London by public transport were to be dispatched to Aldershot. Temporary reception centres were set up at Olympia and Crystal Palace, from where troops were to be sent on to Aldershot.

A dress rehearsal could be said to have taken place between 14th and 19th May with the running of 38 special trains conveying 14,564 Dutch, Belgian and French refugees, who had managed to escape Hitler's clutches.

SR 2-6-0 'U1' class No. 1907 moves empty coaching stock at Ramsgate station in the late 1930s. On the left is the new engine shed with a Cowans Sheldon 15 ton steam crane and the breakdown train stabled alongside. In the middle is the new carriage shed and station to the right.          *A.W.V. Mace, courtesy Mile Post 92½ Picture Library*

Lt Col Simpson and Major Bain met with Mr Dalmahoy and another from the Ministry of Transport during the afternoon of 24th May, 1940 to discuss the provision of 200 motor coaches with civilian drivers to be available at 12 hours notice. These coaches were to report at specific rendezvous in Kent as agreed by Eastern Command, for the purpose of augmenting the rail services and to assist in disembarkation of troops. The officer commanding No. 3 MTSD, RASC, then at Staines mobilized for postings overseas, was instructed to prepare a scheme for operating these coaches. His officers and non-commissioned officers (NCOs) were to control any movements and provide conductors for each vehicle, as well as providing general administration for the personnel and civilian drivers. It was proposed that 100 coaches be assembled in the district of Maidstone as a strategic reserve in the event of destruction of train services, plus another 50 each at Canterbury and Tunbridge Wells for use at the disembarkation points respectively in the East Kent and Sussex groups. The instructions given to all depots of the East Kent were simple - send all the vehicles you can: first coaches, then single-deck buses and lastly double-decks.

No. 4 Ambulance Car Coy, RASC was made available, from which, at the selection of the medical authorities, five motor ambulances were allocated to each of eight disembarkations points, two at each of the two initial 'halte repas' and a strategic reserve held.

On 26th May at the request of Movements Branch special arrangements were made for the provision of motor lorries at Shorncliffe/Dover and the maintenance of 18 lorries daily at Dover until further notice. By 5th June, when the evacuation plan was completed, the hired coaches were released and all special transport arrangements effected were reverted to normal service.

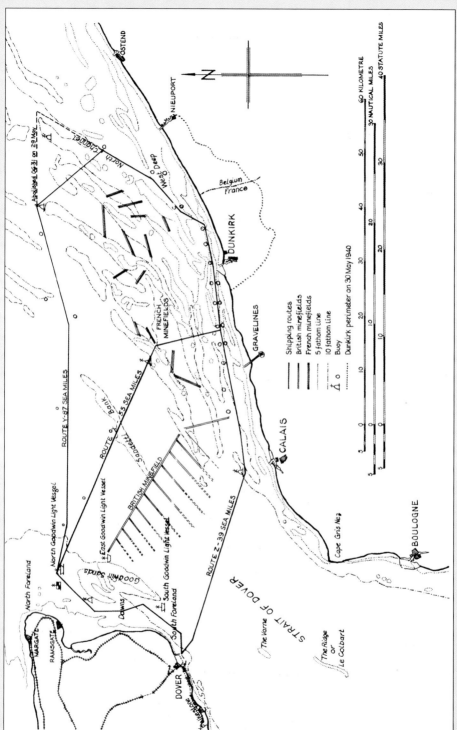

*Figure 4:* The Channel crossing showing the shoals and minefields in the Strait of Dover between the French/Belgian coast and the south-east corner of England. *Author*

# Chapter Six

# Landing and Transporting Troops from the Area

Operation Dynamo had been initiated by a signal from the Admiralty at 6.57 am on Sunday 26th May, 1940 and completed by another signal sent on 4th June which read: Operation Dynamo now completed. This of course may have been so for the naval forces and other vessels engaged in bringing back our forces from Flanders, but it still left an enormous task in sorting out those it had so gallantly returned. These had to be rested, reformed, allowed a brief leave, re-equipped and prepared for battle again against the Nazis, now threatening to launch a marine assault on England somewhere along the east or south coasts.

*Channel Crossing*

Whilst they may not have realised it, the troops' troubles were not quite over once they had slipped out of Dunkirk harbour or sailed away from the beaches. Although only 20-odd miles wide at its narrowest, the English Channel is not a deep water channel for its full width, far from it, and the problems were for the ship's navigators interrupted from time to time by German air attack. Many will be aware of the Goodwin Sands off the coast of Kent between the North and South Forelands, but there are far more extensive shoals lying off the French and Belgian coast stretching from Calais to beyond Ostend. At the best of times the approach to Dunkirk is tricky, running parallel to the French/Belgian coast from either east or west. Furthermore, between 11th September, 1939 and the end of October the Royal Navy, together with their French counterparts, had laid elaborate minefields to bar the main shipping channels to the German and anyone else's vessels, the British maintaining one free channel between the coast and the Goodwin Sands under the British guns.

Before the commencement of the Operation proper, the most obvious and shortest route from Dunkirk to Dover had been past Gravelines and Calais, by the No. 6 Calais bell buoy, to Dover or Folkestone, known as Route Z. By 26th May, when Calais had been captured, this was barred to shipping, however, at least during the hours of daylight, by the activity of German artillery sited on the coast. To reduce the length exposed to gun fire, Route X between the Sandettie Banks and Light FG joining the Z Route between Gravelines and Dunkirk seems to have been available, but perhaps only to shallow draught ships at favourable states of the tide. Otherwise, it was then necessary to take a longer route, Route Y eastwards from Dunkirk, via the narrow Zuydecoote Pass and Middelkerke Bank and thus continue to the north-east round the Goodwin Sands, before heading south for Margate, Ramsgate and Dover, but this too could only be used at night once German guns were located near Nieuport from 28th May onwards. With the sweeping of some mines, a shortening of Route Y was made available from 06.31 on 29th May. This was free of gunfire until the afternoon of 1st June when the Germans brought the final length and the entrance to Dunkirk itself under fire, causing daylight operations to be

As German bombs fall on the port of Dunkirk, the Isle of Man SS *Tynwald* slips out with evacuated troops aboard past the mast and funnel of a sunken vessel in the approach seaway, as the port facilities at Dunkirk, particularly the oil tanks burned in the background.

*Author's Collection*

Destroyers *Icarus*, *Venomous*, *Whitehall* (D94), *Ivanhoe* and *Anthony* lying alongside Admiralty Pier, Dover on 31st May, 1940. As well as the troops crowded on the deck, of what is believed to be HMS *Iracus*, note climbing nets hung from the ship's side and the absence of a boat between the davits.

*Author's Collection*

suspended. All these limitations tended to affect the English ports used by the evacuating shipping and to some extent is the cause of so many troops being landed on the North Kent coast. The use of Harwich on the other hand probably stems from the fact that it was the base for the 2nd and 5th flotillas of destroyers.

Likewise, there was little point in continuing to Folkestone unless Dover Harbour was already full. In any case the working of heavy trains out of Folkestone Harbour station up the 1 in 30 incline was an operating and time consuming nightmare requiring three small banking tank engines before the main line engine could be attached. Margate pier was ill-equipped to cope with vessels of any size or a large influx of troops. Ramsgate harbour is tidal, while the basin was only capable of receiving small pleasure type boats. It and Margate required buses to convey them to the stations, while the Dreamland Park was used as a depot at which to fit fresh clothing to the worst clad men.

A few men also appear to have been landed at Newhaven and Southampton. As it turned out, the landing points of Eastbourne and Brighton were never used, perhaps it was just as well, as the latter two were hardly equipped to land the large number of men that were actually rescued.

By the time of the Operation, it was too late to evacuate non-combatant French, Belgian or Jewish refugees, but it would appear that not a few soldiers took compassion on abandoned French dogs and brought them back with them to England. At least 170 came over, necessitating a special lorry to remove them from the quayside at Dover. Unfortunately, as most men would have been unable to afford the kennel fees during the quarantine period for rabies, they were necessarily put down. It is further reported that one soldier brought back his French wife disguised in battle dress.

### Disembarkation

The control of movement at sea rested with the Vice-Admiral at Dover. A military liaison officer was, therefore, posted to his headquarters with the purpose of notifying the Southern Railway control at Dover and the local movement control (landing control) at the disembarkation points of the incoming ships, thus enabling them to prepare for their reception and onward movement.

The landing stages at Dover consisted of the following:

Admiralty Pier, suitable for large vessels and at which 60% of troops landed, within 200
   yards of hospital and other trains
Prince of Wales Pier, capable of having trawlers and drifters alongside
West Jetty, suitable for destroyers
HMS *Sandhurst*, a destroyer depot ship could have destroyers lying alongside
Eastern Arm, capable of accepting large vessels
Granville Dock Steps, suitable for motor boats and small yachts only
When Dover was already crowded, ships would be redirected to Folkestone

Although the troops were harassed by dive bombing and strafing by the German Air Force while on the beaches, in the port of Dunkirk, or during the voyage back across the Channel, fortunately such aerial attacks were not

The Rediffusion Office in Ramsgate. The cables to subscribers' premises were strung from house to house in quite a primitive way and sometimes crossed over people's roofs lying on top of the slates.

*Ralph Hoult's Old Ramsgate Collection*

pressed home on the English side of the Channel. The time taken to disembark troops off ships and dispatching the trains varied between eight and 20 minutes. A high proportion of troops returned with their rifle or other personal weapon. Early on during the operation, incoming vessels arrived at any time of day, but as the damage caused by enemy action increased, it became necessary to make the crossings during the hours of darkness, which tended to concentrate the requirements for special trains. As well as the movement of special troop trains, coal and oil were required to fuel the ships and special trains had to be slotted in for this purpose.

Back in Dover, the ships crowded the docks, three deep as they unloaded the troops. Both soldiers and sailors were given a heroes' welcome. WRNS Daphne Baker, working as a cipher officer at Dover, recalls that if she and her colleagues had any time off watch during the day, they used to go to the quayside to meet the troops coming off the boats and send off letters and messages to their families for them. She had expected them to be overjoyed to be home, but most walked like automatons, too tired for any emotion. These men did not know then that what looked like defeat would pass into the language as a refusal to be defeated.

Whilst destroyers tended to head for Dover and cross-Channel packets for Folkestone, Ramsgate was used to disembark troops from small vessels, any larger ones being sent on to Margate, or anchored in the Downs from where the troops were ferried ashore. Here, as no doubt elsewhere, the troops arrived miserable and dejected, but were soon made welcome as heroes. Once ashore all were relieved of their personal weapons. Having waded out to small boats off the beaches, some arrived in a virtual state of undress, even walking barefoot down the road. By 1940 Ramsgate had an early cable system (run by Rediffusion) through which residents could receive wireless channels. This enabled the Mayor of Ramsgate, A.B.C. Kempe, to make an appeal for food and clothing, etc., directly into people's radios from the local relay station.

Similar appeals were made in Margate for blankets, which, being a seaside town with many boarding houses, the inhabitants were well able to provide, never realising that unfortunately they were unlikely to be seen again. Thereafter, the men were taken by bus to the railway station.

At Ramsgate some tired troops had to clamber ashore over other moored boats to avoid getting their feet wet. The WVS was on hand at the Royal Victoria Pavilion in Ramsgate which was used for the distribution of food, such as tea and rock cakes, and clothing; and coaches conveyed the troops to the station. Many of the troops who disembarked at Ramsgate were taken by train towards London with people cheering them on the way, feeling that they did not deserve this and that if anyone did it was the Navy for getting them out.

At Sheerness the soldiers were brought from the Docks by bus to the railway station, where the occasional woman was lucky enough to be able to pick out her husband. It is reported that as a special concession the wife of a wounded soldier was permitted to spend a few moments with him, before he was taken by train to London.

The number of troops landed at the various ports is given in the Table on page 70. The maximum during any one 24 hour period was at Dover on 31st May when 36,837 troops were received.

Those soldiers who had suffered the indignity of spending a spell in the sea often received the strangest of garb in their change into dry clothes. Here a pair walk along the quay on 31st May, 1940 clad in amongst other things, an oil skin, a blanket and trousers a size or two too small and sea boots.
*Courtesy British Red Cross*

French troops standing on the platform at Margate before boarding a train made up of LNER corridor stock.                                                          *Author's Collection*

Less welcome was the small number of German prisoners of war captured in France or Belgium and returned across the Channel to spend the rest of the conflict in prison camp. They are seen here under an escort of Royal Military Police, having landed at Dover.          *Courtesy British Red Cross*

## Operation Dynamo - Vessel Arrivals/Troop Landings

| Location | | May 20th-26th | May 27th | May 28th | May 29th | May 30th | May 31st | June 1st | June 2nd | June 3rd | June 4th-5th | Totals 27/5-5/6 | Totals 20/5-5/6 |
|---|---|---|---|---|---|---|---|---|---|---|---|---|---|
| Dover | Vessels | | 8 | 34 | 49 | 83 | 77 | 52 | 42 | 58 | 55 | 458 | |
| | Troops | 22,236 | 6,081 | 13,303 | 24,905 | 31,752 | 36,837 | 25,572 | 13,235 | 11,867 | 14,228 | 177,780 | 200,016 |
| Ramsgate | Vessels | | | 2 | 11 | 22 | 41 | 105 | 56 | 53 | 44 | 334 | |
| | Troops | | | 555 | 2,729 | 6,679 | 6,605 | 10,539 | 5,718 | 3,519 | 3,504 | 39,848 | |
| Margate | Vessels | | | 2 | 13 | 15 | 20 | 26 | 5 | 4 | 10 | 95 | |
| | Troops | | | 482 | 7,041 | 8,170 | 8,040 | 13,867 | 2,525 | 3,758 | 3,889 | 47,772 | |
| Folkestone | Vessels | | | 1 | 4 | 3 | 10 | 11 | | 10 | 7 | 46 | |
| | Troops | 303 | | 494 | 5,127 | 1,367 | 6,313 | 7,067 | | 4,666 | 4,231 | 29,265 | 29,568 |
| Sheerness | Vessels | | | 1 | 2 | | 2 | 9 | 3 | 4 | 1 | 22 | |
| | Troops | | | 656 | 1,212 | | 2,081 | 2,391 | 566 | 1,089 | 470 | 8,465 | |
| Newhaven | Vessels | | 2 | | 3 | 1 | 4 | 1 | | | | 11 | |
| | Troops | 3,276 | 646 | | 789 | 490 | 867 | 122 | | | | 2,914 | 6,190 |
| Southampton | Troops | 2,121 | | | | | | | | | | | 2,121 |
| Harwich | Vessels | | | | | 1 | 3 | | 3 | | | 7 | |
| | Troops | | | | | 567 | 1,910 | | 1,191 | | | 3,668 | |
| Clacton | Vessels | | | | | | | | | | 1 | 1 | |
| | Troops | | | | | | | | | | 27 | 27 | |
| Totals | Vessels | | 10 | 40 | 82 | 125 | 157 | 204 | 109 | 129 | 118 | 974 | |
| | Troops | 27,936 | 6,727 | 15,490 | 41,803 | 49,025 | 62,653 | 59,558 | 23,235 | 24,899 | 26,349 | 309,739 | 337,675 |

## Onward Transportation

The general direction of the emergency plan (Operation Dynamo) to evacuate across the Channel a very large number of troops rested with Movement Control at the War Office. As well as the existing Movement Control points, the additional temporary Landing Controls and Distribution Controls were established by 27th May, all of which are listed below:

**Operation Dynamo - Movement Control Points**

| Type of control | Group | Location | Manned by | PO telephone No. |
|---|---|---|---|---|
| Existing | E. Kent | Dover | | |
| | E. Kent | Folkestone | | |
| | Sussex | Newhaven | | Newhaven 241 |
| | | Southampton | | |
| Temporary Landing | E. Kent | Liaison with Vice-Admiral at Dover | Capt Wright Major Walter | Dover Military East 134 |
| | E. Kent | Ramsgate | Capt Burnett-Hitchcock | Ramsgate 81 |
| | E. Kent | Margate | Capt Evans | Margate 2644 |
| | Sussex | Hastings (2 piers) | Capt Cassells | Hastings 1920 |
| | Sussex | Eastbourne | Capt Hill | Eastbourne 3460 ex. 2 |
| | Sussex | Brighton (Palace Pier) | Capt Baillie, Major Peto | Brighton 6211 ex. 105 |
| Distribution | | Redhill (Control) | Major Neck Major Payne | Redhill 3361 |
| | | Redhill (RTO) | Capt Ridout | Redhill 695 |
| | | Salisbury | | Salisbury 2201 ex. 11 |
| | | Reading | | Reading 60351 |

Banbury could be established at 12 hours notice. A RTO was at Kensington.

Movement Control at Dover was not responsible for disembarkation other than at Dover, whilst other Landing Controls were to communicate direct with the Liaison Officer at Dover and Redhill Control. It was not initially envisaged that points west of Brighton or in the Thames, let alone Harwich would be used other than in an emergency. Landing Controls were instructed to count the numbers disembarked, noting the units and casualties, but without delaying entrainment on this account. As a result the figures returned were in many cases only an estimate. The Landing Control officers were also required to report the departure time, approximate numbers and any useful information to Redhill control by railway telephone. To assist in reporting each train was conspicuously marked by the railway authorities with a code letter for the point of departure and a sequential number, i.e. R3 for the third departure from Ramsgate, see page 74.

Royal Engineer officers Major T.V. Nicholson and J.L. Cambell, one of whom had himself only returned from Calais on 24th May, were directed by Lt Col C.S. Napier of the Q(M) 4 Branch of the Movement Directorate to drive to Dover. There they spent a couple of nights based on the Lord Warden Hotel, which had been requisitioned as a mess. At the Marine station the former liaised with the

Southern Railway, while the other was in contact with Army personnel, to see what could be done to speed up the dispatch of trains. After viewing the feeding arrangements at Headcorn and Paddock Wood, they reported back to London.

Nicholson was then sent to Salisbury to join Southern Command's Movement team to assist in routeing trains once they had passed Tonbridge. For the next fortnight three officers worked in three shifts of 16 hours on duty and eight off to cover the 24 hour day so as to provide two on duty during the day and one overnight. Their duties were to establish, if possible, who the bulk of the troops on a given train were, which reception camp could accommodate the troops and thereby decide on the destination of each train. They then endeavoured to make their requirements known to the railway and local military authorities by means of an archaic overloaded telephone system before the train concerned reached Guildford. Difficulties could arise in making such arrangements especially in trying to make contact with camp adjutants late at night, if a succession of camps were already full, by when the train might have reached Reading, or be held up awaiting instructions.

24 Despatch Rider Section was moved to Dover from where 15 motorcyclists were allotted to Redhill and 10 to Movement Control at Dover. A direct telephone line was installed between the liaison officer with the Vice-Admiral in the underground headquarters within East Cliff below Dover Castle and the Southern Railway Control at Dover. A wireless link was also provided between Movement Control at Dover and Redhill, but not to Ashford or Faversham for the control of empty stock, as had originally been envisaged. The wireless was for emergency use only due to the risk of interception by the enemy.

Many sidings on the routes had been cleared to make way for the special trains of requisitioned carriages held in readiness at such places as: Faversham, Margate, Queenborough and Ramsgate and on the down line from Hothfield to Ashford (West), while single line working was instituted on the up line.

Emergency accommodation for the evacuated troops was to be achieved by doubling the existing barracks or billets as follows:

**Operation Dynamo - Reception Areas for British Troops**

| Reception Area | Capacity | Final destination notified by | To distribution Control at |
|---|---|---|---|
| Aldershot Command | 60,000 | MC Aldershot | Redhill |
| Southern Command: | | | |
| Tidworth | 30,000 | MC Salisbury | Salisbury |
| Warminster | 15,000 | MC Salisbury | Salisbury |
| Dorchester | 15,000 | MC Salisbury | Salisbury |
| Blandford & Bovington | 30,000 | MC Salisbury | Salisbury |
| Devon & Cornwall | 30,000 | MC Salisbury | Salisbury |
| Isle of Wight | 1,500 | | |
| | | | |
| Swindon | 5,000 | Special MC at Reading | Reading |
| Oxford (61st Division) | 10,000 | Special MC at Reading | Reading |
| Tetbury (C Area) | 5,000 | Special MC at Reading | Reading |
| Cheltenham | 5,000 | Special MC at Reading | Reading |
| South Wales | 30,000 | Special MC at Reading | Reading |

| Northern Command | 40,000 | Special MC at Banbury | Banbury |
| Western Command (except S. Wales) | 50,000 | | |

Northern Command was restricted to a line south of Huddersfield to Hull.

General instructions as to the destination areas were given by the War Office to Redhill Control, who routed trains to subsidiary distribution controls farther down the line. In the absence of other instructions, all trains were to be routed via Redhill. Although the eventual destination often seems to have been known, Redhill Control did not need to decide the particular station to which any train was to go, but only the subsidiary control point, such as Aldershot, Salisbury or Reading, who in turn would determine its final detraining station. So far as possible personnel were to be transported by rail at once to the reception areas so as to clear the ports and Eastern Command, but reserves of road transport were held available. To this end 10 coaches each were allotted to the Landing Controls, while 10 spare coaches were held at both Canterbury and Maidstone, with a further reserve of 50 coaches at Canterbury and Tunbridge Wells all under the control of Redhill.

To simplify control and avoid congestion at Redhill, the following instructions were issued:

### Operation Dynamo - Routeing of Trains

| *Departure point of trains* | *Routed to* |
| Ramsgate and Margate | Reading (via Kensington, where there was a RTO) |
| Hastings, Eastbourne, Newhaven, Brighton or Southampton | Salisbury via Chichester |
| Dover and Folkestone | Redhill for distribution to Aldershot, Salisbury or Reading |

The dispatching of trains from the ports and their arrival at Aldershot, Salisbury or Reading was to be reported to Redhill Control quoting the code number of the train, but, to avoid duplication and unnecessary occupation of the telecommunication system, it was recognised that only one channel of communication, either railway or military, would suffice.

To minimize subsequent resorting of men, attempts were made to keep fighting units together as time and the condition of the men permitted. Likewise non-divisional soldiers such as members of the Royal Engineers; Royal Artillery; Royal Army Service Corps; Royal Army Ordnance Corps (RAOC); etc were grouped together as far as possible. Landing Controls aimed to fill the trains with loads of 500 men, but were permitted to exercise discretion in dispatching trains with less than a full load, when no other ships were expected in the short term. The Landing Controls were also to appoint an officer in command (OC) of each train and were to explain to him the general arrangements made.

Considerable responsibility rested on those at Redhill Control to issue whatever instructions experience suggested were necessary to maintain the flow of trains, although matters of policy and general organization were required to be referred to Movement Control at the War Office. It was recognized that the successful execution of the movement of such a large number of troops depended mainly on the initiative and tact of local landing controls. These were expected to liaise closely not only with the station masters, but also with local officers commanding troops. They were entitled to expect assistance from them in regard to administration, guides and to make contact with local welfare organizations, etc. It was recognized that many men would arrive in a state of complete exhaustion and every effort should be made to restore morale by kindness and firmness. The assistance of the Police was to be sought to prevent crowds of the general public assembling.

### Operation of the Trains

The evacuation of some RAF and lines of communication personnel had begun about 20th May, 1940 and numbers gradually increased daily, prior to the drawing up of plans for Operation Dynamo, until they amounted to 24,108 officers and men in 55 trains. Among these a number of French troops were re-embarked immediately at south coast ports and returned to France south of the River Somme.

At 5.00 pm on 26th May, the railways were sent the code word Operation Dynamo and this commenced at dawn on 27th May, 1940. To identify them, each train was allocated a unique reporting number, i.e.: prefixed by the date of departure, e.g. 1 or 2 etc, followed by a letter indicating the point of commencement, viz: Dover – V; Folkestone – W; Margate – M; Ramsgate – R; and Sheerness – S and completed by a sequential number of the train from its departure point. Most trains left in the order of the numbers allocated, but in just a few cases at Dover a small delay in departure may have allowed another to leave in advance of it. Furthermore, some trains were overtaken en route, almost certainly due to their being halted in a loop at a station to enable the troops to be fed, while another train passed. All trains were controlled by telephone as it was not possible, in view of the circumstances, to prepare and issue a printed schedule of timings. In this way, between 7.00 am on 27th May and 4.00 pm on 4th June, the Southern Railway at the time reckoned 319,116 troops were conveyed from ports of disembarkation in 620 trains, conveying on average 546 men each, to the reception areas in all parts of the country.

**Departure Points of Special Trains – Operation Dynamo**

| Departure Point | No. of Troop Trains Dispatched | | | | | | | | | |
|---|---|---|---|---|---|---|---|---|---|---|
| | May 27th | May 28th | May 29th | May 30th | May 31st | June 1st | June 2nd | June 3rd | June 4th | Total |
| Dover | 7 | 26 | 44 | 53 | 65 | 53 | 26 | 25 | 27 | 326 |
| Ramsgate | | 2 | 6 | 16 | 9 | 21 | 12 | 8 | 8 | 82 |
| Margate | | 1 | 12 | 12 | 16 | 17 | 6 | 6 | 5 | 75 |
| Folkestone | | 1 | 10 | 6 | 12 | 16 | | 10 | 9 | 64 |
| Sheerness | | 2 | 2 | | 4 | 5 | 1 | 2 | 1 | 17 |
| Newhaven | | | 1 | | 1 | | | | | 2 |
| Harwich | | | | 1 | 4 | | 2 | | | 7 |
| Totals | 7 | 32 | 75 | 88 | 111 | 112 | 47 | 52 | 50 | 573 |

*Note:* Others landed at Southampton and Weymouth, necessitating 12 and 19 trains respectively.

In due course, when the time came to settle up, the SR submitted an account for £208,000 for its share of the operation.

Despite the intention to route the trains clear of London due to the risk of bombing, a little under a fifth seem to have passed through the fringes of the metropolis. Troops landed at Ramsgate, Margate, Sheerness and other north Kent ports were the more obvious to be sent via the Chatham and the West London lines, but not all. Locomotives on this route leaving the Eastern Section for the Western Section and the West London Extension were sometimes changed at Wandsworth Road, this being handy for Stewarts Lane shed. A few troops were landed at Parkeston Quay, Harwich and their trains were probably sent direct to the Midlands, via Ipswich and Cambridge, or Ely and March etc.

Train movements around Dover Marine station were complicated by the fact that the layout rather precluded reversing empty stock into the station platforms. As a consequence each had to be drawn in by an engine, an additional engine backed on the other end of the train and coupled up before departure. Once the train had departed, the first engine had to be released and sent to the locomotive depot for turning and servicing. Access to the station by ambulances to remove the critically injured from Admiralty Pier involved the use of a level crossing at the landward end of the station which in turn interfered with the unrestricted operation of trains at this critical time.

Unless specifically arranged, all trains from Dover initially set off westwards through Folkestone, at which point a few from the Harbour branch there added to the throng. These continued to Ashford, where they were joined by a small proportion of those from Margate and Ramsgate; and on to Tonbridge and the regulating point at Redhill, where their final onward movement was decided. This was usually on westwards to Guildford from where they could be taken to the Aldershot area, on to Reading, or up the Portsmouth Direct line the short distance to Woking, where they would be reversed yet again for some further destination down the West of England main line.

Redhill station lies on the original line from London to Brighton and is the junction for lines both east to Tonbridge, Ashford and Dover etc., and west to Guildford, Woking or Aldershot and Reading etc. To accommodate traffic, there were platform loops off the up and down through lines, and a further loop on the up side served by an island platform, as shown in *Figure 6* (page 80) By the end of the 19th century, however, the fast through traffic for Brighton and the South coast was able to use the Quarry line from Coulsdon North and Earlswood that bypassed Redhill. Initially during the earlier stages of the evacuation ordinary traffic from Tonbridge to Redhill, Guildford and Reading was merely disrupted, but with the heavy movement anticipated from Sunday 26th May the lines through Redhill were closed to ordinary traffic on the London to Brighton route with all fast and local trains diverted via the Quarry line. The Reigate portions of the Brighton slow electric trains were cancelled and all those otherwise due to stop at Redhill called instead at Earlswood. Passengers for Coulsdon South, Merstham, Redhill and Reigate were bussed to or from Coulsdon North and Earlswood. From 29th May to 4th June, however, the entire service from Tonbridge to Redhill, Guildford and Reading was suspended for the duration of the Operation. The only trains operating into Reading (SR) were the electric-multiple units to Waterloo, via Staines

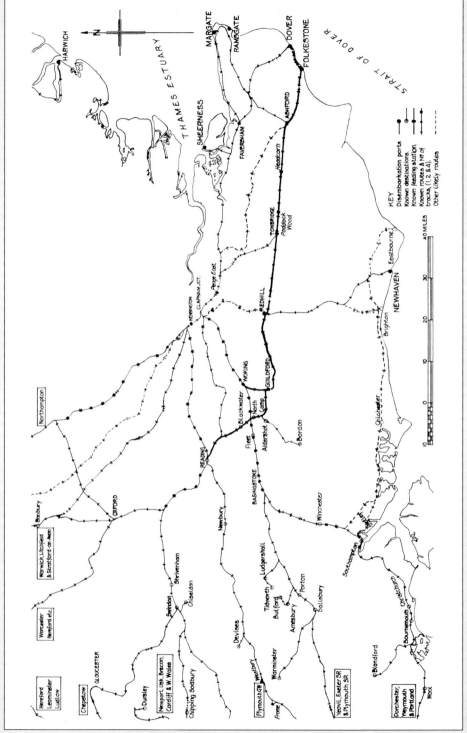

*Figure 5:* Railways of Southern England and some destinations of troop trains.

Author

## Operation Dynamo - Daily Dispatch of Troops by Train

| Period | Port | Personnel British | | Allies | | Totals |
|---|---|---|---|---|---|---|
| | | Fit | Casualties | Fit | Casualties | |
| 27th May | Dover | 3,324 | 300 | 4 | | |
| | Newhaven | | 950 | | | 4,578 |
| 28th May | Dover | 12,360 | 505 | 57 | | |
| | Folkestone | 493 | | | | |
| | Ramsgate | 827 | | | | |
| | Margate | 280 | | | | |
| | Sheerness | 581 | | | | 15,103 |
| 29th May | Dover | 21,897 | 791 | 748 | | |
| | Folkestone | 5,393 | | | | |
| | Ramsgate | 2,508 | | 5 | | |
| | Margate | 6,429 | | | | |
| | Sheerness | 903 | | | | |
| | Newhaven | 326 | 716 | | | 39,716 |
| 30th May | Dover | 24,858 | 527 | 4,319 | | |
| | Folkestone | 667 | | 1,130 | | |
| | Ramsgate | 5,278 | | 2,608 | | |
| | Margate | 5,785 | | | | |
| | Newhaven | 49 | 449 | | | |
| | Harwich | 549 | | 4 | | 46,223 |
| 31st May | Dover | 27,979 | 592 | 8,093 | | |
| | Folkestone | 2,842 | | 2,923 | | |
| | Ramsgate | 5,130 | | 13 | | |
| | Margate | 6,125 | | 1,132 | | |
| | Sheerness | 1,821 | | 82 | | |
| | Newhaven | | 775 | | | |
| | Harwich | 1,896 | 23 | 6 | | 59,432 |
| 1st June | Dover | 15,593 | 1,911 | 15,447 | 795 | |
| | Folkestone | 1,994 | | 4,963 | | |
| | Ramsgate | 5,475 | | 5,730 | | |
| | Margate | 6,001 | | 2,744 | | |
| | Sheerness | 1,694 | | 594 | | |
| | Newhaven | | 111 | | | 63,052 |
| 2nd June | Dover | 8,933 | 122 | 6,896 | | |
| | Ramsgate | 2,793 | | 3,478 | | |
| | Margate | 1,288 | | 1,535 | | |
| | Sheerness | 16 | | 403 | | |
| | Newhaven | 106 | | 41 | | |
| | Harwich | 1,102 | | 88 | | 26,801 |
| 3rd June | Dover | 4,494 | 289 | 9,711 | 101 | |
| | Folkestone | 2,046 | | 2,578 | | |
| | Ramsgate | | | 3,683 | | |
| | Margate | | | 3,166 | 334 | |
| | Sheerness | 15 | | 960 | | 27,377 |
| 4th June | Dover | 2 | | 15,172 | | |
| | Folkestone | | | 4,160 | | |
| | Ramsgate | 5 | | 3,700 | | |
| | Margate | | | 2,673 | | |
| | Sheerness | | | 470 | | |
| | Clacton | | | 27 | | 26,209 |
| Totals | Dynamo | 189,857 | 8,061 | 109,343 | 1,230 | 308,491 |
| | +Pre-Dynamo | 211,267 | 13,053 | 110,877 | 1,230 | 336,427 |

Note: It is thought the small discrepancy between the numbers landed and those dispatched may be due to a few troops sent on by road, marched and/or the wounded being hospitalized locally.

Exhausted troops once aboard their train flake out in the bucket seats of LNER tourist stock, dead to the world. *Author's Collection*

and a few steam-hauled parcel trains. Buses likewise replaced passenger trains between Tonbridge, Redhill and Guildford, together with intervening stations.

Had the disembarkation points of the Sussex Group (Hastings to Brighton) been used, trains for the destinations of Salisbury and points west could have avoided Redhill by being worked along the coast via Chichester and Southampton, another possible landing point, or Eastleigh, while those for further north could have bypassed Redhill Junction by means of the Quarry line. As it was, apart from Newhaven, few if any troops landed west of Folkestone, due to the fall of Boulogne and Calais to the enemy by the time the Operation proper commenced. This meant that the two empty stock trains placed in the proximity of these landing points ready for use will have had to be recovered and redirected to where they were then more urgently required.

Elsewhere in the country some trains, which had been recently organized by the Ministry of Transport for the purpose of allowing parents and others in London to visit their evacuated children in the country, had to be cancelled at short notice. Amongst the special trains from Paddington affected on Saturday 1st June were the 8.50 am to Taunton and 9.00 am to Keynsham & Somerdale. The vouchers intending visitors had obtained for journeys to any of the towns which the trains were to have served had to be regarded as cancelled.

Bernard Holden MBE, as a young man, worked in the Train Supervisory Office (Control) at Redhill at the time of Operation Dynamo. He recalls that while off duty, at 6.0 pm, Mr Horn, the clerk at Burgess Hill station delivered a message instructing him to report for duty at 9.00 pm for a 12 hour shift and to bring some food, as a long stint was expected. Catching the 7.28 pm from Brighton at Wivelsfield station, he and others that had joined the train were

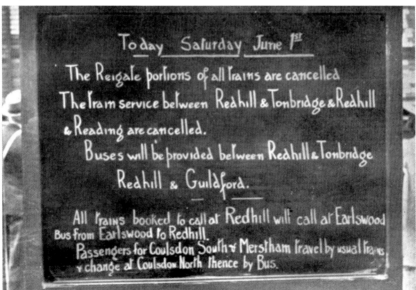

Chalked notice board displayed at Redhill advising the general public of the alterations to passenger train services to avoid congesting the station during this crucial stage of the evacuation.                              *Courtesy British Red Cross*

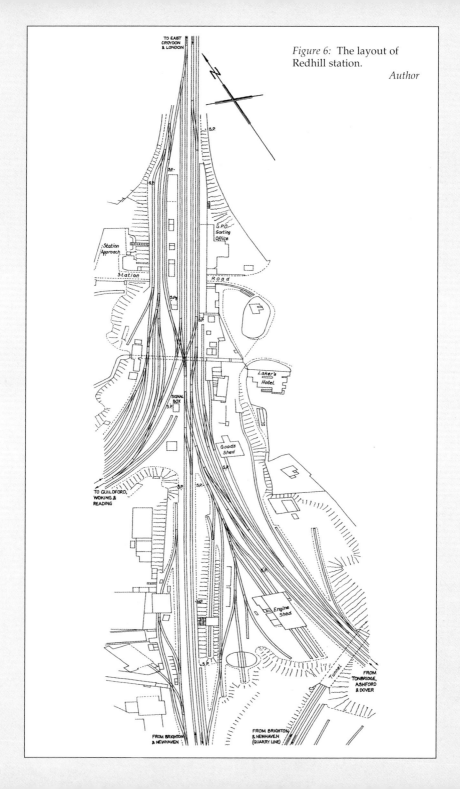

*Figure 6:* The layout of Redhill station.

*Author*

advised at Earlswood station to alight and walk the three-quarters of a mile into Redhill, as the line there was closed to ordinary traffic and their train would be continuing to London by the Quarry line.

Due to the uncertainty of the ultimate destination of the trains at the start of the journey, it had been decided to make Redhill the strategic centre from where trains could be appropriately directed to suit the military authority's requirements. On the Southern these included Aldershot, Salisbury and the West, or otherwise they headed northwards to be exchanged with other companies, mainly through Reading. For this reason from 27th May the Great Western Railway posted Charles R. Clinker, liaison officer for the four railway companies to the Southern Command, and chief inspector G.H. Partridge to Redhill control to enable them to ascertain the direction each train destined to take and where appropriate pass on details. They were found temporary accommodation in an old weighbridge hut. During the next nine days Clinker and Partridge, as Royal trains inspector smartly dressed in a clean wing collar every day, recorded all the trains passing through Redhill, together with some, but not all, of those that took other routes. Those known are listed in *Appendix Two*.

Soon after leaving Dover Marine station the line begins its ascent through the chalk tunnels to pass above Folkestone town to the summit at Westhanger at gradients of around 1 in 250/300, after which it rolls down to Ashford and across the Weald to Tonbridge and Redhill. Assuming the authorities would no more wish to send trains north from Redhill than they already did for trains starting from further east; all trains would be forced to change direction there. This would mean providing a fresh engine, before taking the line westwards through Reigate and follow along the southern flanks of the North Downs before taking the gap through to Guildford.

West of Redhill, however, the gradients for the first 17 miles are severely undulating and include a four mile climb of 1 in 96/100 from Deepdene (Dorking) to a summit at White Hill east of Gomshall, after which they could coast down to Shalford Jn to join the Portsmouth Direct line, through St Catherine's, or Sand tunnel and the Chalk tunnel into Guildford station. While such trains would not have to change direction here, unless destined for the Portsmouth area, it was an important stopping point. Here one or two of the six through lines could be occupied by a troop train for some time, while the men were provided with refreshments and the engine could take water, yet other trains could overtake it on one of the adjacent lines (*see page 84*). If continuing on the Reading line, a further two miles of 1 in 100, initially tightly curved ensued beyond Guildford, all of which will have tested all but the most competent enginemen and their motive power.

On Monday 27th May all seven trains originated at Dover and went to only four different destinations all within the Aldershot/Blackwater Valley military area. By the next day, Ramsgate, Sheerness and Margate, all of whose trains were routed via Kensington presumably for destinations north of London, together with Folkestone were beginning to share in the load, while a few other reception areas were beginning to come on stream, noticeably those with regimental barracks. Nonetheless, Dover and the Aldershot area continued to take most of the load.

Mrs Horne and three evacuees, *left to right*, Kathleen, Dick and Harry Purslow, evacuated from Fulham, where their parents were chemists, stand beside the railway line near Westcott on Sunday 2nd June, 1940 watching a train loaded with exhausted troops just home from Dunkirk. The signal will be the recently installed electrically-operated intermediate block signal, mentioned on page 37. *Miss Horne, courtesy Dorking Museum*

Prior to the war, an unidentified SR 2-6-0 'N' class locomotive hauls the once-daily through restaurant car train along the foothills to the North Downs near Dorking. This train had portions from Margate, calling at Ramsgate, Deal, Dover (Priory), Folkestone and Ashford (Kent); and another section from Hastings, calling at Eastbourne and Brighton. At Redhill these were coupled together before going on to Birkenhead, via Guildford, Reading, Oxford, Birmingham (Snow Hill), Wolverhampton and Shrewsbury. This train, known to railwaymen as 'The Continental', utilized much of the route followed by many troop trains. *LGRP, Author's Collection*

On the whole the operation of the trains ran smoothly until the night of Wednesday/Thursday 29th/30th May, when some hitch appears to have occurred. Ordinarily the journey time from Dover to Redhill over a relatively level route with a limited number of stops should have been about two hours, but from early evening it was becoming extended to four hours or more until the 7.00 pm from Dover (train No. V70) and 6.32 pm from Folkestone (train No. W8) took over 4½ hours and six hours respectively to reach Redhill where they were detained for 31 and 40 minutes before continuing their journeys to Tidworth and Bordon. Fortunately things soon settled down thereafter in the inimitable manner of the Southern Railway. A few further problems, however, appeared to have arisen during Saturday 1st June.

Up until Thursday 30th May, apart from those routed through Kensington Addison Road, all the destinations recorded by Clinker had been on the SR, but thereafter trains were being sent on by other railways to destinations further afield. Other trains, when passing Redhill were indicated only by general area, such as the Salisbury or the Southern Command areas, the final destination being decided further down the line to one of the many camps on Salisbury Plain. Such trains will have required a change of direction at Woking and a 'turn over' engine. By the afternoon, a minor motive power crisis seems to have arisen at Redhill, with a couple of trains held up in one case by more than half an hour waiting for an engine to continue its journey. Later that evening, trains initially intended for Northampton, Devizes and Exeter, were sometime after reversing at Redhill, diverted to Southampton, presumably as a result of a change of plan while they were en route.

By Saturday 1st June troops were being sent even farther afield, mainly to south and central Wales, movement through Reading increasing as a consequence. Also from the same day trains start to resume terminating in the Aldershot area, perhaps because by then many of the troops who had arrived earlier had moved on to their reassembly areas. Should Redhill become congested, there was an alternative route via Faversham and Chatham, which particularly suited trains starting from Margate and Ramsgate, but meant trains passed through the southern and western outskirts of London. Again, despite the policy of trying to avoid the London area, from this day a few more trains from Dover and Folkestone were being routed via Clapham Junction or Kensington, while trains for Weymouth, Plymouth and Salisbury utilized both GW and SR routes. By Monday 3rd June, with most of those landed being French troops, many trains were sent to Plymouth.

The SR was responsible for the movement of empty stock. The intention was that principal stabling points would be in the Ashford area for east Kent and Three Bridges for Sussex. In this way empty trains were held at Queenborough, Faversham, Margate and Ramsgate, together with at one point Willesden, from where they would be called forward to the appropriate point of landing for loading. Completion of the loop line through Margate and Dover, whereby empty trains could approach by the old LC&D lines and depart by the old SER main line helped enormously. Nonetheless, ensuring that there were always empty trains available at Dover was of considerable concern, where the number of troops was sometimes overwhelming, it being policy to have surplus trains to hand near the point of disembarkation.

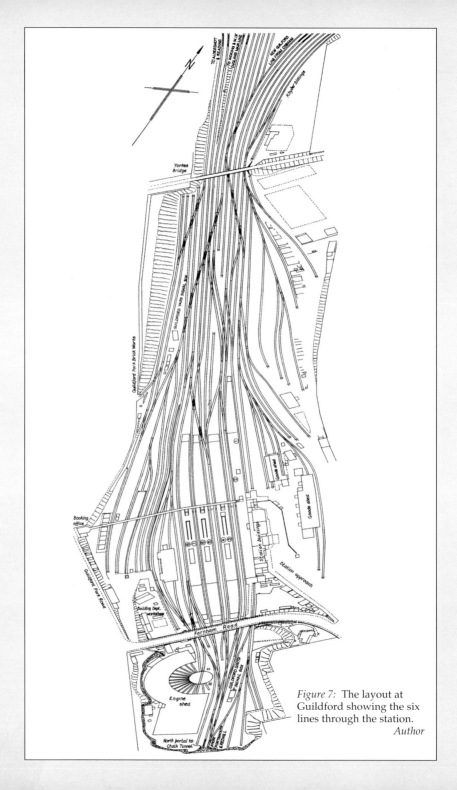

*Figure 7:* The layout at Guildford showing the six lines through the station.

*Author*

On 5th August, 1939, just prior to the outbreak of war, SR 2-6-0 'U' class No. 1611 draws 'The Continental' up from the SR line onto the Great Western main line at Reading. The SR's terminal station is below on the right.  *V.R. Webster, courtesy Kidderminster Railway Museum*

The destination of trains included all the usual locations of military depots in the Southern, Midlands and Northern commands, such as: Chatham, Southampton, Blandford, Dorchester, Weymouth, Aldershot, Tidworth, Ludgershall, Bulford, Salisbury, Warminster, Yeovil, Exeter, Plymouth, Devonport, Devizes, Trowbridge, Frome, Bodmin, Hendon, Formby (Lancashire), Burton-on-Trent, Derby, Peterborough, Doncaster and Catterick. Some trains to the North were routed via Oxford and Banbury for the Great Central line via Woodford and Leicester, others ran via Neasden. Thirty-seven per cent terminated on the Southern, while a like amount passed on to GW and 13 per cent each to LMS and LNER. Only 19 per cent passed through London.

During the period 27th May to 5th June 351 trains loaded with troops plus 26 ambulance trains passed through Redhill Jn, together with 649 empty stock trains heading for the landing points, all of which appear to have reversed there. Each train in either direction required a 'turn over' engine to enable the train to proceed in its new direction. The operation of detaching and shunting out of the way the first engine and bringing to couple up the fresh engine on the opposite end of the train, reconnecting and testing the brakes was achieved on average in four minutes with a best time of 2½ minutes. Arriving engines all detached at London end and had to be held on the down through line until they could be run forward on the Brighton line to the shed at the country end of the junction. Difficulty was experienced with locomotives queuing on the down through line waiting to gain access to the depot between the constant flow of troop trains arriving and departing from the station. There was often further

Two long trains extend beyond the limits of the island platform on the up side of Redhill station with volunteers and soldiers standing in the cess beside the electrified lines and a photographer up the signal bracket. Almost all trains will have reversed direction here, meaning that every one had to have a fresh engine to head off in the new direction. *Courtesy British Red Cross*

Redhill locomotive depot was a relatively small affair with a three-road engine shed. This view, taken on 29th January, 1949, shows ex-LBSCR 4-4-0 'B4x' No. 2072, built in 1901 by Sharp, Stewart and rebuilt at Brighton in 1924, while the nose projecting from the central door is a SR 2-6-0 'N' class No. 3182. Both types worked Dynamo trains. *R.C. Riley, courtesy Transport Treasury*

delay in coping with them once they arrived within its confines. Here they were replenished with water, had their fireboxes cleaned and their ash-pans emptied. Such was the demand for loco coal that special trains had to be run to Redhill and labourers imported from the country around. Three hundred tons of ash was produced, needing special measures to dispose of it, while for a time the demand for water was such to put the municipal supplies under strain.

The pressure on the running shed was so great, that Mr John Pelham Maitland, the shed master at Nine Elms was temporarily seconded to Redhill to assist. It was found expedient to dispatch engines in pairs alternatively to Redhill shed and that at Three Bridges, via Earlswood, 8½ miles down the line for servicing. It is also reported that to reduce congestion on shed and save time, some engines were seen running tender first towards Tonbridge. This might not be quite so unpleasant in the summer as at less clement times of the year but coal dust blown off the tender will still have been discomforting. Mr John Pelham Maitland, who had joined the LBSCR in 1907, was awarded the MBE for his services at Redhill during the Operation.

Elsewhere, the high demand for water at Ashford led to engines continuing as far as Tonbridge where possible. On the Chatham route, water was taken at Faversham, amongst no doubt many other places.

Woking too was a busy spot, as trains from Redhill, via Guildford, were obliged again to change direction as they headed west to the numerous Army encampments around Salisbury Plain, and likewise engines had to be changed. Despite reconstruction of the station three years earlier with four through 820 ft-long platforms and multi-aspect colour-light re-signalling, this will have introduced its own complications. There being no locomotive facilities there, medium-sized engines were worked back to Guildford shed six miles away, where the turntable was of only 54 ft 10 in. diameter. Due to this, unless fitted with six-wheel tenders for use on the Central Section, all 4-6-0s of the 'N15' ('King Arthur') and 'S15' classes, together with other 4-6-0s of the 'Lord Nelson', 'N15X' and 'H15' classes, would have to be turned elsewhere. This could be done by continuing on the up local line to Weybridge station, where it would reverse down the Chertsey branch as far as Addlestone Junction. From here the engine could return via the spur to Byfleet Junction, near West Weybridge station (now Byfleet & New Haw), and rejoin the West of England main line and return to Woking on the down local line. Should a large engine have required any other facilities, it would have been necessary to run up to Nine Elms, Battersea on the outskirts of London, or to Feltham.

The non-preferred route via Chatham was more suited to those trains starting from Ramsgate and Margate, which would proceed along the North Kent coast, via Whitstable to Faversham, where it joined the alternative line from Dover. From here they will have gone on to Sittingbourne, where the Sheerness branch joined, Chatham and probably up the 1 in 100 gradient of the six mile-long Sole Street Bank to Swanley, Bromley, Herne Hill to Factory Jn beside Wandsworth Road station. The route would then be by the West London Extension Joint Railway and the choice at Longhedge Jn would have been either Addison Road, Kensington by means of the Chelsea Bridge over the River Thames for connections to the GWR and LMS railways, or to Clapham Junction. Clapham Jn has three routes passing through, each of four tracks, and the line from

Troops wave from the windows of a train passing through south London.

*Courtesy British Red Cross*

One of the more surprising locomotives associated with the evacuation of troops was an ex-LBSCR 0-6-0 'C2' class observed at Lewes. An example of this type is No. 2435 seen at Redhill engine shed on 21st September, 1946.          *R.C. Riley, courtesy Transport Treasury*

Longhedge joins on the far side of the Windsor lines. So to get to the West of England main line, it was necessary to cross over to the down side of the Windsor lines and proceed for a short distance on through Wandsworth Town and take the connection to East Putney and gain the main line at Wimbledon.

Trains were handed over to the GWR at Reading and at Salisbury, 293 trains containing 1,046 officers and 181,479 men being conveyed by the company. Trains for onward transmission to the LNER ex-Great Central lines travelled either by Reading, Oxford, Banbury and Woodford to Leicester, while others came via the Addison Road, Kensington, Old Oak Common or Neasden and High Wycombe. Those for the LMS also seemed to have worked through Addison Road to Willesden, emphasising the value of the West London Railway and its Extension. Eight trains were run from Harwich Parkeston Quay, mainly to the Midlands, but at least one to Liverpool Street.

The GWR supplied some modern large-windowed and some old clerestory coaches, the LMS stock ranging from modern flush-sided corridor thirds through Midland clerestories to old Lancashire & Yorkshire Railway and London & North Western Railway vehicles; the LNER's was chiefly represented by open tourist thirds with bucket seats in the green and cream livery; and of course the Southern by many types, including a set of LSWR stock.

Locomotives employed included a wide variety of Southern types, as shown in the Table on page 90. The ex-SECR 4-4-0 'D' class were loading up to 12 vehicles, but 9 or 10 were the average load. One train on 4th June was composed of nine NE coaches with three LMS vehicles tacked on the end, and was hauled by class 'D' 4-4-0 No. 1730 – a large load for this somewhat vintage locomotive, and she did very well, too. Nonetheless, one assumes such engines were either only used east of Redhill, leaving the line west thereof in the hands of more capable engines, or they were double-headed. Many of the engines were very clean. SR engines in some cases worked through to Watford or beyond.

Further north, as special trains were observed passing through Bletchley on 2nd June, locomotives included LMS 4-6-0 'Patriot' class No. 5531 *Sir Frederick Harrison* with 10 SR corridor coaches; 4-6-0 '5P5F' 'Black Five' No. 5241 with a similar load; 4-6-0 'Jubilee' class No. 5586 *Mysore* hauling 11 LMS vehicles; and 'Black Five' No. 5325 with about 10 SR coaches, all in the down direction. In the up direction, GWR corridor stock was seen, thus completing the four-company representation; and 'Black Five' No. 5191 of Willesden shed, passed through with 11 SR empty corridor stock.

This monumental effort to disperse the troops evacuated from Dunkirk fell primarily on the SR, particularly on the Eastern Division. Although signalmen were exempt from working very long hours, most other grades of railwaymen during this intense period of the movement, such as locomotive drivers, firemen and guards worked tremendously long periods and led in cases to 18 to 28 hours shifts being worked by some SR locomen.

For the most part only locomotive men from Redhill, Guildford and Reading sheds were likely to have had route knowledge of the Reading branch from Redhill and other routes from Guildford and Woking. Although those men from east of Redhill, plus Stewarts Lane and Bricklayers Arms sheds might know the road to Reading, they would have been flummoxed if at Guildford

## Operation Dynamo - Motive power known to have been employed

| Co. | Type | Class | Designer or re-builder | Introduced /rebuilt | Tractive effort (lb) | Sighted at | Sample Nos. |
|---|---|---|---|---|---|---|---|
| **SR** | | | | | | | |
| SE&C | 4-4-0 | D | Wainwright | 1901 | 17,450 | | 1730 |
| SE&C | 4-4-0 | D1 | Maunsell | 1921 | 17,950 | Reading, Woking | 1492/4, 1509, 1727/47 |
| SE&C | 4-4-0 | E | Wainwright | 1905 | 18,410 | Reading, Woking, Paddock Wood | 1157/9, 1273 |
| SE&C | 4-4-0 | E1 | Maunsell | 1919 | 18,410 | Reading, Woking | 1507 |
| SER | 4-4-0 | F1 | Wainwright | 1903 | 14,491 | Reading, Woking | 1183 |
| SE&C | 4-4-0 | L | Wainwright | 1914 | 18,575 | Woking, Reading | 1770/3 |
| SR | 4-4-0 | L1 | Maunsell | 1926 | 18,910 | Reading, Woking | 1756 |
| SE&C | 4-4-0 | B1 | Wainwright | 1910 | 14,491 | | 1454 |
| LBSC | 4-4-0 | B4X | R. Billington | 1922 | 19,644 | | |
| LSW | 4-4-0 | T9 | Drummond | 1899 | 17,675 | Eastleigh | 708/29 |
| LSW | 4-4-0 | L11 | Drummond | 1903 | 19,756 | Eastleigh | 167 |
| LSW | 4-4-0 | L12 | Drummond | 1904 | 17,675 | Reading, Eastleigh | 417/20/5/34 |
| LSW | 4-4-0 | D15 | Drummond | 1912 | 20,140 | Reading | 465/70 |
| LSW | 4-4-0 | X2 | Adams | 1890 | 16,428 | Woking | |
| LSW | 4-4-0 | X6 | Adams | 1892 | 17,763 | Woking | |
| LSW | 4-4-0 | T3 | Adams | 1893 | 17,673 | Woking | 563, 586 |
| SR | 4-4-0 | V | Maunsell | 1930 | 25,135 | Exeter | |
| LSW | 4-6-0 | H15 | Urie Maunsell | 1914 | 26,240/ 25,510 | Eastleigh | 334, 476/7, 523 |
| LSW | 4-6-0 | N15 | Urie/Maunsell | 1918 | 23,915/ 26,245 | Eastleigh, Headcorn | 749/51/3 |
| LBSC | 4-6-0 | N15X | R. Billington/ Maunsell | 1914 1934 | 23,325 | Eastleigh | 2330 |
| LSW | 4-6-0 | S15 | Urie/Maunsell | 1920 | 28,200/ 29,855 | Eastleigh | 510, 841 |
| SR | 4-6-0 | LN | Maunsell | 1926 | 33,510 | Eastleigh, Clapham Jn | 855/9 |
| SE&C | 2-6-0 | N | Maunsell | 1917 | 26,035 | Woking | |
| SE&C | 2-6-0 | N1 | Maunsell | 1922 | 27,695 | Woking, Reading | 1878 |
| SR | 2-6-0 | U | Maunsell | 1928 | 23,865 | Eastleigh, Clapham Jn | 1614, 1637, 1809 |
| SR | 2-6-0 | U1 | Maunsell | 1928 | 25,385 | Eastleigh, Clapham Jn | 1892/3, 1909 |
| LBSC | 2-6-0 | K | R. Billington | 1913 | 26,580 | Woking | 2348 |
| SE&C | 0-6-0 | O1 | Wainwright | 1903 | 17,325/ 17,610 | Woking | 1109 |
| SE&C | 0-6-0 | C | Wainwright | 1900 | 19,520 | Woking, Clapham Jn | 1113 |
| LBSC | 0-6-0 | C2 | R. Billington | 1893 | 19,094 | Lewes | |
| LBSC | 0-6-0 | C2X | Marsh | 1908 | 19,175 | Lewes, Woking | |
| LSW | 0-6-0 | 700 | Drummond | 1897 | 23,540 | Eastleigh | 350 |
| SR | 0-6-0 | Q | Maunsell | 1938 | 26,160 | Eastleigh | 543 |
| SE&C | 0-4-4T | H | Wainwright | 1904 | 17,360 | Woking | 1177 |
| **GWR** | | | | | | | |
| GWR | 4-6-0 | Manor | Collett | 1938 | 27,340 | Redhill | 7811 |
| GWR | 2-6-0 | 43xx | Churchward | 1911 | 25,670 | Redhill | 5355, 6318/54/5/91/9 |
| **LMS** | | | | | | | |
| LMS | 4-6-0 | Patriot | Fowler | 1930 | 26,520 | Bletchley | 5531 |
| LMS | 4-6-0 | Black 5 | Stanier | 1934 | 25,455 | Bletchley | 5191, 5241, 5325 |
| LMS | 4-6-0 | Jubilee | Stanier | 1934 | 26,610 | Bletchley | 5586 |

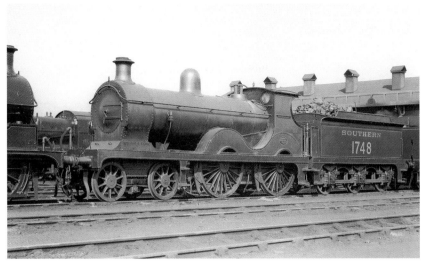

An example of the ex-SECR 4-4-0 of the 'D' class, introduced in 1901, used to haul 12-coach trains during Operation Dynamo. In more peaceful times, No. 1748 of 1903 rests at Ashford engine shed in 1937, unaware of the exertions it will called upon to perform.

*Rail Archive Stephenson/Photomatic*

they had been directed to Woking etc. On the other hand, in the case of Reading, the Great Western had regularly worked to Redhill, so a number of their men were also available and four sets of men were sent to Redhill on the first day to provide relief in their incoming locomotive crews. Men from sheds in Kent, like their locomotives, will have tended therefore not to work beyond Redhill, but to return with empty stock. Some may not have known the road beyond Tonbridge, but made their way anyway perhaps reassured by the advice received that Redhill shed was in view off the country end of the platforms and in the long summer days and fair weather the unfamiliar signals would be capable of being sighted without difficulty.

No borrowed locomotives worked east of Redhill and only GW '43XX' class 2-6-0s and 'Manor' class 4-6-0s were allowed onto SR territory from Reading and had regularly done so before and after the war. At Salisbury shed men were ordered up to the station, there to await arriving troop trains and relieve the crew heading west. This would be fine so long as the destination was on the West of England main line, but there was a large camp at Blandford on the Somerset & Dorset Joint line. Not many Salisbury drivers would be familiar with the routine of coupling up a pilot engine at Templecombe station to be drawn down to Templecombe Junction on the joint line below or have knowledge of the line from there onwards and would likely have required a pilotman. One assumes too that empty stock returning east might also sometimes need relief at Salisbury, as no doubt elsewhere.

Only 2-6-0 and 4-6-0 Great Western locomotives of the '43XX' and 'Manor' classes were permitted to work through to Redhill from Reading. Eleven years after Dunkirk, ex-GWR 2-6-0 No. 6383 of the '43XX' class heads a regular Redhill to Reading train somewhere north of Guildford on 2nd May, 1951.                                           *S.V. Blencowe Collection*

Despite the huge amount of ad hoc working, remarkably few incidents appear to have occurred. The Southern Railway succeeded in operating all its trains without accident, derailment or engine failure, or injury or loss to those conveyed. The only untoward event seems to have been at Clapham Junction on 30th May when V85, an 11 coach train, from Dover to Tidworth unwittingly passed a signal at danger. As a consequence the hood to the colour light signal was adjusted, presumably to improve sighting and avoid a repeat in the future. The Great Western was slightly less lucky when a returning empty stock train from Penally to Reading was involved in a rear end collision at Morlais South at 1.35 am on 2nd June.

Jack Hewitt, a driver at the SR's Reading engine shed, was in his garden when he received a call to go to the shed at once, as the footplate staff prepared to take the troop trains to wherever directed and return with empty stock. Locomotives were regularly changed at Reading, as trains moved from the Southern to Great Western metals, in the return direction possibly by using the tunnel under the main line from Paddington. During the Operation, long shifts were worked with only nine hours off duty. Like others, while standing at Ash, Hewitt encountered one of those lucky coincidences, when he was asked by a French officer on a train heading for Southampton via Aldershot standing on an adjacent line whether they were anywhere near Reading. On receiving an affirmative answer, Jack was requested to pass a message on to the proprietor of Jackson's department store, suggesting that they should meet up at Southampton. It would appear that some years previously Mr & Mrs Jackson's au pair had married the officer, a French Count.

*Motor Transport*

Ten of the requisitioned motor coaches were allocated to the Landing Controls at each of the following ports: Dover, Folkestone, Margate, Ramsgate, Hastings, Eastbourne, Brighton and Newhaven, reporting to the Landing Control for orders, while 10 spare were held at Canterbury and at Maidstone, together with a reserve of 50 coaches at Canterbury and Tunbridge Wells under the control of Redhill. Each coach was capable of carrying an average of 30 troops and intended for local work conveying troops to nearby railway stations.

At Ramsgate and Margate buses were used to transfer troops from the point of landing to rest centres and on to the railway stations. At Southampton Hants & Dorset buses conveyed whole train loads of weary men from Central station to their various rest camps. This necessitated every available driver and vehicle working without rest, sometimes it is claimed for up to 48 hours on end. Even senior staff, such as inspectors, regulators, office staff and maintenance men, all went back to the driving seat to help out in a time of desperate need.

*Evacuation of Children*

Until 10 days earlier, when the military situation in Flanders deteriorated so markedly, children from London had been evacuated to a number of coastal areas, including Kent and East Anglia. Up to that time, South East Kent had been considered safe from aerial attack and was therefore designated as a Reception Area for evacuees. With the strategic situation now drastically changed, rapid arrangements had to be made not only to relocate those evacuated from the cities and towns, but for the local children at risk from invasion within 10 miles all along the south and east coast of England. So as well as the children native to these areas, 8,000 evacuees had also to be rapidly relocated. Nonetheless, wives of those in reserved occupations often refused to leave, and if their children were too young to be separated from their mothers they remained as well.

The evacuation of 48,000 children on 2nd June coincided with the ongoing transport of troops from Dunkirk. So concurrent with Operation Dynamo, these children were moved from Kentish and East Coast coastal towns to safer locations in 70 trains. Those from the east coast of Suffolk and parts of Norfolk went to the Midlands and from Kent to South Wales. The SR contributed 32 special trains from towns such as Margate, Ramsgate, Broadstairs, Sandwich, Deal, Folkestone; together with 6,500 children from the Medway towns of Rochester, Chatham, Gillingham and Sheerness. The total amounted to 22,238 and included 1,500 persons from Dover who departed from Priory station for Ebbw Vale, Caerleon and Bedwelty in Monmouthshire. The LNER provided 25 trains to carry 17,881 passengers. On the receiving end, the GWR accepted 31 trains as part of the movement. The resulting additional demands for staff and motive power tended generally to disrupt freight services and the occasional passenger service.

Amongst the trains imposed on the system at this critical time were at least eight which passed through Redhill, as shown in the Table below, on top of the 38 trains run in connection with Operation Dynamo that day.

**Evacuation of children trains from East Kent**
**passing through Redhill on 2nd June, 1940**

| Train No. | From | To | Times at Redhill arr.    dep. | Remarks |
|---|---|---|---|---|
| Evac 100 | Sandling Jn | GW via Reading | 9.58am 10.03am | 11 bogie coaches |
| Evac 101 | Folkestone | GW via Reading | 10.33am 10.39am | 12 GW bogie coaches |
| Evac 102 | Sandwich | GW via Reading | 11.30am 11.35am | 12 GW bogie coaches |
| Evac 103 | Folkestone | GW via Reading | 11.53am 12.01pm | 12 GW bogie coaches |
| Evac 104 | Deal | GW via Reading | 12.14pm 12.xxpm | GW coaches |
| Evac 105 | Folkestone | Caerphilly | 12.28pm 1.06pm | 12 GW bogie coaches |
| E.2 | u/k | Pangbourne | 1.26pm 1.31pm | 11 bogie coaches |
| Evac 106 | Deal | Merthyr | 1.33pm 1.38pm | LMS coaches |
| Evac 107 | Folkestone | Abergavenny via Reading | 2.40pm 2.47pm | GW coaches |

Of 37 LMS trains run in connection with schoolchildren's evacuation that day 12 had commenced their journey on its territory. Nine of the 26 that set out from the LNER were transferred by means of the LMS to the GWR via the Cambridge-Oxford line. Six of these were observed passing through Bletchley, all composed of LNER stock of 13 to 15 vehicles (including GE coaches), the average weight of trains being 400 tons. All were hauled by LMS 2-6-0s of both Fowler and Stanier types.

In the expectation of the bombing of the metropolis, a further evacuation of children was to take place from London during the period 13th to 18th June in which 42,391 children and their attendants were conveyed in 84 trains. On the Southern 38 electric trains fed children to main line train departure points at Waterloo, Vauxhall, Clapham Junction, Earlsfield, Wimbledon, etc., from where they were taken to places in the West of England and Berkshire, 21,000 being transferred in through trains to the GWR. Parties of children were grouped by the school at which they attended. At intermediate stopping points some nurses from local hospitals would be in attendance to deal with any minor ailment, while voluntary organizations provided the children with refreshments. On arrival at their destinations, fleets of motor coaches would be on hand to convey the children to their new homes in the allocated village.

# Chapter Seven

# Provision of Sustenance on the Journey

With the issue of instructions on 24th May for the planning of Operation Dynamo, the War Office's Directorate of Supplies and Transport (ST4) was faced with an unusual and for the Army exceptionally large and widespread catering task, which had to be in operation in a minimum of time and under improvised conditions throughout and with the utmost secrecy. With the uncertainty of numbers, timing and location, to ensure that, as well as putting food and water on the ships which were returning to collect more personnel from across the Channel, food also had to be made available at the disembarkation points and during the journey to the reception camps.

## A Snack at the Port of Disembarkation

In view of the decision to avoid congestion, no sorting of personnel or the provision of cooked meals would take place at any of the ports. On landing buffet type feeding, pending entraining, was arranged at Harwich, Dover, Folkestone, Ramsgate, Margate, Hastings, Eastbourne, Newhaven and Brighton. Instead brief halts of just 15 minutes were arranged on all the rail routes to be traversed.

Although some troops had been lucky enough to receive a bully beef sandwich and a mug of hot tea on board the larger vessels while returning to England, many had not had an adequate meal for some days. Upon disembarkation troops were offered various forms of cold sustenance by the WVS, Salvation Army, Church Army, etc. immediately on landing, such as at Dover Marine and initially at Folkestone. These good souls also took great jugs of tea and coffee down to the crews of the smaller boats, or the wounded men waiting to be carried from the point of landing. Elsewhere men had either to walk or be taken by bus to a nearby centre, like a school or cinema, or straight on to the railway station, where they might be given a bun and an apple each.

At Dover home-coming men were met by those wonderful ladies of the Women's Voluntary Service, who plied them with hot tea, sandwiches and pork pies, or a bun and a banana. One teenage girl was holding a big tray of sandwiches, or others with five Woodbine cigarettes and a bar of chocolate. Likewise at Sheerness ladies handed out sandwiches and cups of tea.

## Haltes-repas

Altogether 14 official stopping points along the rail routes were opened to provide more substantial refreshment. General arrangements for these 'haltes-repas', as they became known in Army circles, were planned verbally with Commands concerned and a detailed arrangement carried out by the latter. No delaying of the trains was permitted and distribution of food had to be undertaken within the time limit. The staff to man these had to be hurriedly assembled, equipped and provisioned, and preparations made for making and cutting sandwiches, distribution etc. One of the major problems was the provision of cups as the troops had no utensils. Several hundred thousand waxed paper cups were eventually produced after a hurried comb-out of all possible means and sources. Six teams of cookery instructors and Emergency Cookery Training Centre (ECTC) students, together with cooking equipment, were hurriedly dispatched, four from the London School of Cookery and two from the ECTC at Guildford. All Eastern Command catering advisers were detailed to the various 'haltes-repas' and Aldershot Command catering advisers supervised the messing arrangements at reception camps.

Initial plans seem to have been for stops at a limited number of feeding stations, as follows:

For trains from east Kent at Headcorn, Paddock Wood or Faversham
For trains from Sussex at Horley or Chichester

It was hoped to provide one hour's notice to these stations of the intended stop for feeding by the troop trains, nonetheless, they were expected to be organized to cater for trains arriving without warning. Those at Headcorn and Paddock Wood were already established by 27th May and were about to be provided at Faversham, Chichester and Salisbury at that date. It was recognised that further refreshment halts might be necessary at Swindon Junction,

A troop train halted for refreshment at an unknown location. Note the cauldrons stretched out along the platform with soldiers distributing food and drink.     *C.G. Maggs Collection*

Leicester and Birmingham. At each halt a hot drink and a sandwich was issued, together with cigarettes and matches. This was supplemented by hard-boiled eggs, fruit, etc. as conditions improved.

At one stage trains were actually coming through at the rate of one every eight minutes at some locations. Paddock Wood, Faversham and Addison Road experienced a flow of trains so great that the 'haltes-repas' staffs had to be supplemented. As a consequence assistance was sought and given to the Commands by volunteers at many of the 'haltes-repas'. For example, Messrs Horlicks of Slough supplied and issued at Paddock Wood and Addison Road gifts of Horlicks malted milk. Some 120,000 bag rations of fruit and chocolate were provided by NAAFI. The refreshment halts continued their valiant work until 5th June when, as a result of the completion of Phase 1 of the evacuation, personnel and equipment were withdrawn and the halts closed down.

Due to the encirclement of the Allies in the Dunkirk enclave, the extent to which troops were landed at the Sussex points, apart from hospital ships at Newhaven, was extremely limited and it seems unlikely that there was much call for feeding facilities at Chichester or Horley. On the other hand numerous either ad hoc or other feeding stations added later have been recorded. As well as those mentioned above, feeding stations were also located along the routes at Tonbridge, Guildford, Woking, Basingstoke and Salisbury, at all of which four or more tracks enabled other trains to continue past them; together with Redhill, Penge East, Wandsworth Road, Addison Road Kensington, Westbury, Frome, Leicester, Peterborough and Grantham. Sandwiches, sausages, meat pies and hard boiled eggs were washed down by vast quantities of tea and coffee, during these brief stops.

Guildford and Leicester were along those that provided ablution benches on the platform to give the men a chance to wash, whilst Redhill had a barber's service available to give the men a shave and Salisbury and Penge East offered musical entertainment.

Helpers came in the form of members of the WVS, who like others plied cups of tea and cigarettes, or shoved troops into reception centres hastily set up in cinemas, churches and halls and where many of them fell fast asleep. Women rolled them into lines, removing equipment, their boots and socks, revealing many feet bleeding, bathing them as they lay there, washing their socks and then returning them. WVS centre organizers in ports and important railway junctions were asked at short notice to arrange canteens, usually with the assistance of others such as members of the Association of Friendly Societies, Rotarians, Church of England and free churches, British Red Cross, Round Table, Salvation Army, Toc H, Church Army and fire brigades, with the FANYs and men of the RASC in the background supplying food in some cases. Free postcards were distributed to the returning troops to enable them to inform their loved ones of their safe arrival back in England. These could be written on the train and collected by volunteers and posted at a subsequent station stop.

Headcorn dealt in this way with 207 trains, out of the 351 trains that passed that way. On the London-bound (up) platform of the station of this Wealden village, 40 soldiers from the RASC, assisted by about 50 volunteers, working in eight hour shifts to provide cover all day and night, dispensed food and drink to the troops on the train during its brief halt. Nineteen stoves were set up along the platform to

Regular troops of the Royal Army Service Corps prepare hot food and drink in a number of vast cauldrons behind the platform of Headcorn station. *Courtesy British Red Cross*

Home-based soldiers still in service dress hand out food and drink to tired and hungry troops aboard a train bringing them from their point of landing to reception and rest camps further west. Two SR non-corridor carriages appear to have come straight from the works having just been overhauled. *Author's Collection*

produce hot drinks, while food was prepared in the large barn of Rushford Manor in the centre of the village, where it seemed the whole village joined in, offering whatever they could spare. Adjacent to the station open trenches were dug over which to spit-roast beef. For their part the local bakers worked non-stop, to provide up to 2,500 loaves of bread a day to be sliced and buttered (or more likely margarine was spread). Sandwiches were filled with sliced meat or some of the 5,000 boiled eggs, or grated cheese, by women and girls, supplemented after work by men, while young girls looked after the babies and toddlers. Once completed the sandwiches were conveyed by hand cart pushed by boys to the station. At the station, food and drinks, together with cigarettes and fruit, were dispensed by women to the troops on the briefly-halted trains, watched by evacuee children and those of the neighbourhood. In addition some 100,000 cups of tea were dispensed, except that, due to a lack of sufficient cups, tin cans were substituted. This had the advantage that as the train drew out, the shout would go out 'Throw them out on the platform', so they could be collected washed and used again for the next train.

At night the Good Samaritans at Headcorn would thump on the outside of the steamed-up carriage windows to awaken the tired occupants with trays of steaming hot cups and mugs of tea. On being advised of the location, a few men with local connections were able to ask for their families to be informed by telephone of their safe return in one piece. In recognition of her services in organizing the refreshments at Headcorn, Mrs Joan Kempthorne was awarded the British Empire Medal (BEM).

At Tonbridge it was reported that troops returning from Dunkirk were disembarked from trains, where milk churns of water were positioned along the platform, filled by means of a garden hose run out from the refreshment room. Here they were given a meal, funded by collections from the public; donated cigarettes were freely available and they were given the opportunity to bathe for the first time for days at nearby breweries where empty vats were filled with hot water. Despite the imperative to avoid delay as the trains changed engines at Redhill, refreshments do appear to have been offered there as well.

Miss Helen Lloyd was born in 1899 and by 1920 her family had settled in Weston Lodge, Albury. In 1938 she joined the WVS and was quickly made responsible for arrangements concerned with the reception of children evacuated from London to Guildford Rural District Council's area, soon becoming one of the two WVS County Evacuation Officers. Nonetheless, it was only by chance that Miss Lloyd heard that the BEF troop trains were stopping at Guildford station. Weary soldiers had been seen on the platform searching for water, some even drinking from the fire buckets. After a struggle with the authorities, permission was granted, late on Thursday evening 30th May, for the WVS to be admitted to the platform.

It was difficult for them to do much that night beyond providing clean drinking water, as the supplies of fruit and cigarettes from the station stalls had quickly been exhausted. But the next morning, as well as recruiting her niece, 19-year-old Margaret Bray, together with Margaret's cousin Lily Bray, urgent calls were made for helpers and emergency canteens quickly set up. Mollie Liddell of was one of many contacted and she was asked to provide two helpers. The idea was that the WVS should run things during the day from 8.0 am to 8.0 pm and that the Rotary Club should take on the night shift. It was a hectic time for a while as an attempt

The ladies of Headcorn come together to slice loaves of bread, butter these and insert one of a variety of fillings to produce sandwiches by their thousands.          *Courtesy British Red Cross*

More ladies and a few soldiers hand food to hungry troops in the trains.
*Courtesy British Red Cross*

was being made to build up an organization. Trains were arriving and had to be dealt with at intervals of as little as quarter of an hour. Members' duties were to give to the soldiers passing through drinks, cigarettes and postcards upon which to write brief messages home. Those who could speak the French language were much sought after, because by this stage increasing numbers of French troops were going through. It all started on a very small scale and in a surprisingly short time the platform had been transformed, until the operation reached tremendous heights by the night of Saturday 1st June.

The two small waiting rooms were turned into a larder and a pantry and there, without ceasing, some seven or eight people cut, spread and buttered, until before long loaves were being used at the rate of a hundred in a couple of hours. On the platform numerous canteens sprang up in haphazard fashion, some manned by organizations, others by private individuals, but no one seemed to quite know either who was responsible for them or who was in charge. Soon the platform was littered with porter's barrows, trestle tables and railway benches on which were arranged an assortment of drinking vessels, enamel jugs, tins, jam jars and cardboard cartons. Beside them stood huge urns full of hot tea and steaming coffee, the latter provided specially for the French. At intervals down the platform were placed milk churns filled with lemonade which was kept cool by blocks of ice which chinked refreshingly as the churns were emptied. Rows of improvized trays, such as box lids, parts of packing cases, hat boxes and sheets of corrugated cardboard, were laden with meat and lettuce sandwiches, buns and hot sausages, while baskets of sliced oranges and trays of cigarettes were placed in readiness. 'Hand them out singly' were the instructions 'or they will all go to one carriage. The French have a liking for English cigarettes'.

At the conclusion, station staff look on at the detritus. *Courtesy British Red Cross*

Troops leaning out of the windows of a GWR clerestory coach at Redhill as lady volunteers standing at track level reach up to pour liquid refreshment into soldiers' billy cans.

*Author's Collection*

A policeman assists as an old barrel is filled with water straight from the locomotive water column.

*Author's Collection*

Volunteers scurry around on the platform at Redhill as two trains stand at the station awaiting 'turn over' engines to head in the westerly direction towards Guildford etc.

*Courtesy British Red Cross*

On the human side, seeing the first train was a heartbreaking affair, it did not seem possible that men could be so weary. A great many did not even wake up when the train stopped. A cry would echo down the platform, 'A train coming', in response to which there was instant turmoil. Trays of food and drink, heavy jugs, baskets of fruit and boxes of cigarettes were hastily snatched up and the line of helpers ran down the train. It was apparent before the trains drew into the station whether they were carrying French or British troops. The English soldiers were leaning out of the carriages waving enthusiastically; the French soldiers, also standing at the windows, mostly did not wave, but gave the 'Thumbs up'. Many of the faces were dirty and unshaven and scarred with lines of fatigue, some looked half-dazed, others, deep in sleep, sprawled on the seats in an abandonment of weariness. But in spite of their exhaustion most of the men were laughing and eager to talk.

Snatches of conversation were audible above the din: 'It was terrible over there'. 'It is only by a miracle that I am here.' 'England has never looked as good as it did today.' An aeroplane flew over the station. 'That is the first British bomber I have seen for weeks. We must have more machines.' And then, with deliberate understatement, 'We haven't much of an opinion of the Belgians, you know'.

A sergeant, an oldish man wearing medal ribbons of the last war, was in expansive mood. He talked of Dunkirk and told how destroyers could not put in to the quay and the troops had to line up on the shore. He smiled as he described how, while they were waiting, some of the men played leap frog on the sands. Then after an interminable wait the men had to wade out to sea breast deep and clamber into small boats from which they were transferred to the destroyers. He went on to tell how on the beaches were bombed and then shelled and at times the bombardment was so intense that the men had to retire and take cover and wait for nightfall before returning to the shore.

Later in the week a different story was told. An officer described how he belonged to the detachment that was sent to carry out the evacuation. He told how they had built jetties of lorries, motor cars and carts, anything they could lay their hands on, to enable the boats to come alongside; and then when the jetties were blown away, they built them up again. He described how heart-rending it was when men were shelled and killed on the jetties only a few yards from safety. 'How long ago is it?', he said, looking at his watch, 'Five hours! Only five hours since we were all in the thick of it. It seems like a dream'. Then, with an apologetic gesture towards a group of helpers, 'You can't think how queer it is to see these girls in pretty frocks!'

A sailor got out of the train and was loudly cheered by the troops. A gruff voice called out from a carriage as he passed, 'If it wasn't for you we shouldn't be here, mate'. Likewise, a bearded Frenchman, spotting a sailor on the platform, jumped from the train and gave the blue jacket a bear hug.

The centre of an interest sprung up around a man with a small black and white puppy in his arms. 'He's half French, half Belgian and I'm taking him home' the man explained as with a grin he stuffed the dog back into his pocket. There were other souvenirs. Some of the men clutched children's toys, a teddy bear, a trumpet, a child's bucket and spade, all picked up on the beaches of Dunkirk.

There was an eager demand for newspapers. The entire stock of the town was bought up and given away in an hour. The men had received no news for days, some of them did not even know of the capitulation of the Belgian Army. A frequent question asked by the French was 'Are the German planes here?' A French soldier was overheard asking the guard where they were going, and when told near Tidworth, asked anxiously if Tidworth had been bombed. The answer 'No' brought a heart-rending look of relief to his face.

The different nationalities had different needs. Many of the French and Belgians were ravenously hungry – one man was given so many buns he said he felt like an elephant – and their favourite drink was café au laît. The British preferred lemonade, though many of them asked for water - 'We can't get it over there', said one, 'For two days we didn't have a drop to drink.'

The rows of washing tubs and clean towels provided at either end of the platforms were popular and were always surrounded by a throng of men. 'Guildford is the only station that has thought of this' was their comment. It was a great disappointment when the washing tubs were removed by orders of the railway company who feared that the impromptu bathroom might delay the trains.

There were a few men without shoes or socks, others with torn battledress, but on the whole it was astonishing how neat and clean were the uniforms of the British troops. Many of these men had not had a good night's sleep for a month, some had only a handful of biscuits to eat for four days, yet their spirit was magnificent and they were all keen to go back after they had had a rest.

The most welcome service possible was to help the men to inform their families of their safety. Some of their messages were very moving. A sheaf of telegraph forms, all handed from the same carriage window, began in the same way – 'Darling, I'm safe'. A boy of 19 or 20 asked for a telephone message to be sent his father – 'Gilbert is in England, please be sure to let mother know'.

Postcards were provided by the tens of thousands for the men to write home and posted free or if local even delivered by volunteers on their way home. A signature and the address was all that was required, and the postcards, filled in, were showered out of the trains as they pulled out of the station. Major Starling of the Salvation Army was inspired when he had some printed in French which gave great joy. *'Je suis bien arrivé en Angleterre et vous ecrirai bientôt'* (I have arrived safely in England and will write to you soon). The French were so delighted with their welcome - nearly all their postcards home spoke of the wonderful reception they were having. One when being consoled with the fact that, although he was out of Dunkirk, he was not at home said, 'England and France - they are all the same to me now'. Unlike the British they did not know whether they would were returning to their home country. 'We do not know the fate of our families' said one young soldier with trembling lips. The contents of the platform post box bore tragic evidence to this truth for many of the letters addressed to homes in territory already occupied by the enemy.

Some amazing coincidences took place. A young Frenchwoman wrote to some cousins in Surrey: 'I have returned to my mother in the South of France. Louis made me leave Boulogne and I got away on the last train to depart from the town. What has happened to Louis I do not know but I doubt if I shall ever see him again'. Before this letter was delivered, her husband had already passed through Guildford with the French troops. He asked a volunteer helper who was offering cigarettes, 'Do you know a village called Peaslake?' 'I do.' 'Do you by chance know a lady there, Miss Paine?' 'I do.' 'She is my cousin, give her my love and tell her I am in England.' Amazingly Miss Paine was billeting officer for Peaslake and the question was asked of one of the few people at the station who knew her well.

Another surprising incident happened to helper Miss Liddell who while talking to an officer in the Durham Light Infantry mentioned her anxiety for a friend in the Northumberland Fusiliers. The man's name was Jones, and she felt slightly foolish at making enquiries for him but the officer she was talking to turned out to be his best friend!

A Guards corporal only a few hours since holding an outpost in France, being evacuated under cover of a naval bombardment had escaped from the beach under machine gun fire and falling bombs to a small boat and then twice had destroyers sunk from beneath him. On asking who was paying for the refreshments, was assured that it was 'A small token of our gratitude to you all from the people of this town'.

Towards the end of the week the number of unofficial helpers became embarrassing and the crowd on the platform was chaotic, so much so that it was difficult for the canteen workers to get near the trains. In due course a system of passes was instituted but was not easy to enforce especially as now and then a passenger train left from the platform otherwise reserved for troops. At times there was a panic that supplies were running short. It was difficult to gauge the requirements as sometimes there were gaps of several hours between the trains while at others they followed at a short interval. Also there was no co-ordination between the different canteens; each group of people made their own catering arrangements without consultation with the others. But in spite of the chaos the work was done and the men were fed.

There was unfortunately a good deal of ill feeling between several groups of people doing this catering. Cow & Gate, the baby milk formula producers in Guildford, provided a tremendous amount of tea but insisted on keeping their end of the platform which meant that the opposite end of the train never got any tea. The people who had brought things on their own resented the authority of the WVS. There was no coordinated method of buying in supplies. Suggestions for improvement if such a thing ever happened again were that one central body such as the WVS be asked to organize the whole thing in conjunction with other organizations; that passes should be very strictly issued; that all resources i.e. money, food, etc should be pooled; and that one competent person should be responsible for the ordering. The co-operation of the Salvation Army, particularly Major Starling, was invaluable. Far greater use could have been made of the Royal Army Service Corps, now part of the Royal Logistics Corps. A Quarter Master Sergeant and four men were there for some time on Sunday and they were excellent. Male help was essential when moving heavy churns of water, tea, etc. Despite all the chaos, the men were very well provided for and they were most grateful.

Once the operation got under way, general members of the public were kept out of the station, unless travelling, and congregated instead on the roads round about overlooking the scene. Those not involved on the station looked down from the Farnham Road overbridge at the country end of the station, as they did elsewhere all along the line. People were unbelievably generous and immense sums of money were given and spent. £30 alone was collected from the people watching from the Farnham Road Bridge over the railway line, and two of the spectators on the platform just handed over £5 notes. Money was collected from here, there and everywhere and spent just as fast as it came in, leading the Mayor, Robert H. Tribe, to write a letter to the *Surrey Advertiser* seeking contributions to refund the cost of purchasing refreshments. The supplies could not have been kept going without the enthusiastic support of the Guildford tradesmen who were willing to be knocked-up at all hours of the night and who gave goods often at a discount of 60 per cent.

Ambulances waited at the station entrance to take away any wounded not already separated out at the point of disembarkation, or whose condition had worsened during the journey.

At some point the station master asked that no more food should be handed out, so only lemonade, oranges and cigarettes were given and there was still a big demand for postcards. On Sunday night the Rotary Club, who had definitely undertaken to man the station until 8.00 am, decided to pack up and either returned or gave away all the food, leaving only porters on the platform to give the men water. On Monday, however, as the trains continued to arrive, the WVS had to start from scratch all over again although only with drinks, fruit and cigarettes.

Until the afternoon of Sunday 2nd June the numbers of English and French soldiers were of about equal proportions. Thereafter, except for a little bunch of Englishmen including two generals on Monday morning, they were almost all French until the trains stopped about 6.00 pm on Tuesday.

Looking back the week seemed a confused dream of trains continuously rushing through the station full of tired, bearded dirty men with hands clutching food and drink and yet how glad everyone was to be able to do anything, however small, for these men whose deliverance can only be described as a miracle. Two things were absolutely outstanding in the men's conversation, their bitter hatred of the Belgians and the feeling that our Air Force had let them down. They kept complaining of the waves of German bombers and, to them, never a plane of ours in sight. There were examples of men with neither shoes nor socks. And yet their spirit was magnificent and they were all ready to go back after they had rested. But it was an inspiring and deeply moving experience and those who were present counted it a high privilege to have been there.

As a 10-year-old, Judith List has memories of the evacuation of troops from Dunkirk. Her family lived in the North Lodge originally part of Langton Priory outside Guildford. One imagines that as an avid reader of Enid Blyton, a 'secret path' at the bottom of the garden led down to beside the Portsmouth Direct line between St Catherine's Hill tunnel and the Chalk tunnel. From here she recalled witnessing the troops returning from Dunkirk, and almost every train was held up in the Valley between the tunnels. Only the ambulance trains appeared to get a straight run through. Ladies from the Women's Institute also found their way down to the line past the Valley cottages. At first they may have taken trays of sandwiches, but as it was difficult to feed a whole troop train. On the other hand, the men were desperate to get news home to their families so as each train came in the WI members walked along the side of the tracks with large baskets handing out postcards and pencils and then collecting them up again for posting.

As many of the trains arriving at Woking came via Redhill and Guildford, they will have had to stop at the station while the engines were changed before heading off in a westerly direction. This gave an opportunity for the WVS to organise the handing out of tea and buns on the platform. Once it became clear that increasing numbers of French troops were passing through on their way to

A view of Guildford station from the Farnham Road bridge showing six through lines and associated platforms. From here a collection was made from members of the public watching the trains stopped in the station for the purpose of feeding the exhausted troops.

*R.K. Blencowe Collection*

A huge heap of empty cartons and orange boxes piled up against the stairway to the footbridge at Guildford station with the station master and some volunteers looking on. *Courtesy British Red Cross*

The view that might have been witnessed by 10-year-old Judith List of Langton Priory. The signals for Shalford Junction, south of Guildford are in the background, where the line from Redhill joins the Portsmouth Direct line to head northwards through the Sand and Chalk tunnels into Guildford station itself. This train, probably photographed shortly before the war, shows SR No. 1802, formerly 2-6-4T 'K' class *River Cuckmere* built in August 1926 and rebuilt two years later as a 2-6-0 'U' class, hauling a Redhill to Reading train.                                              *Transport Panorama/Author's Collection*

return to France from ports further west, the need for French speakers became evident. A regular passenger known to the station master, Mr Avery, was Eric Davenport, who had commuted from Woking station to the City since 1933, but currently chained to a desk in the Adelphi as a 'temporary civil servant' in the Ministry of Supply. Somehow it was discovered that he was fluent in the French language, so he and some friends found themselves on liaison duties.

At Basingstoke, then only a country town, the Mayor with the assistance of an energetic lady of the town quickly assembled a group of volunteers and, with the help of a contribution of £100 from the staff of Thornycrofts Works, raised and expended £500 on providing refreshments for the troops as they paused at the station while on their way to some Southern Command camp. Around a hundred, mainly lady, helpers, drawn from local churches, the Rotarians, the Fire Brigade etc., were roped in to prepare food and drink, while bakers and confectioners in the town worked overtime to provide the necessary ingredients.

On the alternative route from the coast the station master's wife at Penge East rose to the occasion, quickly supported by volunteers, with chocolate, fruit and cigarettes. As one of the first troop trains paused there that Sunday, a Salvation Army band happened to be passing along the road and were invited by the station master to come and play to the troops. That evening the band returned to raise funds at an impromptu concert in the goods yard, assisted by the station master on the clarinet, songs from a guard accompanied by a railway clerk on the Station master's piano, and other local artists. Some of the excess funds raised on that occasion were used to provide fruit and tobacco to wounded soldiers in Orpington and Farnborough (Kent) hospitals over the next eight weeks.

Not all trains passed through Redhill, especially those from the north Kent coast which were frequently routed through south London heading for Addison Road, Kensington and on to the LMS lines for the North and West. At Faversham, a British soldier on the platform hands cigarettes across to a French comrade in arms.
*Courtesy British Red Cross*

The school playing fields of the Beckenham & Penge County Grammar School for boys at Penge in South London backed onto the railway line between Penge East & Kent House immediately adjacent to Kent House station. Trains carrying French troops rescued from Dunkirk were frequently held at signals adjacent to the playing fields of, it is thought, this school.   Soon the boys had made contact, scrabbling up the slippery embankment to offer gifts of sweets, chocolates and biscuits to these unshaven, weary and dusty men.  In due course, convoys were organized to bring them water, cakes and fruit. One soldier scribbled on the back of a packet of cigarettes *'Nous n'oublierons jamais cet accuiel chalereux. Merci!'* (We will never forget this warm welcome. Thank you). One of the masters had, probably highly illegally, taken a cine film, which after the war would be shown to the boys in the main hall. This showed troop trains and hospital trains held at signals near the playing fields carrying men recently returned from Dunkirk.

At one south London station used as a 'halte-repas', a Mrs Watkins, the wife of the station master scoured the faces of every soldier she could in the hope of spotting her 19-year-old son, Cyril, without success until eventually he shouted 'Hello mother' from one that was only passing through, rather than stopping.

The YMCA ran canteens at Charing Cross, Victoria, Waterloo, London Bridge, Euston and Liverpool Street stations. The Salvation Army was also operating at King's Cross and St Pancras while the Church Army was fulfilling a similar function at Paddington station. Margaret Henry of the British Red Cross recalled the trainloads of troops pausing at Derby station during the night, as their trains made their way north. Here also the young soldiers were plied with cups of tea.

At an unknown location discarded paper cups litter the cess.          *Courtesy British Red Cross*

A wounded corporal and a veteran of earlier conflicts, leans on the shoulder of a naval petty officer and is assisted from behind as they ascend the gangplank by which to reach Dover quayside on 31st May, 1940.

*Courtesy British Red Cross*

# Chapter Eight

# Treatment of Casualties and Ambulance Trains

At the start of the campaign the planned return of the wounded from France was undertaken via Dieppe, where a medical base had been set up, to Newhaven. In the early days of the war, up to eight hospital trains were based at Newhaven, from where they could move to the north, or westwards. In the latter case, due to the constraints of the layout at Brighton, arrangements were in place for the train to arrive in the terminal station from the direction of Lewes, when a pilot engine would be attached at the rear. This would then draw the train back about a mile and a quarter along the main line to Preston Park, from where the train would resume its journey in a westerly direction via Hove and on towards Chichester etc.

With the launch of Operation Dynamo, the number of hospital beds available in the south-east of England was clearly going to be inadequate and anyway the threat of invasion made them inappropriate for all but the most serious and urgent cases. The plan was, therefore, to move the wounded away from the south-east as quickly as possible and for this purpose hospitals far and wide were cleared of non-urgent cases. In the event ambulance trains were taking men to places as far away as Lancashire and Leeds. By this time the condition of some of the patients' wounds had deteriorated markedly stretching the nursing resources at the reception hospitals to the extreme.

Medical reception centres were organized by the War Office through Eastern Command at each point of disembarkation. A few motor ambulances were made available at each point, together with a reserve pool, for clearing lying cases to hospital. The walking wounded were to be made as comfortable as possible on the trains. A medical officer and staff were to be in attendance at each official feeding station to deal with casualties who could not continue their journey.

### Operation Dynamo
### Hospital Ships Arriving at Newhaven

| Date | Time | Name of ship | No. carried |
|------|------|--------------|-------------|
| 27th May | 04.35 | Isle of Guernsey | 346 |
| | – | Worthing | 300 |
| 29th May | 08.35 | Dinard | 271 |
| | 16.53 | St David | 118 |
| | – | Paris | 400 |
| 30th May | 11.15 | Isle of Guernsey | 490 |
| 31st May | 17.47 | St Julien | 247 |
| | – | Dinard | 90 |
| | – | Paris | 230 |
| | – | Worthing | 300 |
| 1st June | 07.14 | St Andrew | 122 |
| | | Total | 2,914 |

Once the BEF and its allies were cut off from the rest of France, the wounded were often brought to Dover. Here the walking wounded are proceeding along the quayside to waiting trains. As well as the one man with a stick being assisted, notice the labels tied to each man, no doubt detailing the medical diagnosis and treatment already administered.

*Picture Service/Author's Collection*

A nurse tends to a stretcher case on the quayside before being loaded into a waiting ambulance train for transport to an inland hospital. *Courtesy British Red Cross*

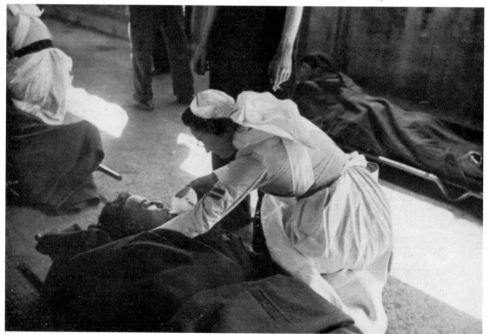

Once the BEF and its allies were encircled and cut off from the rest of France, the use of Dieppe was no longer possible and the wounded were necessarily evacuated from Dunkirk. Here some of the wounded waited three nights before being taken out to the mole to board a hospital ship. While waiting, they lay four abreast inside a wall of cotton bales for protection from the shelling. Once the ship was alongside, boards were put down for people to walk, or crawl onto the boat, while others had to be carried aboard on stretchers. Upon arrival at Dover, Newhaven, or elsewhere they were transferred to a hospital train.

To deal with the critically wounded, Buckland Hospital on the outskirts of Dover was commandeered and other patients were taken to Folkestone Hospital. Those troops well enough to travel were sent to numerous hospitals all over the country, including: Tidworth Military Hospital; Salisbury Royal Infirmary; Sutton Emergency Hospital; Botley's Hospital, Ottershaw; Southampton; Queen Elizabeth Hospital, Birmingham, the train travelling by the Didcot, Newbury & Southampton line; the Derby Royal Infirmary; and Yorkshire. The Emergency Military Hospital, Burntwood, Lichfield, received 500 mostly injured and shell-shocked. Royal Victoria Military Hospital Netley once again saw its bed strength increase at the outbreak of another World War. During World War II it treated casualties throughout the war which included patients from the Dunkirk evacuation in 1940, later being used by the Americans.

Some wounded were taken by train to Hendon, where sandwiches and a cup of tea were handed out by guardsmen and ladies of the WVS, while civilians arrived at the station with gifts of food and cigarettes. In this case the train continued to Southport Infirmary, where patients remained for a week while the medical staff sorted out all the patients according to their injuries. They were then transported onwards to the selected hospital, sometimes by bus.

Surgeon Captain A.R. Fisher, as Senior Medical Officer at Dover, reporting on the organization for the reception of casualties, stated that prior to the evacuation starting he had at his disposal five medical officers (MOs) and 19 sick bay staff. These were drawn from the sick bays of the Royal Naval Sick Quarters; HMS *Sandhurst*, a destroyer depot ship at Dover, an ex-merchant ship *Manipur*, built by Harland and Wolff, Belfast; and the Dover Patrol Sick Bay. At their disposal were two four-cot motor ambulances and two hand-powered ambulances. To man these, two stretcher parties each of a petty officer and eight men had been trained and kept available at HMS *Lynx*.

Upon receipt of information on expected casualties, the senior MO at the RN sick quarters would make arrangements for the wounded to be received at the landing stages. All ships carrying wounded were met by a team of one MO and two sick bay attendants equipped with a Neil Robertson stretcher, a field service valise, a haversack of first aid and an ambulance. The MO would immediately board the vessel to ascertain the number of casualties, establish the ambulance transport required, assess the need and prioritize patients. From a practical point of view it was found expedient to let the fit troops vacate the ship prior to landing casualties, while the MO rendered first aid to the more seriously wounded if necessary. This included morphia injections, dressings applied with least disturbance to cover wounds, offering hot drinks and keeping the patient warm. On the other hand no blood transfusions were administered on the quayside. In this way urgent cases were taken to a nearby hospital; the non-urgent stretcher cases sent farther afield, mainly by ambulance train; and the walking wounded to either a train or nearby sick bays. Labels were attached where necessary to pass on information about the condition and the treatment already dispensed.

For more serious cases, the specialist Neil Robertson stretcher was found invaluable in containing the patient as he was removed from the vessel and transported to where he could be treated. Unfortunately this vital piece of equipment was in such short supply that patients had to be transferred to field or ARP stretchers as soon as practical often on the quayside. At first minor cases were sent to the RN Sick Quarters of HMS *Sandhurst*, whilst the more serious were taken to one of the following hospitals:

### Hospitals for Serious Casualties in Dover Area

| Name | Location | No of Beds | No of surgical teams | Distance (miles) |
| --- | --- | --- | --- | --- |
| EMS Casualty Hospital | Dover | 100 | 2 | 1½ |
| Royal Marine Infirmary | Deal | 150 | 2 | 9 |
| Military Hospital | Shorncliffe | 200 | 3 | 11 |
| Royal Naval Hospital | Chatham | | | 43 |

There was co-operation between the various medical services. Agreement was reached between the military and civil authorities to pool resources. By this means the number of motor ambulances initially available was five from military sources and 14 from civilian, the latter made up of four regular ambulances and 10 converted vehicles. Their efficient use, however, was not helped by difficulties in communication between the Naval and Royal Army Medical Corps (RAMC) transport when the offices were two miles apart and with a telephone system which at the time was grossly over-loaded.

Initially only a few minor naval casualties were dealt with largely by naval resources. From 10th May refugees began to arrive from the Netherlands, followed by refugees of various nationalities and troops from Boulogne and Calais, amongst whom were some casualties. Once the evacuation got into full swing, it soon became evident, however, that local medical staff were more usefully employed rendering first aid to minor cases, while leaving the more seriously injured to be transported to hospital. To establish their ability to receive fresh cases, base hospitals were asked to provide estimates of their capacity twice daily and, as the operation progressed, hospitals further inland became involved. To cope with the influx hospital staffs were augmented.

On 25th May additional staff, two ambulances and a converted motor bus were transferred on loan from Chatham. By this time also the RAMC was established at Dover Marine railway station and organized the ambulance trains and convoys of motor ambulances. As a consequence, it was arranged that the RAMC would cope with all the casualties landed at Admiralty Pier, while naval staff dealt with those brought ashore elsewhere, regardless of the Arm to which the patient belonged.

Naval medical facilities at Dover worked at high pressure coping with up to 200 cases a night. Most were wounded, but some had suffered immersion or nervous exhaustion, the treatment for the latter being a hot meal, a dose of bromide and a good night's sleep. Most stayed no more than a night or two before being discharged to either a rest camp or to hospital. At one port in the south-east a hostel was operated by the WVS for the next of kin of seriously wounded men who had been landed in the vicinity. Out of the 177,780 troops landed at Dover between 25th May and 5th June 6,880 were casualties requiring hospital treatment, the peak being about 1,200 on 31st May. Many were transferred to Buckland hospital where teams of surgeons worked day and night saving the lives of all but fifty. A constant stream of stretcher bearers was required to convey the injured from the ships and boats to the ambulance trains.

A mortuary was set up in New Customs shed at Dover, while the old one was used as a clothing store for those poorly clad. Members of the ATS/FANYs were on hand in requisitioned lorries kitted out as ambulances to convey the injured to hospital. From end of May until 10th June over 31,000 casualties were carried by ambulance trains for admittance to military and emergency medical hospitals throughout UK.

Similar collaborative arrangements were put in hand at Ramsgate, and no doubt other landing points. Surgeon Lieut B.H. Palmer RNVR of the Naval Sick Quarters at Ramsgate reported that the Merrie England base, and former entertainment complex, was used as a casualty clearing station, supported by the Naval Officer in Command. The wounded were rapidly cleared from the ships as they berthed. A naval and a military doctor were always available at the pier head from some time before and after high tide, when many of the larger vessels entered the harbour. Medical personnel rallied at the pier head where stocks of dressings, stretchers and medical essentials were kept. Ambulances were available from military, ARP and St John's.

Many cases of both simple and compound fracture of the thigh and leg, together with other severe mutilations, due to bomb blast, were encountered resulting in shock as they were moved from confined spaces aboard the ships, especially if they had also been subjected to prolonged immersion in the water. At the height of the emergency the Port Medical Officer at Dover sent over two naval surgeons to Ramsgate, although one, with stores and first aid material, was promptly dispatched to Margate to carry out similar duties there. The additional MO at Ramsgate enabled one to put to sea and make contact with the wounded aboard vessels which may have broken down or could not make the harbour for various reasons. About a dozen wounded enemy soldiers and airmen were attended to on the pier. At the peak approximately 170 wounded were dealt with within a 24 hour period, leading to those engaged in their care suffering from nervous strain and lack of sleep.

Large numbers of wounded military personnel were dealt with at the base and removed by military ambulance to various destinations. Of the naval and mercantile marine personnel, two naval ambulances took 32 wounded to the Royal Naval Hospital at Chatham; 20 matelots and four French sailors to Ramsgate Hospital; and six RN, two merchant and one French sailors were moved to the Holy Cross Hospital in the town. Fourteen less serious cases were treated at the RN sick quarters in Ramsgate, together with 50 more naval ratings with minor injuries to enable them to travel. Owing to the need to keep local hospitals near the coast clear of patients not too ill to travel, due to the risk of invasion, many were soon transferred to more inland hospitals, such as: Tunbridge Wells; Preston Hall, Maidstone; Dartford; Canterbury; and Farnborough, Kent.

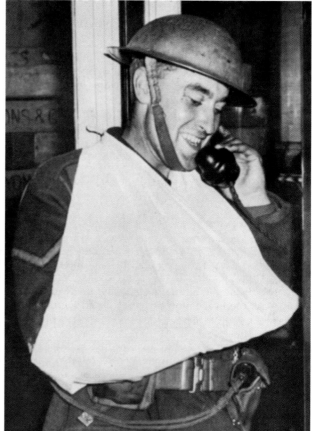

*Right:* This lance-corporal with his arm in a sling is able to telephone home to report his safe arrival back in England.

*Courtesy British Red Cross*

*Below:* Photographs of ambulance trains in service are extremely rare, but the date of 27th May, 1940 of this one suggests that it might just have been running in connection with the early stages of the evacuation from Dunkirk. It shows LNER 2-6-0 'K3' class No. 1307 heading past Low Fell Junction towards Newcastle.

*W.B. Greenfield, courtesy NELPG*

In the military context the value of anti-shock treatment was already appreciated and radiant heat and/or blood transfusions were carried out prior to transfer to the operating theatre. In those days the wounded were issued a smart blue uniform. Such was the sympathy of members of the public that such a uniform often resulted in goods and services being offered at no cost.

Within a period of a fortnight, it was the sad duty of the Senior Chaplin at St Mary de Castro, the Saxon church within Dover Castle, to bury over 140 of those who had succumbed to their wounds. Due to the difficulty in travelling at the time, this often took place in the presence of only the wife or even without any of his family or friends at all, in attendance as mourners.

### Ambulance Trains

During 1939-40 home-based ambulance trains: HAT Nos. 59, 60, 61 and 62 were stationed at Newhaven and these undertook 52 journeys to various destinations all over the country. Likewise HAT Nos. 55, 56, 57, 58, 63, 64 65 and 66, during the first year of the war made 55 journeys from Southampton.

As the evacuation progressed and the military situation in France dictated that more of the wounded were landed at Dover, rather than Newhaven, one ambulance train was kept on platform 3 at Dover Marine station in the process of being loaded, with another in a siding close at hand and a third 12 miles inland at Ashford. Some 4,646 wounded men are understood to have been moved in the course of the whole evacuation from Dover. During the evacuation the following ambulance trains were dispatched from SR stations:

| | |
|---|---|
| Newhaven | 17 |
| Dover | 8 |
| Ramsgate | 1 |
| Margate | ? |

Of these 26 travelled via Redhill.

Many of the wounded were taken to the Royal Victoria Hospital at Netley, access to which was via a branch from the Southampton to Fareham line. Because there were no locomotive turning facilities at Netley, the train engine had to be at the rear of the train and this was therefore assisted by the provision of an ex-LBSC 0-6-0 'E1' class tank engine to help the train over steep gradients and led the train on the return journey.

With the arrival back in Britain of large numbers of sick and wounded 2,800 mobile VADs, who had yet to be posted, were released so that they might join the Civil Nursing Reserve and staff the over-stretched EMS hospitals.

The GWR dealt with 52 ambulance trains. Following the end of Operation Dynamo, casualties initially placed after landing in local hospitals were gathered up into civilian evacuation train CET 18, made up of Gresley stock, on 10th June, 1940, the train being staffed by VADs from the British Red Cross and the St John's Ambulance Brigade and leading to the train being nicknamed Knight Errant.

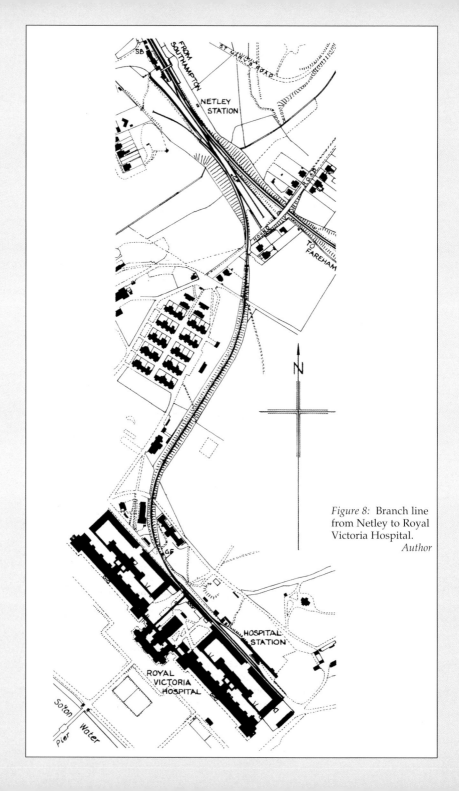

*Figure 8:* Branch line from Netley to Royal Victoria Hospital.
*Author*

# Chapter Nine

# Reception Areas

The staffs of the Command headquarters, in which Reception Areas were located, were responsible for the initial sorting out and onward dispatch of personnel to the Divisional Areas in the case of divisional troops and Corps and GHQ troops to Re-organisational Centres. To assist them in their task, officers from GHQ 'A' were dispatched, together with clerical personnel, three officers reporting to Aldershot Command and four to Southern Command to work under the orders of the General Officer Commanding (GOC) concerned. To facilitate reference to the composition of divisions of the BEF, orders of battle were forwarded by special motorcycle dispatch rider to the command, divisional, corps headquarters and GHQ with a view ultimately to reassembling troops in their divisional and corps areas as shown in the order of battle.

The sudden arrival of such a large number of men presented a considerable problem to the Directorate of Ordnance in the matter of meeting the need for accommodation for the troops and the provision of large quantities of cooking stores at very short notice.

Although some did arrive as a unit, or part of one, no attempt was made in Phase 1 to sort out men into their units on landing. Instead the priority was to get them away from the coast out of the way of possible shelling or aerial bombardment. They were, therefore, sent to reception centres set up at camps all over the southern half of the country to be rested and cared for. Here a roll call of names, numbers, rank and units would be taken. The troops were given a hot meal, an opportunity to change out of soiled clothing, followed by the issue of a clean towel, shaving and washing kit with the opportunity for a hot shower or bath, and rest in a bed, often under canvas.

Members of the Royal Army Pay Corps furnished officers in charge of units or sub-units with cash and acquittance rolls to enable immediate payment to be made, or to pay individual 'other ranks' whose units or officers were not present, with which to make small purchases in the NAAFI. Under orders issued by the Chief Paymaster at the War Office, sufficient staff were arranged to be able to deal with up to 20,000 men at each Reception Area. The possible loss of AB 64, Part II, the Army pay book, was anticipated and arrangements made for 'other ranks' that arrived without pay books and could establish their identity to be issued with a replacement.

A few posts at likely landing places had been established in the hope that ordinary stores might be collected from any of the men who might have got away with technical equipment such as gun sights etc., but all that was collected were a some rifles, pistols, grenades and some blankets. Each post consisted of a small party from the Royal Army Ordnance Corps (RAOC), with an officer for every four or five posts, at such places as Margate, Ramsgate, Dover, Hythe, Folkestone and Newhaven. If not already relieved of their rifles or other arms and grenades on landing in the country, this was done upon arrival at the first rest camp. Many rifles were in poor condition anyway after having been used to dig foxholes in the dunes behind the beaches. There was therefore a need to recondition all such equipment before being reissued.

The initial reception areas were intended to tide over the immediate accommodation problem, but within a few days personnel were sorted out by each Command and sent by rail to areas where units were being reformed. In Phase 1 upon arrival each man was issued with one blanket, plus another on temporary loan, while a further blanket was issued on arrival at the divisional areas in Phase 2, after which clothing and equipment were replaced. Officers of formations accommodated in the London area had to find their own lodgings for which a 'detention allowance' was authorized for eight days.

Great pressure was brought to bear on the War Office to allow each man to send a free telegram upon arrival in England, but this was considered impractical. Instead arrangements were made for one free-post field service postcard to be issued to each man upon arrival at reception centres and passed in bulk to the nearest GPO, deliveries of blank pre-printed cards having been dispatched by passenger train to Command headquarters to arrive on the afternoon of 29th May.

Corporal Richard Holborow records that at Eastville Park in Bristol, where the Gloucester Regiment was quartered in tents, for some days the camp had been reorganized in anticipation of receiving evacuated troops. Amongst other things trenches were dug by the resident troops and screens erected to provide extra latrines. When the survivors arrived they were in a most exhausted condition not least because most were from front-line fighting units. They were tired, dirty and short of most of their kit. Very few of them had come back with their weapons and from the haunted look on their faces one could tell that they had suffered a great deal during their traumatic experiences of the previous few weeks. After a good feed, wash and sleep the majority perked up quite well and they soon were fitted out with replacement kit. Due to the pressure on the railway system, leave for home troops had been suspended and it was only possible to send evacuated men home on leave after some wait. In compensation, however, the Bristolians were anxious to take them into their homes for entertainment and often to stay for a few days. Eventually they dispersed to their reassembly areas, while at Eastville Park the temporary arrangements were removed and returned to normal.

Just prior to the fall of Dunkirk, an ATS company was transferred from a requisitioned country house in Narborough in Leicestershire to a newly-built military camp in Ramsey, Huntingdonshire. Here, following the evacuation, uninjured troops, about 100 at a time, were marched into the camps exhausted and in tatters, some wearing legless trousers and armless jackets or even less. As a consequence of their arrival, members of the ATS unit were stretched to feed and provide for them. All had to help in the kitchens preparing food, such as peeling potatoes, cleaning other vegetables and washing up. Camp beds and blankets had to be provided, and the quartermaster had to re-equip the soldiers with suitable clothing.

L/Cpl D. Dutton of the RAMC had similar experiences at Beckett's Park Barracks in Leeds, where he helped take particulars and issue blankets and meals to a batch of 250 BEF troops, who had arrived at 03.45 hours in the morning of 31st May. Further parties of men turned up in groups of 50 to 60 at a time at intervals during the afternoon and evening up until 9th June. After staying 24 to 48 hours earlier batches were sent to billets in private houses around Leeds, so as to make room for further arrivals. By the end of June these had all moved on and the routine at the barracks returned to normal and the possibility of leave was reinstated.

On the Sunday morning in Cricklade an officer knocked on front doors of houses to ask if the occupants had a bathroom, and, if so, could a couple of men from France have a bath? These duly arrived in their dirty clothes and somewhat smelly as they would not have been changed since sometime before leaving Dunkirk. The officer informed the soldiers that once in the bathroom they were to throw their dirty clothes out the window and put on the clean clothes in their kitbags. Needless to say the men were very grateful for the opportunity of a bath and change of clothes. At Devizes men slept on a mattress on the floor in a school gym. After two or three days the men were gradually returned to their units. There, at last, they were able to exchange their salt-encrusted battle dress and be issued with a hat, thereby enabling them to go out on the streets again and have a pint of beer.

Obviously, with so many soldiers returned from France, it took the authorities a little while to sort them out, so some spent a few days kicking their heels, until orders came to post them to where their regiments were being reformed. Nonetheless, in the meantime most men had recovered from their fatigue, were much fitter and back to their old selves.

In fine weather all over the south of England men relax in the sunshine and recover their energy, here with tented accommodation in the background.    *Courtesy British Red Cross*

*Above:* An English lady of mature years responds to Gallic flattery as she dispenses much needed drinks from a large enamel jug to a crowd of French soldiers shortly after their arrival on British shores.

*Author's Collection*

Right: A wounded French soldier has his ankle treated while waiting for the train at Ramsgate station.

*Courtesy British Red Cross*

# Chapter Ten

## Reception of Allied Troops and return of French Troops to France

The French 1st Army had fought alongside the BEF on the right flank to the south and west, and many of them too had been cut off by the German thrust to the sea. In France, the perceived preference of the Royal Navy for evacuating British forces at the expense of the French led to some resentment. At high level a certain degree of mistrust seems to have set in between the Allies following the enemy's break through and the combined failure to mount satisfactory counterattacks, when maximum cooperation was required to restore the desperate situation. Instead, once the lines of communication were cut and with supplies of food and ammunition running short, evacuation through Dunkirk was considered as the only option open to the British and in their view to their Allies in North Eastern France also. Furthermore, the First Army's commander General Blanchard was forced to take up command of the First Group of Armies following the tragic death of General Billotte in a road accident on 21st May, only for the former's replacement General Prioux to be captured by the Germans eight days later. As a consequence leadership of the BEF's French comrades was somewhat shaken and damaging to morale, leading in a few cases to a breakdown in order.

The first part of the evacuation consisted mainly of British troops, but on 29th May formal orders were given for the French to evacuate as well, when on 31st May Churchill instructed that French and British troops should be embarked in equal proportions. At the conclusion a few thousand French forces eventually surrendered, but only after the evacuation effort had been extended for a day to bring a further 26,175 Frenchmen to Britain on 4th June.

Initial plans had been made to assemble the various allied troops at specific reception centres and in this case 5,000 each had been allowed for the French at Tidworth; the Belgians at Tenby; and the Dutch at Haverfordwest. But it soon became evident that many more French troops than originally anticipated might reasonably be expected to arrive on British shores. General Lelong, Chief of the French Mission in London estimated that this might amount to between 50,000 to 100,000 men, as larger numbers than at first predicted fought their way to the coast. Scarcity of shipping made it essential that they should be brought back to England in the first instance instead of moving direct to French ports south of the Somme.

The more than 100,000 evacuated French troops were disarmed, in the same manner as the British despite protestations in some cases, and efficiently transported, to camps in various parts of south-western England where they were temporarily lodged before quickly being repatriated.

Once in Britain larger parties of foreign troops were to be escorted en route by our troops drawn from local units. Smaller parties were to be taken over by the local Officer Commanding, the War Office being informed by telephone of the strength and nationality of each party and accommodated locally until a sufficient number had been collected to justify a special train. In the meantime they were to be confined to barracks and kept under close watch and interpreters obtained from Military Intelligence if really necessary.

Early arrivals included members of the Terrestres Anti-aériennes (FTA) who at 4.00 pm on 28th May landed at Folkestone, from where they were sent to London and spent the night at St Stephen's Service Club before moving on to Tidworth the next day. Three days later they were to be followed by 800 taken by train directly to Tidworth and later others to the vicinity of Ludgershall, before being taken to the south coast and shipped back across the Channel.

As the influx rapidly increased towards the conclusion of the Operation, clearly more radical measures were necessary. In a stoke of genius, it was decided to invite the mayors of certain southern seaside towns, no doubt currently denuded of the usual summer visitors in their hotels and boarding houses, to ask their citizens to house the evacuated French soldiers. In return for which arrangements would be made for increased rations, such as canned beef, bread or biscuit, tea, sugar, milk, cigarettes and matches, to be available in bulk through military channels to the local authority in those towns for use by people accommodating French troops. The mayors responded readily, some even using cars with loud speakers to tour their towns to enlist the help of residents, and agreed to take the following:

| | |
|---|---|
| Southampton | 15,000 |
| Bournemouth | 25,000 |
| Weymouth | 5,000 |
| Plymouth | 15,000 |

As it turned out the last three towns largely exceeded the numbers promised.

In response to the telephone call to the Mayor of Bournemouth asking the town to accommodate a number of French soldiers, a conference with the military was set up at which the town was requested to receive more than the number initially indicated and that the first train load was expected within a few hours. The Mayor called in the Town Clerk, the heads of the Corporation transport, education, medical, catering; and the Borough Engineer; together with the Police, the British Red Cross, St John Ambulance Brigade, war service, commercial and charitable organizations to arrange for their assistance in the great task.

As well as providing space in the Town Hall and the service of the staff at the disposal of the authorities, the Council Chamber was used by the French for their conferences. It was decided to close several educational establishments and other communal buildings to accommodate the influx. Headmasters were placed in charge of arrangements at each of their schools. They were warned to expect some men to arrive imminently, when they were to provide food and drink and other facilities. Further batches arrived in the coming days and dispatched to various places for accommodation.

Space was found at the local council schools, including the Bournemouth School for Boys, which took 2,500 troops; Bournemouth School for Girls; Malmesbury Park School; Winton; Moordown; and the Municipal College where between two and five o'clock in the afternoon of 30th May the school was transformed into a barracks. Following the Mayor, Alderman Reg Hayward's appeal, people flocked in their hundreds to local schools to prepare beds and food, while the pupils gained an unexpected holiday. Majors A.F. Page and S.C. Jones organized their reception from Bournemouth Town Hall, while feeding the men was the responsibility of Mr L.H. Harker the Borough's Deputy Food Officer. Preparing food was undertaken centrally with the Corporation's Catering Department, marshalling all the resources of the Pavillion to find sufficient food for the men until the arrival of Army rations. From headquarters in Westover Road, allocations of bread, tins of corn beef, milk, etc. were put together by soldiers aided by Boy Scouts and distributed, along with blankets, to the feeding centres, such as Dean Court football ground and the Christadelphian Hall. The resources of the Bournemouth Gas and Water Company were called upon, whose fitters working through the night installed 100 cookers and 68 wash coppers in the district by 8.30 am the next morning. Likewise the Auxiliary Fire Service assisted in laying on emergency water supplies. Upon departure of the French troops all this work had to be undone and the parts returned to the showrooms and stores.

Members of the St John Ambulance Brigade administered first aid treatment for long periods. For their part members of the town's Cercle Francais found a cause worth working for and provided numerous interpreters to settle men into their billets, prepare literature and supply French flags. Appeals for clothing and soap were met in abundance enabling such things as clean underwear, new shoes and socks to be handed out.

**Items dispensed by the War Service Organization from their Comfort Depot**

| | | | |
|---|---|---|---|
| Shirts | 3,152 | Boots & shoes | 101 |
| Socks (pairs) | 3,153 | Berets | 700 |
| Pants | 1,472 | Towels | 1,068 |
| Vests | 512 | Handkerchiefs | 1,096 |
| Soft slippers | 202 | Miscellaneous | 136 |

In addition to this, 12,000 cigarettes, stationery, razors, sweets, tooth brushes and paste, shaving brushes, playing cards, boot polish and brushes and other necessaries were collected at short notice and handed out.

On Sunday many residents of the town entertained one or two French troops at their homes, where they would be given a meal and after a sleep, offered a bath, or taken out to cafes, while others enjoyed playing on the beaches yet to be mined and barricaded off against invasion. Having been on the battlefield for so long, there was a great demand for haircuts, while at the YMCA free shaves were also on offer, along with recreation activities. Not surprisingly, there was a run on French dictionaries in the town.

The new premises of the Bournemouth School for Boys (grammar) in East Way had been opened as the war broke out. With the arrival of French troops nine months later, Jim Bartle, a teenage pupil, remembers this being taken over for use as accommodation for French troops. During their stay there, Jim and his school friend Bertie Love, as Boys Scouts attended to some of the soldiers' feet, cutting off their boots where the blood had otherwise made it impossible to remove then. They also had a couple of French soldiers back to his mother Lillian's bungalow in Broadway Lane, Throop for tea, during which they

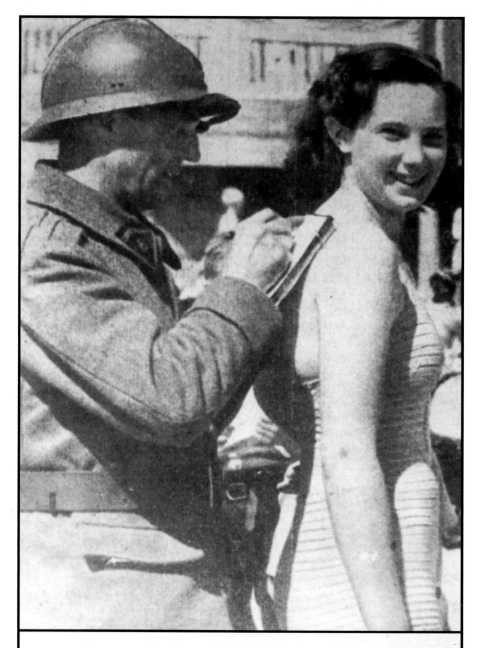

# FROM THE FRONT TO THE BACK!

Here's a Poilu who does thing in style and you'll agree he's selected a snappy line in writing desks! Just another delightful little Entente Cordiale cameo seen everywhere in Bournemouth this week.

A cutting from the *Bournemouth Evening Echo* for 14th June, 1940 showing a French soldier writing in his notebook rested on the back of a pretty girl. *Courtesy Bournemouth Echo*

gathered confidence in the use of their schoolboy French. They promised to keep in touch, but nothing further was heard, reluctantly leading to the conclusion that perhaps the worst had happened to the pair either during or following their return to France.

For their part the French troops laid a floral tribute of pink and white carnations tied with red, white and blue ribbon with a suitable inscription on the Bournemouth War Memorial in the Lower Pleasure Gardens in thanks to the townsfolk and in remembrance. At a reception in the Council Chamber, official thanks for all the hospitality received was expressed to the Council and a sum of 1,000 francs donated for charitable disbursements for the benefit of our own troops. Elsewhere more unofficial thanks were expressed by the men, such as a message scrawled on a school blackboard reading: 'We were strangers and you took us in and when we are back in France we will remember the happy days we passed with you. *Vivre l'Angleterre'*.

In Weymouth they had already received evacuee children at the outbreak of war, followed by mariners shipwrecked as a result of striking a mine or being struck by torpedo. Then from 21st May, 1940 civilian refugees arrived from Belgium and France, as they were, later from 19th June, from the Channel Islands. A procedure was in place for each to be medically examined upon arrival and sent as appropriate to hospital, isolation hospital, maternity home, cleansing station, or temporary accommodation to be fed and rested, before being moved on by train to reception camps.

So when on 31st May, the Town Clerk received the message from the Government calling upon the residents to receive about 5,000 or more French soldiers and that the first batches were already on their way, he issued a circular to the head school teachers in the Borough of Weymouth and Melcombe Regis informing them of the situation. He requested them to close their school and send the children home. All teachers were asked to report at 2.30 pm at the Welcome Club in King Street to be briefed on distributing the soldiers to residents within a district allocated to them. A loudspeaker van toured the town during that afternoon to warn members of the public what to expect and to elicit their support and asking them to give food and shelter to their guests for a night or two.

The first of the French troops arrived in the early hours of the next day at Weymouth station from where they were conducted to Christ Church, offered sustenance in the form of corn-beef and half a loaf of bread, after which they either walked a short distance to their accommodation for the night, or were taken on by bus to outlying villages. The schools and public halls were used first to accommodate a substantial number of the French and Moroccan troops. They stayed for considerably longer than the two or three days initially envisaged and the schools did not reopen until 17th June, 1940. Great hospitality was shown throughout, with food, including coffee, freely provided. Interpreters were found to translate where sign language failed, all of which was much appreciated. During this period 73 French and Colonial soldiers were treated at the St John's Ambulance First Aid Post, while members of the Brigade also acted as guides, attended to sore feet and generally made themselves useful.

Jim Bartle and his school friend Bertie Love in Boy Scout uniform standing beside two French Chef Corporals being entertained at the Bartle's home in Bournemouth. *J. Bartle Collection*

The same two poilus standing each side of Mrs Lilian Bartle. *J. Bartle Collection*

At Southampton many men were messed by the transit camp which already existed. The provision of canned beef, bread or biscuit, tea, sugar, milk, cigarettes and matches was arranged through military channels for issue in bulk to town authorities, who distributed to billeters. Women of the WVS staffed 15 out of the 20 schools used to accommodate troops, including Manor Road School in Bitterne Park. At one such school local residents handed sandwiches and cakes to the French troops through the railings. Before they left, the French indicated their gratitude to the British for their organization of the evacuation and the welcome received and again even chalked up their thanks on the blackboards of more than one school. A transit camp was also used and as well as being provided with food, somehow sufficient red wine was obtained to be able to make an issue. While waiting to sail back on 7th June, they were entertained to a show of singing and dancing. Elsewhere barbers offered free haircuts and others free use of shoe shining equipment.

Further afield, to assist in the welfare of foreign troops billeted in the area, the WVS set up an Allied Information Bureau in Edinburgh, catering amongst other things for soldiers who spoke little or no English. French, Polish, Norwegian, Dutch and Czech speaking ladies were enrolled into the WVS specially for the purpose of being able to assist these visiting troops. Later, as the war progressed, other centres opened to cater for foreign guests, such as for the Poles in Cambridge, while the Malvern Centre, as no doubt at many centres elsewhere, coped with numerous requests.

Arrangements were made by the Director of Movements to ship French soldiers back to France south of the River Somme at the rate of 15,000 a day and which was only just achieved. British ships seem to have sailed to Cherbourg and French vessels to Brest. It was proposed that on 1st June three British ships together with a further three Dutch ships should sail each with 3,000 men to Cherbourg, after which five British ships carrying 5,000 men should sail to Cherbourg on the understanding that they should return from France with as many British troops, as part of Operation Cycle, see below. Likewise it was proposed that French troops would sail from Plymouth to Cherbourg on 1st June and from then on from Plymouth to Brest, while British ships continued to serve Cherbourg, but from Southampton. In essence, much of this plan was adhered to, crossings being made without attack, due probably to the Royal Navy's control of the waters. For the repatriation of French troops blankets and cooking stoves were provided for use on board ship.

Upon their arrival back on French soil, many were moved to such locations as: Rennes, Caen, Thury-Harcourt, Liseux, and in the region of Paris for regrouping, although more than half are estimated to have failed to resume combat duties prior to the signing of the Armistice on 22nd June. As a result many were taken prisoner. In the event, a valuable political gesture and magnificent organizational achievement it may have been, but they might have done better for the Allied cause had they stayed in Britain! For many French soldiers the Dunkirk evacuation was not a salvation but represented only a few weeks delay before being made POWs by the German army after their return to France.

On the other hand, those wounded French troops who required treatment lasting any time, naturally failed to return to France before the signing of the Armistice. Of

A group of less seriously injured, with large labels attached giving details of their medical treatment, give the thumbs up as they prepare to move on. *Author's Collection*

Those French troops remaining in Britain faced a stark choice, either join General de Gaulle in the Free French Army, or be interned. Contrary perhaps to the myth probably deliberately cultivated at the time not so many took the former course. Some of those that did were inspected by the General on 14th July, 1940, Bastille Day, at the Cenotaph in London. *Author's Collection*

these some were treated in Warren Road Hospital, Guildford (later known as St Luke's). As a French speaker, Anne Shelley volunteered her services as an interpreter and was able to reassure some patients regarding their situation and the possibility of communicating with their families. Most were not seriously wounded and in due course were able to accept invitations to tea in the home of the people of Guildford, while appeals were issued for French books and magazines.

When the German Army broke through at Sedan on 15th May, General Charles de Gaulle was given command of the recently formed 4th Armoured Division. He attacked the German panzers at Montcornet on 17th May with his 200 tanks. But lacking air support, he made little impact on halting the German advance. On 28th May, however, he was more successful at Caumont, when he became the only French commanding officer to force the Germans to retreat during the German Invasion of France.

On 5th June, 1940, the French prime minister, Paul Reynaud, sacked Edouard Daladier as his Minister of War and appointed Charles de Gaulle in his place. As part of his duties to liaise with the British, he visited London. When on 16th June he returned to France, however, he discovered that Henri-Philippe Petain had ousted Reynaud as premier and was forming a government with a view to seeking an armistice with Germany. Not prepared to accept defeat so readily and in danger of being arrested by the new French government, de Gaulle hurriedly returned to England. On 18th June he made a radio broadcast calling on the French people to continue with the fight against the German Army. Winston Churchill refused to recognize Vichy France and backed de Gaulle as leader of the 'Free French'; by this time, however, most of the French troops evacuated from Dunkirk were already back in France.

France's accommodation with Hitler and Nazi Germany radically altered the relationship between the British authorities and those troops still remaining in this country. De Gaulle was considered a traitor by the Petain Government and as a result those that went over to his cause were few in number. Unlike the troops of other Allied forces who had found refuge in Great Britain along with their governments in exile, the British had to ask themselves, where did the allegiance of the remaining French troops and refugees lie? As a consequence, much to their disgust, they were interned.

At 4.00 pm on 17th June the French fleet had sailed from Brest, most of it turning south heading for Casablanca and Dakar, with only a small number of ships making for Britain. Nonetheless, despite the terms of the armistices between France and Germany and Italy and assurances from Admiral Darlan, the French Navy Minister, doubts remained as to the security of the French naval forces and the risk of these falling into Nazi hands. This resulted on 3rd July, 1940 with a series of co-ordinated actions by the British Royal Navy. French warships in British ports and likewise Alexandria, Egypt were boarded and the crews interned. In the western Mediterranean a task force arrived off Mers-el-Kébir in French Algeria and delivered an ultimatum offering varying options to place the French fleet under British control, or face action. Regrettably negotiations faltered and an attack was launched, leading to 1,297 French sailors being killed and about 350 wounded. This resulted in much ill feeling among the French everywhere.

French sailors being escorted onto a train at Waterloo station, following their internment on 3rd July, 1940.                          *Courtesy British Red Cross*

Back in Britain, the authorities were faced with the problem of the remnants of the French Army evacuated from France, mainly those who had been wounded, together with the sailors forcibly removed from French vessels. Some 2,500 wounded men were at White City and Crystal Palace, while the rest were located in large camps, generally in the north-west of the country, such as 13,600 at Aintree, 5,530 at Trentham Park and 1,900 at Arrow Park, together with some at Blackpool. The intention was to repatriate them in French ships, currently in British hands, to French Africa, such as Morocco from where the French Government would be responsible for them. As an alternative, they were given the option to continue the fight by joining the Allied ranks, but few of them chose to join de Gaulle's Free French Forces. Instead morale sank among the remainder as attempts to repatriate them dragged on and Britain was subjected to German air raids. Finding suitable means of passage was no easy matter, especially after one vessel was sunk by a German E boat and two British ships were impounded by the Vichy Government. After much delay, soldiers from White City sailed from Liverpool on 18th September. In November it was arranged for the remainder, the majority French sailors, to be repatriated in French ships to be released from American ports, to sail to Marseilles until by Christmas 1940, the remaining 6,574 officers and men had been returned in this way, allowing the French camps to be closed down.

# Chapter Eleven

# Redistribution and Reorganization Areas

The initial steps of Phase 2 of the Operation were put into operation on 30th May with the earliest arrivals taking part in the redistribution and regrouping. By 30th May accommodation was available at Aldershot for 20,000 men and another 10,000 at Tidworth, mainly under canvas with improvised outside ablution facilities. Until individual units were issued with field catering equipment, the RASC was responsible for organizing their catering services.

With the completion of Operation Dynamo for the evacuation of troops from Northern France on 4th June, the full emphasis was then placed on re-equipping and re-forming all the elements of the British Army as soon as possible. COs of Reception and Reorganization areas were ordered:

a)   To assemble by units all troops received by them for early dispatch to Reorganization or Divisional areas.

b)   To report to Command headquarters very early the figures for the previous midnight of the numbers of GHQ and Corps troops who were available for move to their final destinations so that Command Movement Control can arrange for movement by rail. A similar report was to be made by Reception Areas under Phase 1 of parties available to move to Divisional or Re-organizational areas under Phase 2 and 3.

c)   To grant leave from Re-organizational Areas only to certain personnel.

Division and Corps areas were designated and fighting units redirected to these, while GHQ and Corps troops were allocated locations at which to re-assemble. It would seem that a greater emphasis was placed on motor transport to achieve these movements and on 4th June the various Commands were ordered to assemble pools of road transport available at Reception and Reorganization areas in their commands with a view to the utmost use being made of road transport for moving troops to their final destination.

**Phase 2, Redistribution of Troops (Part 1 - Divisional Troops)**

| Command | Division/Unit | Area | Location |
|---|---|---|---|
| - | GHQ | London | |
| Northern | 1 | Yorkshire | Leeds & Sheffield |
| | 2 | | Bradford, Halifax & Huddersfield |
| | 12 & 42 | Northumberland | |
| | I Corps | North Midland | Nottingham, Leicester & Derby |
| Scottish | 5 (including | 9th Divisional | Elgin - Aberdeen |
| | 25 Infantry Brigade) | | |
| Southern | 3 | GL | Warminster |
| | 4 | J | Dorchester |
| | 23 | M | South Western |
| | 44 | South Midland | Oxford |
| | II corps | | |
| | French troops | H | Wimborne |
| Western | 46 | | Pembrokeshire |
| | 48 | | Hereford area |
| | 50 | | Shrewsbury-Chester |
| | III Corps | | |

A sergeant returns home on leave to lift up his daughter and give her a kiss.

*Courtesy British Red Cross*

## Phase 2, Redistribution of Troops (Part 2-Corps & GHQ Troops)

| Arm/Unit | Area/Command | Location |
|---|---|---|
| RAC – Tank battalions | Aldershot | Aldershot |
| RAC – Divisional cavalry & yeomanry | Southern | Imber |
| RA – Horse & field artillery | Southern | Okehampton |
| RA – medium & heavy | Southern | Larkhill |
| RA – Heavy AA | Western | Aberforth |
| RA – Light AA | Southern | Penhale |
| RA - SLs | Southern | Taunton |
| RA - remainder | Western | Transfyddyd [Trawsfynydd?] |
| RE – Army & Corps field coys | Northern | Newark |
| RE - Army field workshop & field park | Northern | Ripon |
| RE – Chemical warfare coys | Southern | Barton Stacey |
| RE - Railway units | Aldershot | Longmoor |
| RE – Field survey coys | Southern | Fort Southwick, Portsmouth |
| RE _ Tunnelling & road construction | Western | Chester |
| RE – General construction coys | Southern | Plymouth |
| RE – Miscellaneous | Northern | Ripon |
| Royal Signals – GHQ Signals | Northern | Catterick |
| Royal Signals – Corps Signals | Western | Prestatyn |
| Pioneer, overseas garrison & M/G bns | Southern | South Western area |
| RASC | Southern | Swindon & Burford areas |
| RAMC | | Leeds |
| RAOC | | Chilwell |
| RAPC | | London area |

Although the Dunkirk evacuation had saved the lives of many, nonetheless many thousands of soldiers were casualties, being killed, wounded or missing, and the British Army had left most of its equipment on the beaches. June of 1940 was a time when battalions hurriedly re-formed, re-equipped and trained as best they could in an atmosphere in which German invasion was thought imminent and the weaknesses of the British Army was apparent to all. While individuals got on with their lives and the British 'stiff upper lip' led few to complain, the situation was nonetheless precarious.

It was necessary for administrative support to be provided to recreate Field Records and establish who were safe and those who were killed, missing or prisoners of war, so that the next of kin could be informed.

Replacement personal equipment was sent in bulk to Command Ordnance depots on the assumption that at least 75 per cent of this equipment would have been lost. In fact it was found that, even those who brought their equipment back with them left it at the reception units who in the first place played hosts to them and practically 100 per cent issue was needed. Five divisions were re-equipped in this way during the month of June and the remainder in July.

The condition of the men's clothing was in many cases in a sorry state, a few even that of rags and of course the clothing of men who had been in the water would have been soiled and had probably been discarded at some stage during their journey. The returned BEF and Allied troops were therefore initially re-clothed to home scale, less one suit of battle dress and one shirt. Within a few months, however, not only had the BEF men been brought up to the full home scale, but the Allied troops as well. The latter were provided, either by the War Office or the forces concerned, with worsted titles such as France, Norge, Poland etc. sown to the shoulders of their uniforms. The BEF troops were also issued with two vests and two pairs of shorts for physical training.

After a few days under canvas and by then fitter many men were re-formed into other types of unit than that they served in the BEF, typically anti-tank regiments, and posted to possible locations for a German invasion. Within two days of arriving at a reception centre some were moved by truck or rail to join other members of their unit. For instance a party at Aldershot went to Marlborough, others from Blandford to Codford St Mary, Halifax or Monmouth.

At Frome women of the WVS provided cars and volunteer drivers to enable Major-General Bernard Montgomery's staff officers to keep in touch with their units until such time as their replacement transport became available in about two weeks. This soon developed into a roster to cover from 09.00 to 21.00 hours in shifts, plus other times by arrangement.

With the BEF at home the volume of personnel and operational movement became considerable, and the Quartermaster (Movements) became responsible for all inter-Command movement of this type in Britain, and for feeding troops and equipment to ports for the convoys running from the Clyde and Mersey to the Middle East. The work involved much consultation and co-ordination with the four main-line railways whose operating headquarters were at Dorking, Aldermaston, Watford and Gerrard's Cross. For each unit it was necessary to establish the actual location from which the numbers of troops would arise, their equipment and if any special loading arrangements, like end-docks or cranes were required, and then go into the matter with the railwaymen who were familiar with their railway's facilities and capabilities.

Kington Camp was used as a re-grouping point for several battalions following their evacuation from Dunkirk, it having been prepared for military occupation by the Royal Engineers in May 1940. The troop trains with the first Dunkirk survivors began to arrive at Leominster in early June where the wounded were disembarked and taken by ambulance to Hergest. The fit ones were put on local trains for Kington, where they were met by townspeople who helped in the transfer of men to the camp. Many soldiers walked the two miles from Kington station to Hergest. Their uniforms were in tatters, many walked barefoot and people remember how pale and weary they looked.

At the camp, the troops were housed under canvas in tents placed around the field edges, each tent surrounded by a ditch and small ridge of earth to protect the occupants from low flying shrapnel from exploding bombs. Bren gun positions were prepared near Mahollam and Arrow Court farms. Field kitchens were set up for cooking, water for washing being taken from the Arrow River, while drinking water was taken from the Kington Town supply. The 180th Field Ambulance Battalion was stationed at the Camp for three months manning a field hospital. While most troops were accommodated in the camp, a small number were billeted in various empty properties scattered around the town, for which purpose a canteen and recreation room was opened in the Church hall. In this way Kington families provided accommodation for soldiers, some with their wives who also came to stay.

The battalions trained intensively and kept fit. Some undertook long route marches, while others daily climbed Hergest Ridge to keep a watch for parachute landings. As they crept along the hedges, the training soldiers sometimes surprised local people. Due to a lack of equipment the battalions used mainly civilian vehicles and, sometimes with civilian drivers, many of the vans still displaying the names and occupations of their owners.

Entertainment at the camp was laid on by the local inhabitants, while dances were held in the Kington Church Hall with music supplied by local people. Kington's cinema (in Bridge Street) was given special permission to open on a Sunday and a marquee was erected at Mahollam where a concert party regularly played to a packed audience.

Amongst those that arrived in Kington was the 8th Battalion of the Worcester Regiment. They had left for France in January over 900 strong, but returned to England on 1st June with the ranks reduced to 151. They only stayed for a month before moving on to Castle Cary. During this time clothing and equipment was issued, the drafts of men from various depots received and reports written and submitted on the five different rearguard actions during the withdrawal. By the end of June the battalion was up to strength and had collected a considerable number of small arms, some of great antiquity, creating the feeling that, given the time to train, they could again give a good account of themselves.

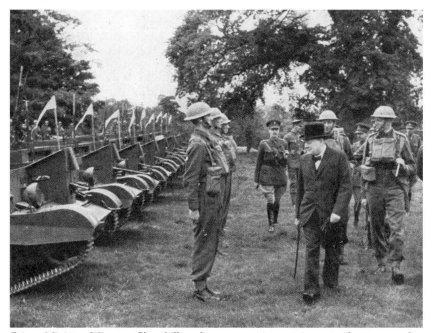

Prime Minister Winston Churchill and entourage inspect inspects the troops of a reformed unit, as they stand in front of their Bren gun carriers.        *Author's Collection*

During this period of rapid reconstruction of the British Army following a severe set back, morale boosting visits were made by royalty, ministers and other notables. For instance King George VI with the Duke of Gloucester toured the Aldershot Command on 6th June and visited Salisbury on 14th June. His consort Queen Elizabeth visited several hospitals during which, amongst other things, she spoke to wounded officers of the Tank Corps and RAF in Hertfordshire as well as talking in excellent French to some Poilu. The Duke of Kent also undertook such visits to the troops and, once back in Britain, General Montgomery took the opportunity to address the men and to present medals to those who had shown conspicuous bravery.

King George VI's brother, the Duke of Kent, in the uniform of an Air Commodore of the RAF, inspects the guard of honour during his visit in January 1941 to the Queen's Own Royal West Kent Regiment, of which he was Colonel-in-Chief, somewhere in Scotland.
*War Office, Author's Collection*

# Chapter Twelve

# Subsequent Evacuations from France

Although before the war the original intention had been for the BEF to take up position on the Franco-Belgian border, the threat of sea and air attack in the Straits of Dover largely precluded the use of the shorter sea crossing and instead ports from Le Havre to Nantes were employed. This led to long lines of communication from the point of landing men and equipment, such as ammunition, petrol, food for rations and a mass of other materials, and a series of base camps across Northern France to the front line. As a consequence, it meant that following Operation Dynamo there were large numbers of support troops still left in Western France, not yet directly endangered by the German successes in Flanders and north-east France.

The intention had been to reform, re-equip and return a smaller British fighting force to France in support of our Allies as soon as possible. These included the 52nd Lowland Division sent across to France between 7th and 12th June followed by some of the 1st Canadian Division the next night, who joined the remnants of the 1st Armoured Division and other units still there. General Alan F. Brook returned to France on 12th June to command British forces there. Nonetheless, as the number of men remaining elsewhere in France had been reduced from over half a million to a little under 200,000, surplus men and material in the supply lines were shipped back to England. For instance, the railway staff at Boulogne left on 23rd May and the medical stores were cleared from Dieppe by 31st. Further shipments were made from Le Havre, Cherbourg, Brest, St Nazaire and La Pallice. However, during the closing stages of Phase 3 of Operation Dynamo and within 12 days of the last troops being evacuated from Dunkirk, the progress of the German advance was so rapid that it soon became necessary to undertake a second evacuation to lift the northern base troops.

*Operation Cycle*

Although much of the BEF escaped from Dunkirk, the 1st Armoured and 51st (Highland) Divisions remained south of the Somme when the Germans reached Abbeville. The Germans had crossed the River Somme on 5th June and drove the Allies towards the River Seine at Rouen, threatening British forces north of Rouen. British and French units began to head for the port of Havre, sending an advance party to secure the port. Operation Cycle was therefore launched at 13.20 hours on 9th June, 1940, under the direction of the Commander-in-Chief Portsmouth Admiral Sir William James to rescue some 20,000 men from the area. The British vessels sent that day stood off to allow the French to undertake their evacuation.

Troops of the 51st Division, who had been on detachment to the front at Saar in the French sector, but by now having been pushed back from the Somme and

This is a scene of troops of a British infantry regiment, most aboard three lorries, south of the River Somme on about 8th June. Although huge quantities of artillery, equipment and supplies were lost at Dunkirk, the subsequent evacuations were carried out with sufficient opportunity to also ship back significant amounts of military hardware. This will have been of some comfort to those desperately trying to re-equip the units reforming after their return from Dunkirk.

*Photographic News Agencies Ltd, Author's Collection*

In contrast to the evacuation from Dunkirk and the adjacent beaches, the need for evacuation from Western France was anticipated with just sufficient time to enable troops to reach a properly equipped ports before the vital facilities were bombed or under serious attack by the Germans. This enabled the loading of almost all the heavy equipment. Here lorries have brought the troops to the quayside at Cherbourg thus allowing them to go straight aboard the ships. *British Official Photograph, Author's Collection*

cut off from Le Havre, were isolated at the small coastal town of St Valery-en-Caux. Withdrawal during 10th/11th June was delayed and only 50 wounded and a few fit soldiers were lifted that night. When, however, British destroyers returned the next night, they found the Germans had reached the coast during the day and were manning the shore batteries. Unfortunately enemy artillery and sea fog prevented rescue, leading to surrender on 12th June at St Valery. Nonetheless, 2,137 British and 1,184 French troops, together with 34 seamen and civilians did escape at Veules les Rose four miles along the coast.

Elsewhere, by 15.30 the next day, 8,837 men at our base in Le Havre had been transferred from there to Cherbourg, while another 2,222 British troops were taken by the Royal Navy direct to England, all without loss of any ships. The latter troops were billeted in transit camps around Southampton pending information on the situation at Cherbourg and their disposal. Many were in small formed bodies and a decision was awaited as to where these units were to be reformed. Even as late as 14th June, British reinforcements had been arriving in western France.

**Operation Cycle – Troops Transferred in France or Disembarked in UK**

| Port | 10th June | 11th June | 12th June | 13th June | Totals |
|---|---|---|---|---|---|
| Cherbourg | | | 5,920 | 6,533 | 12,453 |
| Portsmouth | 5 | 615 | 7 | 93 | 720 |
| Southampton | | | 1,450 | 420 | 1,870 |
| Poole | | | | 435 | 435 |
| Totals | 5 | 615 | 7,477 | 7,481 | 15,478 |

## Operation Aerial

Even so, following closely on this operation, with the rapid overrun and culminating in eventual fall of France, it became evident that the evacuation of all the remaining British troops in that country was inevitable. In view of the French Army's reported inability to organize resistance and a divergence of opinion about the British Government's approval of a proposed defence of Brittany, late on 14th June General Brooke received notification from the Secretary of State that he was no longer under the authority of the French. He was, nonetheless, to continue to co-operate with them and start to withdraw his force to United Kingdom. From 15th June surplus men and material were shipped back to England.

This further plan, coded Operation Aerial, provided for the evacuation of about 160,000 troops remaining south of the River Seine and a then unknown number of Allied troops, including French soldiers and sailors, Belgians, Dutchmen, Poles, Czechoslovaks and members of the Foreign Legion. The evacuation of men and equipment was undertaken from various ports and harbours, including Cherbourg, Granville, St Malo, Brest, St Nazaire, Nantes and La Pallice, later even extending as far south as the River Gironde, Bayonne and St Jean de Luz on the Spanish border.

There was slightly more time to prepare for this operation and, as a high proportion of men was of base and lines of communication units, it was hoped

During the closing stages of Operation Aerial, once France sought an armistice, large numbers of Polish troops were rescued from south-west France. Here Polish troops are seen disembarking from a large vessel at some British port, determined to continue the struggle for the liberation of Poland. *Author's Collection*

to bring back the majority of British troops as formed units. Orders were issued by the Director of Quartering setting out the units and the locations to which they were to be sent. Accommodation for each British unit was arranged with the various Commands, who then prepared to receive them. Operation Aerial was initiated on 14th June, with activities in the Channel again under the command of Admiral James, while Admiral Sir Martin Dunbar-Nasmith C-in-C Western Approaches at Plymouth directed affairs in the Bay of Biscay. Most of the 52nd Division embarked on 15th-17th June, followed on 18th June by fragments of other formations. 30,630 troops, including 9,000 moved from Havre during Operation Cycle, and all but one gun were lifted from Cherbourg by 15.00 hours on 18th June. The 1st Canadian Division embarked at St Malo on 16 June until by the end of the next day 21,474 troops had been shipped from St Malo all without loss of life or shipping, while a further 32,584 were transported from Brest to England. Only on 17th June, with the collapse of the French Armies and the French Government's request of the Germans for an armistice were the last British division and RAF squadrons fighting with the French able to extract themselves and make for the coast.

By 16th/17th June 12,000 troops from Nantes were embarked in six large troop transports anchored in the roadstead at the mouth of the River Loire, when at 15.48 ex-RMS *Lancastria*, requisitioned as a troopship, was bombed, set on fire and sank. There were 2,477 survivors, but tragically an unknown number of between 3,000 and 4,000 perished. Nonetheless, by the next day some 23,000 troops from St Nazaire sailed in 10 ships for Plymouth, followed a little later by 2,000 Polish troops. Farther south at La Pallice 10,000 men were embarked in a number of requisitioned cargo ships and they sailed on 18th June for Britain. This was followed the next day by another 4,000 Poles. From 16th June further batches of Poles and Czechs, who were prepared to fight for the Allied cause, were brought off from Bordeaux followed by the British Embassy and Consular staff, together with the President of Poland and influential Poles on 19th June.

Sailors look on as their destroyer edges forward to rescue such men as they can from the water as the HMT *Lancastria* is about to sink on 17th June following German bombing.
*Author's Collection*

### Operation Aerial including from Channel Islands, ships arriving in UK

| Date / Port | Jun 15 | Jun 16 | Jun 17 | Jun 18 | Jun 19 | Jun 20 | Jun 21 | Jun 22 | Jun 23 | Jun 24 | Jun 25 | 26 Jun to 4 Jul | Totals |
|---|---|---|---|---|---|---|---|---|---|---|---|---|---|
| Portsmouth | | | | 1 | | | | | | | | | 1 |
| Southampton | 3 | 12 | 13 | 22 | 2 | 4 | 10 | 1 | 2 | | | | 69 |
| Poole | | 4 | 1 | | 7 | 1 | | | | | | | 13 |
| Weymouth | | 1 | 9 | 10 | 2 | 8 | *13 | 26 | 10 | | | | 79 |
| Plymouth | 1 | 3 | 6 | 8 | 12 | 15 | 9 | 3 | 2 | 1 | 2 | 2 | 64 |
| Falmouth | 1 | | | 7 | 4 | 3 | 4 | 2 | 2 | | | 1 | 24 |
| Bristol Channel | | | | | 2 | | | | | | | 1 | 3 |
| Milford Haven | | | | 1 | | 1 | 1 | | | | | | 3 |
| Liverpool | | | | 2 | | | | | 1 | 1 | 3 | 5 | 12 |
| Gibraltar † | | | | | | | 1 | 1 | 1 | | | | 3 |
| Totals | 5 | 20 | 29 | 51 | 27 | 34 | 38 | 33 | 18 | 2 | 5 | 9 | 271 |

*Notes:* * includes one at Portland.  † for transfer from Gibraltar

Although the magnitude of those brought from France post-Operation Dynamo may not be as great, this time a substantial amount of equipment was also recovered and the sailing distance involved was of a different order than slipping across the Straits of Dover.

### Operation Aerial, Troops and Equipment Landed

| Port | Troops British | Troops Allied | Motor transport | Artillery | Ammunition (tons) | Stores (tons) |
|---|---|---|---|---|---|---|
| Southampton | 48,543 | 2,757 | 2,268 | 266 | | 45 |
| Poole | 2,162 | | | 1 | | |
| Weymouth | 6,015 | 112 | | | 150 | |
| Plymouth | 53,325 | 17,492 | | 36 | | 12 |
| Falmouth | 16,871 | 2,654 | 14 | | | |
| Newport | 2,303 | 98 | | | 2,720 | 28 |
| Barry | | | | 7 | | 1,698 |
| Port Talbot | | | | | 544 | |
| Milford Haven | 1,031 | | | | | |
| Liverpool | 7,342 | 3,825 | | | | |
| Unknown | 2,210 | 19,577 | | 5 | | |
| Totals | 139,812 | 46,515 | 2,282 | 315 | 3,414 | 1,783 |

Although the French Government announced that evacuation must cease on 25th June, the evacuation of foreigners went on for several months from ports further south and proved to be extremely complicated. A number of Allied troops used the French Mediterranean ports. The principal difficulty was that the only warning of probable commitments came from diplomatic or intelligence sources that there was a certain number of a given nationality in a given port. For reasons of security ships could not advise in advance by signal the nationality and numbers aboard and this information only became known once they reached port. The most elastic arrangements, therefore, had to be made by commands, resulting initially in contingents being accommodated almost entirely under canvas upon arrival in United Kingdom.

By 14th August the eventual numbers received were as follows:

**Operations Cycle and Aerial - Numbers of Personnel Received**

| Operation | | Cycle | Aerial | Totals |
|---|---|---|---|---|
| British | | 4,359 | 139,812 | 144,171 |
| Allies | French | 1,184 | 17,062 | 18,246 |
| | Poles | | 24,352 | 24,352 |
| | Czechs | | 4,938 | 4,938 |
| | Belgian | | 163 | 163 |
| Totals | | 5,543 | 186,327 | 191,870 |

Personnel who arrived as formed units or portions thereof were so far as possible sent direct to their final destination. Those who landed as mixed parties or not as formed units were sent to transit areas on the same principle as in the Dynamo Operation and subsequently dispatched to their divisional area or specialist unit. Mixed parties and those without an officer were wherever possible superimposed on an existing unit or formation. Billets and scattered accommodation were, if possible, only used for organized formations under command of an officer. In this case individual Commands were responsible for arranging transport in conjunction with Movement Control to be available at each port.

The maximum numbers of Allied troops which might have been expected to arrive in Britain, based on the numbers known to be operating in France, were formidable, viz: Poles 100,000; French unknown; Dutch 5,000; Belgians 10-15,000 and Czechs 15-20,000. As the anticipated numbers were so vague, the arrangements made for the reception of the allied troops were on a broad basis, but it was decided that each nationality was to have a separate reception area. Instructions were therefore issued that accommodation on an elastic scale was to be prepared as follows:

**Operation Aerial - Distribution of Allied Troops**

| Nationality | Command | Location |
|---|---|---|
| Poles | Scotland | |
| French | Western | South Lancashire |
| Dutch | Western | Porthcawl |
| Belgians | Western | Tenby |
| Foreign Legion | Western | Trentham |
| Czechs | Western | West Lancashire |

As before orders were issued by the Director of Quartering for arrangements to be made for medical facilities to be available at ports and for the transport of casualties to local hospitals for treatment. It was realised that some unformed units might be without cooking utensils and Commands were to ensure that improvised arrangements, if necessary, were made for neighbouring or parent units to provide facilities. Arrangements were made for representatives of the Royal Army Pay Corps (RAPC) to be on hand at transit camps and areas to provide funds for units to enable them to pay their troops, or to make payment to individual other ranks whose units or officers were elsewhere.

The transit areas prepared for British troops were as follows:

### Operation Aerial - Transit Areas

| Port(s) of landing | Camps etc. | Capacity |
|---|---|---|
| Portsmouth, Southampton, Weymouth & Poole | Southampton Transit Camp, billeting with subsistence in Southampton, Bournemouth & Weymouth | 20,000 |
| Plymouth, Falmouth & Fowey | Plymouth & 23rd Div area around Launceston | 15,000 |
| Avonmouth | Tetbury area and Bristol | 5,000 |
| Liverpool | Aintree, 50th Div area & Blackpool | 15,000 |

In this case a significant quantity of heavy equipment was brought out and landed at Southampton, Plymouth, Falmouth and Avonmouth. Arrangements were made with the RASC and RAOC for this to be collected into depots and reissued to units. Those units which arrived with their motor transport were dispersed to their assembly locations in road convoys. Although 76,697 tons of ammunition was expended in battle, destroyed or captured, 32,303 tons safely made its way home and was moved by rail to Command Ammunition Depots.

During this period, rest centres were set up and staffed by the Red Cross at numerous locations, including Southampton, Ringwood and Bournemouth.

British divisional troops were accommodated in the following areas:

1st Armoured Division at Longbridge Deverill, near Warminster, Southern Command
51st Division in Dumfries-Ayrshire area, Scottish Command
52nd Division in Ely area, Eastern Command
1st Canadian Division in Aldershot Command

Non-divisional troops were accommodated in a wide variety of locations, depending on to which arm they belonged.

As a consequence, their distribution involved the running of another 260 trains. Of these, 221 passed over GWR metals conveying 102,667 officers and men. A total of 123 trains were received by the LMS, many on their way to other areas in some cases, as far north as central Scotland.

Many assorted craft, bringing back the exhausted soldiers, slipped silently past RAF Calshot into Southampton Water. To meet their needs, as much clothing as possible was assembled from the stores, loaded up in station transport vehicles and proceeded to an Embarkation Unit in Southampton Docks. Here on a very hot day, aircraft women worked flat out, handing out clothing replacements to these exhausted men. Unwashed for days, sleeping rough, and begrimed, some were half naked and was a deeply distressing sight. Most had lost all or nearly all their belongings. The floor was strewn with discarded wet clothes, together with a few photographs and personal memorabilia in disarray.

# Chapter Thirteen

# Final Redistributions

Phase 3 of the Operation Dynamo was formally put into effect from 8th June, 1940, although a start had already been made to reassemble, reorganize and rearm those units with men who had been early arrivals from France and had largely recovered. During the 10 days from 6th June, 565 trains were run in the second and third phases of the operation to redistribute 330,000 troops to military depots for the regrouping and the re-equipping of units, together with returning over 110,000 French troops to the ports for embarkation for Western France.

A daily census of the number of officers and other ranks in each reception area ready for redistribution with their destinations was furnished by each command to Movement Control who then consulted with the railways on the movement of troops. Troops were therefore to be redistributed with the minimum of delay, subject to rail movement into reception areas retaining absolute priority.

For various reasons, there were quite a few men who did not rejoin their original units. Once reassembled in their units after such an ordeal, it was natural to look around for their mates only to discover that some had either failed to make it back to England, or had been transferred to other units, but there was no way of knowing which. Depleted units were either made up to strength by drafts or otherwise absorbed into other units. In either event, cohesion and comradeship had been lost and a new round of training was necessary. They were issued with new battledress, rifles and equipment, consisting of a webbing belt and strapping to support a pair of ammunition pouches in front and a small over a big pack on the back.

No leave had been permitted from the reception areas, but once personnel had reached their final destination, it was considered only right that they should be afforded special leave. Once there men were paid and usually given a well-deserved 48 hour leave pass, thus imposing a further burden on an already over-stretched railway network. Although granted leave to enable them to re-establish contact with and reassure their loved ones, initially the War Office was reluctant to issued warrants for free rail travel, the troops having to pay a single fare plus a third for their return journey. Soon, however, the War Office relented and issued passes to those who had not already used two within the previous year. Those hard-worked sailors in the Royal Navy involved in the operation were also given leave.

The first to be redistributed were the staffs of Corps and General Headquarters (GHQ) and line of communication troops. No movement of divisional troops was to begin until Movement Control had been informed by the Quarter Master General that each divisional area was ready to receive them, when detrainment stations will have been selected. In the early stages of the evacuation it was intended to refit the 3rd and 4th Divisions, so as to include some seasoned men, starting as soon as possible with the 3rd Division and

Troops pass through Victoria station, London on their way to rejoin their proper units.
*Courtesy British Red Cross*

return them to France. General Alan Brooke was put in command. He foresaw risking a second disaster and although, as recounted above, he crossed back to France briefly, all too soon his worst fears were realised and following the fall of France most remaining Allied forces returned to Britain.

Once it was clear that Britain was on its own, units were dispersed to defensive positions throughout the British Isles, ready to repel any possible invasion. On the LNER typical movements included Addison Road and Wood Green to Clacton and from Crystal Palace and Liverpool Street to Southend. With Eire an unknown quantity, the fear of the Germans using Ireland as a stepping stone, led to the strengthening of the garrison in Northern Ireland. To this end, large scale movements of troops took place between 16th and 19th June, 1940, requiring 23 trains from the south of England to Stranraer, where they were ferried to Larne. The LMS steamers were commandeered, resulting in normal services being suspended during this movement, while another large one took place in February/March 1941. Subsequently many of the units that escaped from Dunkirk were dispatched to the Western Desert.

It has long been recognised that mail from home is an important element in maintaining morale. The operation of a mail service for members of the British Army had, therefore, been undertaken by a dedicated team, the Royal Engineers (Postal Section) - RE (PS). Because units were often moving about and for reasons of security, rather than using a geographical address, BFPO numbers were allocated and it was the job of the Postal Section to locate the units to which the letter, packet or parcel was addressed. The rapid return of the

BEF from France, however, threw the BFPO into disarray. At the Home Postal Depot in Bournemouth huge quantities of mail arrived from the GPO, much of it associated with correspondence regarding casualties, while all the post returned from France was received there as well. Without knowledge of where the units were now located, mail began to accumulate in large quantities. Only slowly was it possible to restore order and to deliver the mail to the intended recipients.

Although 338,000 men had escaped from Dunkirk, 68,111 were lost to the Army as casualties killed, missing in action, taken prisoner or wounded and a further 599 died of their wounds after being returned to the United Kingdom. The RAF lost 1,526 from one cause or another. The BEF left behind, however, 416,000 tons of stores, 165,000 tons of Petroleum products, 63,879 vehicles and 2,472 guns, together with the loss of 931 aircraft. All of this had to be replaced, therefore, before the reformed units could contribute to an effective fighting force to repel the anticipated German air and seaborne assault. Likewise, the shipping lost included nine destroyers, three of which were French; nine personnel carriers; five minesweepers; a hospital ship; 20 trawlers; and over 200 smaller vessels. The loss of so much material meant that the British Army needed months to re-supply properly and some planned introductions of new equipment had to be delayed while industrial resources concentrated on making good the losses.

The enemy having swept through the mainland of Western Europe within a couple of months, the overriding thought throughout this period was the possibility of the Germans trying to follow up with some form of invasion or infiltration. Everyone was on tenterhooks awaiting the code word 'Cromwell', which would have indicated that the German assault had begun. The need to re-equip units with any kind of motor transport was therefore paramount. At the same time the Army Ordnance supply side was pulling out all the stops to find armament, instruments and small arms, not to mention clothing and everything else that an army requires when it has lost the lot. The shortage of army vehicles after Dunkirk was so acute that the Royal Army Service Corps was reduced to retrieving and refurbishing numbers of obsolete bus and coach models from scrapyards across the country in order to press them into use as troop transports. The vehicles obtained varied from baker's vans to 10 ton lorries, which in those days were heavy vehicles. At the opposite end of the scale, 150 or 250 cc motor cycles for dispatch riders, or occasionally a 750 cc Triumph Speed Twin would turn up, which again in those days was really big. These were then issued to the fragmented BEF units all over the country then trying to reform.

In July 1940 the War Office estimated it needed 412,000 bed-spaces, which existing military barracks could in no way accommodate. Although the requisitioning and enhancement of civilian buildings led to a massive reduction of tented sites, as winter approached the question of suitable winter quarters became acute. Nonetheless, a peculiar problem was presented by a number of French personnel in tented camps in Western Command, principally sailors, who facing the prospect of remaining under canvas all winter, were bitterly complaining. It was decided that, as a large number of British troops would also perforce still be under canvas during the early winter, their number should not be increased merely to provide accommodation for men unwilling to continue the fight. Instead arrangements were made to repatriate them.

All through this period of adjustment and re-equipment in camps with limited facilities, the auxiliary and voluntary organizations did their best to ease the lot and provide for the comfort and entertainment of the troops. The WVS reported:

> Tea at an hour's notice for any number between 40 and 400 became common place. Baths, laundry, salads, RAF pullovers and socks for men, altar flowers for chaplains, floral decorations for officers' messes, interior decorations for the same, together with the upholstery of chairs and sofas, provision of furniture on a hire purchase system, cakes and sandwiches for special Sunday teas, fresh fruit, arrangements for concert parties, billets for wives and children, constant supervision of the welfare of AA sites ...

Ready to fight again. Refreshed and re-equipped a couple of soldiers put on a brave face and a smile for the camera.                                     *Courtesy British Red Cross*

# Chapter Fourteen

# Public Perception

In Britain at the time, a Defence Advisory Notice, called a D-Notice, was an official request to news editors not to broadcast or publish items on specified subjects for reasons of national security. By this means, under the aegis of the Ministry of Information, newspapers and broadcasters were under strict Government instructions to report events in a positive light to keep up public morale. The casualty figures from the campaign in Flanders, France and Norway announced by the War Office were hidden away in small print among the harmless public notices. Although the dire position of the BEF was common knowledge, at first the fact that a full blown evacuation of our troops from Northern France was underway was kept from the population and it was not until 6.00 pm on 31st May, 1940 that the BBC broke the news, after which the national newspapers were permitted to reveal what was going on.

Yet on 26th May, the British Cabinet had been so concerned at the situation in Northern France that they seriously debated how they might take advantage of a possible approach by the French Government to Mussolini. The French were seeking Britain's sanction to set aside the obligation under the treaty between the two countries by inviting Mussolini to intercede with Hitler to obtain terms for France's surrender. At that time the conclusion was reached that Britain should await the outcome to Operation Dynamo when a clearer picture of her ability to defend herself would be apparent. By the next day the Cabinet decided that so long as Britain was able to maintain some superiority in the air, she should continue to fight on alone.

After a bitter winter, the late spring weather during much of Operation Dynamo was beautiful and anticipated a fine summer. Had they been awake enough to notice, the returning troops would have witnessed a glorious sight as they passed through the Garden of England. The radio, or wireless as it was known in those days, put out the music of the orchestras of Billy Cotton, Geraldo and Sid Lawrence, while at midnight, the National Anthem would be played with the BBC closing down. By mid-way through the Operation it broadcast regular news of the evacuation, interspersed by broadcasts from Duff Cooper, Minister of Information, while the ordinary member of the public remained calm as they thought of the men still in France.

Prior to the completion of the operation, the prognosis had not been at all positive, with Winston Churchill, recently installed as Prime Minister, warning the House of Commons to expect hard and heavy tidings. Subsequently, he referred to the outcome as a miracle, and the British press presented the evacuation as such a turnaround, that on 4th June Churchill, in a speech to the House of Commons, had to remind the people of the country that 'we must be very careful not to assign to this deliverance the attributes of a victory. Wars are not won by evacuations'.

British propaganda later very effectively exploited the successful evacuation of Dunkirk in 1940, and particularly the role of the work of the 'little ships'. For

BLACK-OUT 9.36 p.m. to 4.20 a.m.
Sun rises 4.51 a.m.
sets 9.6 p.m.
Moon rises 3.9 a.m. tmw.
sets 5.16 p.m.

DAILY SKETCH, SATURDAY, JUNE 1, 1940.

# ITALY BREAKS OFF TRADE TALKS: BACK PAGE

## Daily Sketch

No. 9,694  (E*)  **SATURDAY, JUNE 1, 1940**  ONE PENNY

# B.E.F. REARGUARD FED BY 'PLANE

## GORT, SLEEPLESS, DOES MARVELS: Full Story Page Three

Coming ashore at a British port yesterday are B.E.F. heroes from Flanders. Their gallant battle against the heaviest odds has won the world's admiration. On pages 7, 8, 9 and 10 are wonderful pictures of the men who fought their way through.

---

The front page of the *Daily Sketch* newspaper projecting the positive image of a troops cheerfully returning from Dunkirk. Those officers and men in battle dress and wearing tin hats, crossing from the deck of one ship to another, are the exhausted troops, whereas those in flat hats and service dress are likely to be on reception duties. *Author's Collection*

many decades after the war, the term 'Dunkirk Spirit' stood for a popular belief in the solidarity of the British people in times of adversity. The public was indeed thankful that so many of their men had been rescued from Germany's clutches. With our backs against the wall and spurred on by Churchill's rallying speeches, a determination grew to see that Great Britain welcomed its men home and prepared them to resist any attempt at invasion. Although the events in rescuing our troops from Dunkirk gave a great boost to British morale, they also left the remaining French to stand largely alone against a renewed German assault southwards. German troops entered Paris on 14th June and the French accepted surrender on 22nd June.

Following the sinking of the *Lancastria*, the immense loss of life was sufficient to cause the British Government to ban any public announcements of the disaster. On 26th July, however, the news broke in the *New York Times* and *The Scotsman* newspapers and subsequently the British press did then cover the story. Nonetheless, due to the imposition of the D-Notice and the threat of the Official Secrets Act, survivors and the crews of the ships that had gone to the aid of HMT *Lancastria* kept quiet about the disaster at the time due to the fear of court martial.

British Pathe News produced some uplifting newsreel reports for showing in public cinemas, such as *Evacuation of Dunkirk - June 1940*, *Men of the BEF resting*, *Run rabbit run* and *2nd BEF home again*. To a background of martial music, singing and the strains of 'Land of hope and glory', viewing them today, they seem jingoistic, with a commentary declaring that the troops had returned to defend Great Britain, our island fortress, and no mention is made of the sinking of the *Lancastria*.

The need to acquaint the public with information on the progress of the war and in an attempt to generate a 'feel good factor' in difficult circumstances led to the production of a number of small publications. Some were, within the limits of censorship, purely factual or pictorial, while a few others were more fictional, often introduced or written by well know authors and poets. Among these was *Home from Dunkirk*, a photographic record in aid of the British Red Cross and St John with an introduction by J.B. Priestley, a 32 page booklet issued in 1940. Also to appear that year was *Return via Dunkirk* by Gun Buster, alias Capt Richard Austin, relating the experiences of Y Battery in *Boys' Own* style. The same year, naval author Edward Keble Chatterton spun his version in *The epic of Dunkirk*, based on sanitized official information available at the time. In March 1941 John Masefield contributed *The nine days wonder (Operation Dynamo)*, a tale dedicated to Vice-Admiral Sir Bertram Ramsey, KCB, MVO, together with the officers, warrant officers and ratings and all others who bore a hand in the operation. More fictional was Paul Gallico's touching romance, *The snow goose – a story of Dunkirk*, first published in November 1941, which ran to many editions, from December 1946 illustrated by Peter Scott, who incidentally as a naval officer entered St Valery-en-Caux on 11th June.

All of these were of course precursors to a steadily growing literature, which after the war was to expand into a series of films and television programmes and thrives to this day.

### Spiritual Aspects

Due to wartime censorship, and the desire to keep up the morale of the nation, the full extent of the deteriorating military situation in Flanders and Northern France was not widely known. However, as early as Friday 19th May, the rapidly declining fortunes of the Allies in Flanders led King George VI to have an official announcement issued from Buckingham Palace reading as follows:

> It is the desire of the King that Sunday 26th May should be observed as a Day of National Prayer on behalf of the Nation and the Empire, of their Allies and of which they are united.

At 9.00 pm on the evening of 24th May, Empire Day, the news bulletin on the British Broadcasting Corporation Home Service was preceded by the King's broadcast of a programme entitled 'Brothers in arms'. This was followed at 9.20 pm by 'A national call to prayer' given by the Very Revd W.R. Matthews, the Dean of St Paul's.

As well as the Archbishops of Canterbury's and York's invocation to the Anglican Communion, Cardinal Hinsley of the Roman Catholic hierarchy of England and Wales and the Revd Robert Bond, Moderator of the Federated Council of Free Churches addressed similar letters to their people. The call was also taken up in Australia. As a consequence on that day most churches throughout the country were filled to capacity with local dignitaries, such as the mayor and councillors, council officers, members of the British Legion and cadet forces in attendance, as Britain faced the darkest hour in its history and people prayed for a miraculous delivery. At Westminster Abbey a service attended by King George VI and Queen Elizabeth, together with the Prime Minister and many dignitaries was broadcast on the radio. The Archbishop of Canterbury led prayers 'for our soldiers in dire peril in France'. Similar prayers were offered in synagogues and churches throughout Britain that day, confirming the public's suspicion of the desperate plight of the troops.

That evening towards closing time a parson entered a suburban public house in London crowded with people and suggested to the customers that on that particular night it might not be out of place to pray for peace, even in the front of a counter swimming with spilled beer. One man banged his can down with indignation and left the building. The rest remained silent until the parson began to recite the Lord's Prayer. They joined in that and then silent again, while he spoke a prayer of peace. Finally they joined in full throatedly when he led them in 'God save the King'. The parson said 'God bless you all' and left.

Elsewhere, the Revd Francis Boyd, the Rector of Beckenham, had at the time been in the habit of addressing the audiences in two large cinemas every Sunday night and did so with particular meaning on the Day of National Prayer.

On 4th June the King issued a message to members of the Armed Forces. The next day the Lord Mayor's National Flag Day was launched in aid of the Red Cross and St John Fund for the sick and wounded in the war. Following the evacuation of so many, Cosmo Cantuar (Archbishop of Canterbury) called for a special day of prayer on 9th June to express thanksgiving in response to the Day of National Prayer, two weeks earlier.

# Conclusion

There can be no denying that the Battle of Flanders was a significant defeat for the Allies, but it could have been a great deal worse. More than 35,000 French soldiers were taken prisoner. For every seven soldiers who escaped through Dunkirk, one man was left behind as a prisoner of war. Nevertheless, in the nine days from 27th May to 4th June, 338,226 men escaped, including 139,997 French, Polish and Belgian troops, together with a small number of Dutch soldiers. It was not therefore, for the British at least, a rout and this is due in a large part to General Gort's timely anticipation of the enemy's moves leading to the issue of the orders necessary to maintain contact with adjacent units on both flanks. This can only be achieved by discipline and training, together with adequate communication both up and down the lines. The success of Operation Dynamo was that, whilst the BEF lost all its heavy equipment, a quarter of a million trained and by now battle-experienced soldiers returned to England.

### Comparative Losses in France, Belgium and Holland in 1940

| Item | British | French | Belgian | Dutch | German |
|---|---|---|---|---|---|
| Killed & died of wounds | 11,014 | 90,000 | | | 27,074 |
| Wounded | 14,074 | 200,000 | | | 111,034 |
| Missing/Prisoners of War | 41,338 | | | | 18,384 |
| Total | 66,426 | 290,000 | 23,350 | 9,779 | 156,492 |

### British equipment and material lost in north-east France and Flanders in May/June 1940

| Type | Item | Lost |
|---|---|---|
| Artillery - Field | 25/18 pounder | 704 |
| | 18 pounder | 216 |
| | 4.5 inch howitzer | 96 |
| Artillery - Anti-Tank | 2 pounder | 509 |
| | 25 mm | 98 |
| Artillery - Medium | 6 inch howitzer | 221 |
| | 4.5 inch/60 pounder | 32 |
| | 60 pounder | 18 |
| Artillery - Heavy | 6 inch gun | 13 |
| | 8 inch howitzer | 13 |
| | 9.2 inch howitzer | 27 |
| | 9.2 inch gun | 2 |
| | 12 inch howitzer | 4 |
| Tanks | Light VI | 331 |
| | Matilda I | 77 |
| | Matilda II | 23 |
| | Cruiser | 184 |
| Vehicles | | 63,879 |
| Small arms | Rifles | 90,000 |
| | Bren guns | 8,000 |
| | Ant-tank rifles | 400 |
| Ammunition (tons) | | 7,000 |
| RAF planes | Fighters | 477 |
| | Bombers and other planes | 454 |

The rescue of the bulk of British Expeditionary Force from Dunkirk provided a psychological boost to British morale. Since, once they were back, the United Kingdom retained the ability to defend itself against the threatened German invasion, any possibility that we should seek peace terms with Germany was ended. Only once the threat of invasion receded, were any significant numbers transferred overseas to the Middle East and other theatres. It was this Army which grew and subsequently provided the nucleus of the military forces, which with the support of our Allies, returned to France in 1944 and eventually after a horrendous struggle in Europe and the Far East overcame the Axis Powers in 1945. For their part several high ranking German commanders concluded in retrospect that the failure to eliminate the British Expeditionary Force by an all-out assault on Dunkirk was one of the major mistakes the Germans had made in the Western Theatre.

One lesson learnt that summer was that fixed fortifications tended to inhibit the flexibility to movement necessary to respond quickly to the now highly mobile enemy's advances. Having invested financially and emotionally in the Maginot Line, the French were too committed to it at the cost of adequate resources to meet the threat in the north. Their thinking was still locked in the horrors of the largely static war of 1914-1918, whereas the Germans had taken note of advances in military sciences, particularly in tanks and mechanized mobile forces, which so speedily overran the Allied forces.

Britain with its Empire now standing alone against the Axis menace resulted in the Dunkirk Spirit. Britain's humiliating ejection from the Continent and the subsequent Battle of Britain demonstrated clearly that as never before the whole population of the country was affected and therefore involved. This brought about a coming together of the whole community, particularly the women, now subjected to bombing, to meet the need of the hour.

During the Battle of Britain in August and September 1940 Hugh Dowding's Royal Air Force saw off Herman Goering's Luftwaffe. Whereas, previously the Luftwaffe had been largely unopposed and had therefore been able unhindered to inflict its punishment on the cities, towns and military formations below, without command of the skies over Britain and the surrounding seas, the Royal Navy remained a potent force to repel any threat of invasion. In any case the Germans had never had many destroyers and of those they had many were lost in Norway only month before.

It has been contended that the evacuation of our troops from Dunkirk was a glorious feat of improvisation and of course to a considerable extent it was. Nonetheless, the hastily created organizations set up under the imminent threat of war, due in large part to their flexibility, rose to the occasion by enabling others to contribute in time of need to marvellous effect. A general was heard to remark that he wished that 'the Army could operate with as few written instructions as the Southern Railway does in an emergency'.

After the war the Committee on the Grant of Honours, Decorations and Medals was set up in 1946 to make recommendations on awarding, amongst other things, campaign medals. It did not recommend either the issue of a star or a bar to a campaign medal for either the campaign in France and Flanders, or the evacuation in 1940. However, service at Dunkirk has since been recognized by extending the eligibility criteria for the 1939-1945 Star. In 1948 the Dunkirk Commemorative Medal was established by the French Government under the patronage of the town of Dunkerque. Ordinarily medals given by foreign governments may not be worn alongside or in line with medals or awards instituted by the Sovereign unless express permission is also given. In 1970 the Queen gave authority for this medal to be awarded to British personnel who served in operations at Dunkirk in 1940. This medal was first made available to veterans of the Dunkirk evacuation and later administered in respect of British forces by the now disbanded Dunkirk Veterans Association. It was created by the French National Association of Veterans of the Fortified Sector of Flanders and Dunkirk and awarded in recognition of the sacrifice of 30,000 combatants between 29th May and 3rd June, 1940. In 1986 further representations were made in Parliament for the institution of a bar to the 1939-1945 Star recognising service at Dunkirk, but the Government of the day declined to be moved.

One of the consequences of the German rapid advance across the Low Countries and France, particularly the use by the Germans of parachutists and fifth columnists dropped behind the lines to cause alarm and disrupt communications, was a move towards the creation of local defence force. So on the evening of 14th May, 1940, after various unofficial attempts to start arming men too old for conscription to carry out such duties, Anthony Eden, the Secretary of State for War, announced on the radio the formation of the Local Defence Volunteers (LDV) and appealed for volunteers to join the force. In his announcement, Eden called on men between the ages of 17 and 65 in Britain, who were not in military service but wished to defend their country against an invasion, to enroll in the LDV at their local Police station. The announcement was met with much enthusiasm, with 250,000 volunteers attempting to sign up in the first week and by July this number

Even before the news of the evacuation broke officially, one suspects members of the public living along the lines used by the troop trains began to realize that something was up, especially if they had any contact with those transporting or feeding the troops. Here a small group wave at a passing train from a foot crossing. *Courtesy British Red Cross*

had increased to 1.5 million. These were mostly those that were too old (over the age of 40) or too young (under the age of 18) to serve in the forces and of course later became known through the BBC's long running television series as 'Dad's Army'. Never a prosaic term, the LDV, quickly derided as 'Look, Duck and Vanish', was officially renamed the Home Guard on 22nd July.

The men were issued an armband with the letters LDV, to show that they were members of this force, and in due course with a uniform of the by then Home Guard. Members of the public were asked to donate any rifles, pistols or shotguns that they might have to provide the members with weapons. Those that were not provided with weapons made makeshift weapons from pieces of pipe or knives. Most of the men had full time jobs and trained in the evenings. As well as preparing themselves to be ready to fight off a German invasion, the Home Guard guarded buildings that had been bombed to prevent looting; helped to clear bomb damage and to rescue those trapped after an air raid; guarded factories and airfields; captured German airmen that had been shot down; and set up roadblocks to check people's identity cards.

One of the reasons arriving troops had to be placed with host units was the current arrangements for feeding other ranks in the Army. Between the wars the battalions had their own cooks, some of whom might have been trained in one of the two cookery schools at Aldershot and Poona in India. Trade pay was introduced in 1936, but equipment was still poor and in many units meals were collected in bulk from the kitchen for consumption in the barracks rooms. By the late 1930s, aware of the difference in standards of catering in the two other services, the Army Board looked to making improvements in cooking and food service by providing, training and a career structure for cooks. An Emergency Cookery Training Centre appears to have been set up in Guildford. It is interesting, however, that it was not until 27th July, 1940, that the Quartermaster General raised the issue of setting up an Army Catering Corps, one can only presume that the feeding of the returning troops highlighted deficiencies. The Army Catering Corps was formed on the 22nd March, 1941.

With the isolation of Britain from the Continent, further rationing restrictions were introduced. In July 1940 a complete ban was put on the making or selling of iced cakes, and in September the manufacture of 'candied peel' or 'crystallised cherries' meant the death knell for the traditional wedding cake. On 1st December, 1941 the Ministry of Food introduced the points rationing scheme for items such as canned meat, fish and vegetables at first. Later items such as rice, canned fruit, condensed milk, breakfast cereals, biscuits and cornflakes were added. Everyone was given 16 points a month, later raised to 20, to spend as wished at any shop that had the items wanted.

This momentous effort on the part of the railways and its employees brought forth letters and telegrams from a multitude of sources, including the Chairmen of each of the railways' Board of Directors, together with their General Managers. Amongst the Government officials who likewise expressed their gratitude were: Anthony Eden, Secretary of State for War; Sir John Reith, Ministry of Transport; Gilbert S. Szlumper, Director General of Transportation and Movements at the War Office; R.H. Hill, Railway Control Office at the Ministry of Transport; together with tributes in the newspapers, see *Appendix Three*.

# Epilogue

During his few days stay resting in Aldershot, no doubt in an attempt to place the traumatic events in context, my father put pencil to paper and wrote the poem *Dunkerque June 1st 1940*, reproduced below. Partly because on landing troops were promptly loaded on the first train available without necessarily keeping units together, only about 50 of his battalion found their way to Aldershot. In addition, a paddle steamer, thought to be the *Medway Queen,* also lying alongside the mole at Dunkirk disembarked its troops at Ramsgate from where they will have been taken to one or more different rest camps. On 5th June those at Aldershot were sent by train to the 4th Division's Reception Area at Yeovil and the following day by coach on to Crundle Court, Milborne Port, near Sherborne, where most of those who had made it duly turned up during the day. Three days later they were sent on four days' leave.

When the 1/6th Battalion of the East Surrey Regiment had landed at Cherbourg on 5th April, 1940 it numbered 28 officers and 643 other ranks. By the time it finally reassembled at Milborne Port, by 14th June, Lieut-Colonel Armstrong's battalion had been reduced by 59 per cent to 13 officers and 262 other ranks. Of course, the Army only counts fit men able to resume the fight and the shortfall would be accounted for by those who had been wounded, sick or captured, as well as those who had sadly made the ultimate sacrifice. Two weeks later they were defending the beaches around the Witterings in West Sussex awaiting the signal 'Cromwell', which would have announced the invasion of Britain by the Germans.

The CO's leading of the battalion and personal conduct in the field of battle resulted in his being awarded the DSO (Distinguished Service Order) for which the citation read:

> He led his battalion with unflagging energy and by his personal example of courage and coolness under fire, inspired all with whom he came in contact. Under, and by reason of, his gallant command, his young Territorial Battalion carried out most efficiently all the tasks allotted to it throughout the operation.

Likewise the Captain (D) of the 16th Destroyer Flotilla noted that this was the third occasion recently that HMS *Venomous* had done well in action and considered that credit was due to her Commanding Officer. As a result Lt Cdr John Edwin Home McBeath, RN was also awarded the DSO on 27th August, 1940 for his part in commanding this ship during Operation Dynamo.

On the other hand, regrettably in the final stages of the battle an officer of the battalion was found four miles behind the lines, having deserted his post. On return to United Kingdom, this 2nd Lieutenant was, at Horndean on 18th October, 1940, charged with leaving his post. At a General Court Martial on 5th December he was found guilty and was sentenced to be cashiered and to serve a term of imprisonment. While no others faltered in the face of the onslaught, once it was over not surprisingly the horrors of the vicious fighting during the previous three weeks in Flanders began to take its toll on some in the form of what these days we would call post-traumatic stress. For not a few during the previous World War I, the inability to respond as ordered was deemed to be 'cowardice in the face of the enemy' and sadly led in a portion of cases to their being court martialled and shot. Fortunately a few in the medical profession thought otherwise and began to recognize the serious mental effects exposure to such horrors could result in the

161

Tel. No.—Whitehall 9400.

> Any further communication on this
> subject should be addressed to:—
> The Under-Secretary of State,
> The War Office,
> London, S.W.1
> and the following number quoted.

THE WAR OFFICE,

LONDON, S.W.1.

CHELTENHAM.

17th January 1941.

P/93465/4 (M.S.2.b.)

Relinquishment of Commission on account of ill-health.
2nd Lieutenant A.Tatlow, The East Surrey Regiment.
Territorial Army.

Sir,

I am directed to inform you that as the medical board by whom you were examined on 2nd December 1940, pronounced you as permanently unfit for general duty, it is regretted that there will be no alternative but to gazette you as relinquishing your commission on account of ill-health with effect from 1st February 1941.

The requisite notification will appear in the London Gazette on or about 31st January 1941.

I am to take this opportunity of thanking you for your services in the Territorial Army, and to express regret that ill-health should prevent your continuing in the Service.

I am to add that the Employment Bureau for Ex-Officers of the Army exists for the purpose of assisting ex-officers to find suitable employment in civil life, and should you wish to have the advantage of its service, I am to request you to write or call on:- The Secretary, The Employment Bureau for Ex-Officers of the Army, Watergate House, York Buildings, Adelphi, W.C.2. Telephone No, Temple Bar 6043.

In order to enable you to obtain the civilian ration card it will be necessary for you to register under the National Registration Act, which you proceed to do immediately, pending your ceasing to be actively employed as above.

I am,

Sir,

Your obedient Servant,

W. Dumfbard. Captain.

for Lieutenant-General,
Military Secretary.

2nd Lieutenant A.Tatlow,
 The East Surrey Regiment,
  Craigmore House,
   Craigmore,
    Rothesay.

Copies to:- Scottish Command, Officer i/c Army Pay Office, Manchester,
 and Financial Adviser and Auditor, Western Command, Chester.

A letter dated 17th January, 1941 informing 2nd Lieutenant Alan Tatlow of being invalided out of the Army due to ill health.
*Author's Collection*

minds of the more sensitive. Whilst there was still a long way to go in the understanding and treatment of such a condition, it was accepted that not all otherwise ordinary fit men were capable of coping with the extreme stresses of war.

Among these was my father, who was admitted to Queen Alexandra Hospital Cosham on 23rd June and discharged on 11th July, 1940. A month later he was sent on attachment to the 10th Infantry Brigade on staff duties and on 7th October posted to the East Surrey's Infantry Training Company. By then my mother and grandmother had taken my brother and I to the Isle of Bute in the Firth of Clyde to escape the blitz and I can recall my father coming up occasionally on leave. As a consequence of an examination during a medical board on 2nd December, 1940, he was declared Category E, i.e. permanently unfit for duty and sent on leave to await War Office instructions. As he was no longer capable of being of use to the Army, he was invalided out on 1st February, 1941. His commission was relinquished due to ill health on the same day, notification appearing in the *Supplement to London Gazette* on 3rd February, 1941.

He resumed his peacetime job as an architect in London dealing with bomb damage and a little over a year later, with the worst of the blitz over, the family reassembled in Cobham. Here we saw the war out, apart for a short absence while the 'Doodle Bugs' ('V1' flying bombs) were at their worst. During this period my father, as a member of the Auxiliary Fire Service, carried out fire watch duties from the roof of Unilever House by Blackfriars Bridge looking out for flying bombs.

As the war progressed, toys became increasingly scarce so for recreation my father took to making model toys for my brother and I, including a battleship, aircraft carrier, castle, sword, helmet and shield, passenger liner/oil tanker, and tommy gun, each. He also constructed a model farm set of Meikle Kilmory farm on the Isle of Bute, where my mother, brother and I had spent the summer of 1941 in a rented 'butt and ben', while later he assembled a clockwork Hornby Dublo railway train set for us. Such were the boyhood pleasures of having a father on hand and led to an absorbing pastime for all three of us. Interestingly he also made a model of HMS *Venomous* for himself.

Nonetheless, I recall he had recurring problems with his stomach, for which the solution was a dose of paraffin and, like many of his generation he was regrettably a heavy smoker. Whether all of this and wartime experiences affected his health in the long term, I cannot say, but I suppose, compared with some, I was lucky to have known him as I grew up until it was my time to serve in the Forces, fortunately during the Cold War. Nonetheless, following a brush with cancer and a nervous breakdown, he joined his Maker totally white-haired at barely aged 50.

On the other hand, my aunt Hester continued in the FANYs and on 3rd September, 1940 was taken on as driver to Brigadier D.J.R. Richards at the time in charge of 49th Brigade anti-aircraft artillery in central London, later Major General of the 1st AA Division. She was granted an Emergency Commission on 27th November, 1941 and as a subaltern No. 216971 was posted to the Chilwell Group, Nottingham. In April 1945 she was posted out to the Canal Zone, Egypt. A year after leaving the Army, on a skiing holiday she met her future husband Charles Hopkins, an Australian doctor, about to be discharged from the RAMC. Following their marriage she emigrated with him and set up home as a GP's wife in Mornington, Victoria brought up three daughters and at the time of writing she is still alive, aged 93.

*Dunkerque June 1st 1940*

We fought our way like heroes
From Brussels to the coast,
So they said, so let's believe 'em.
A betrayed and battered host -
We didn't fight for victory
Or glory, but for life.
In every march was discipline,
There was coolness in the strife -
But through that bloody struggle
A star above us shone,
It was our nation's honour
Upheld when hope was gone.
So after miles of hardship
T'was in the dawn's grey murk
We battled through the shell fire
To the beaches of Dunkerque.
Before us stretched those beaches
Bestrewn with kit and dead.
La Panne in flame behind us
Dunkerque ten miles ahead.
And in all that weary distance
Was no cover worth the name.
And there, like hordes of locusts,
The German warplanes came -
Their guns aflame raked o'er us,
We scattered 'neath their storm,
But ere the droning vanished
The order came 'reform'.
Then on to face the bombers
That 'pasted' Bray Les Dunes
To see our shipping vanish
To those missiles spiteful tune-
But they didn't pass unchallenged
For as they zoomed o'erhead,
From desperate men with rifles,
They met a storm of lead.
So up in threes we mustered
And on tired and blistered feet
We marched along the foreshore,
Asweat in the evening's heat.
T'was thus we entered Dunkerque;
Our goal in ruins stood
We couldn't smell the glory.
We could only smell the blood
Of those who'd gone before us,
Whose labours were in vain,
For there mid desolation
Forsaken lay the slain.

The final phase, the greatest test
Before us lay the 'Mole'.
And down it weary warriors trudged
Towards the ships - their goal.
It lay just like a ribbon,
Just holding four abreast.
Without a scrap of cover
We stood upon the crest -
And so we stood and waited
Our turn to go aboard -
But God! We made a target.
Our only shield - the Lord.
God must have had compassion
For in that flame lit dark
Although the Jerry shelled us
He never made his mark.
And so by the light of morning,
We made the Dover Roads;
Set foot at last in England,
That land of curious codes,
Which make nations brands us
As madmen – but they're blind.
For the battle had been won for us
By those we left behind.
We were just the lucky ones,
We'd played a risky game
And fought a rearguard action
Which bore of unheard of fame -
For cut off, part surrounded,
Starving, weary, short of guns,
Of men and ammunition,
We had left for our son's sons
The story of a miracle,
A truth we almost doubt,
Of how by God's great mercy
The B.E.F. fought out.
And now we rest in England,
Whose smiling acres roll,
And the care of many thankful hearts
Revives a shattered soul.

*Alan Tatlow (2nd Lt)*
*1/6th East Surrey Regiment*
*5th June, 1940*

# Appendix One

# Abbreviations and Glossary

| | |
|---|---|
| AA | Anti-aircraft, or ack-ack (guns) |
| ARP | Air raid precautions |
| Arr. | Arrive |
| ATS | Auxiliary Territorial Service (women) |
| BBC | British Broadcasting Corporation |
| BEF | British Expeditionary Force (to France) |
| BEM | British Empire medal |
| BFPO | British Forces Post Office |
| Bn/Bns | Battalion/battalions |
| Bovril | Salty meat extract paste, often made into a drink |
| Bren (gun) | Light weight .303 inch calibre automatic gun |
| CBE | Commander of the British Empire |
| CET | Casualty evacuation train |
| C-in-C | Commander-in-Chief (naval) |
| CO | Commanding Officer (of a battalion) |
| Coy/Coys | Company/companies |
| Dep. | Depart |
| Div | Division (Army) |
| DSO | Distinguished Service Order (medal) |
| ECTC | Emergency Cookery Training Centre |
| EKR | East Kent Railway |
| EMS | Emergency Medical Services (hospital) |
| ESO | Embarkation Staff Officer |
| FANY | First Aid Nursing Yeomanry |
| ft | Foot/Feet (= 305 mm) |
| GE | Great Eastern (railway) |
| GHQ | General headquarters |
| GN | Great Northern (railway) |
| GOC | General Officer Commanding |
| GPO | General Post Office (Royal Mail) |
| GWR | Great Western Railway |
| HAT | Hospital ambulance train |
| HQ | Headquarters |
| HMS | His Majesty's ship |
| HMT | His Majesty's troopship |
| IB | Intermediate block (railway signalling) |
| in. | Inch (= 25.4 mm) |
| Jn | Junction (railway) |
| K&ES | Kent & East Sussex (Railway) |
| LBSCR | London, Brighton & South Coast Railway |
| LC&DR | London, Chatham & Dover Railway |
| L/Cpl | Lance Corporal (Army) |
| LDV | Local Defence Volunteers (later Home Guard) |
| LMS(R) | London Midland & Scottish (Railway) |
| LNER | London & North Eastern Railway |
| LPTB | London Passenger Transport Board |
| LSWR | London & South Western Railway |

| | |
|---|---|
| Matelot | RN sailor |
| MBE | Member of the British Empire |
| MC | Movement Control, or military cross |
| M&D | Maidstone & District (bus company) |
| M/G | Machine gun |
| MO | Medical Officer |
| NAAFI | Navy, Army & Air Force Institute (welfare facilities) |
| No. | Number |
| OC | Officer commanding |
| OPC | Oxford Publishing Company |
| Other ranks | All those soldiers other than commissioned officers |
| Oxo | Brand of stock cube and yeast extract, sometimes made into a drink |
| oz | Ounce (weight = 28 gm) |
| Poilu | Term for French soldier, equivalent to British Tommy |
| POW | Prisoner of war |
| PRVC | Princess Royal's Volunteer Corps |
| QAIMNS(R) | Queen Alexandra's Imperial Military Nursing Service (Reserve) |
| RA | Royal Artillery |
| RAF | Royal Air Force |
| RAMC | Royal Army Medical Corps |
| RAOC | Royal Army Ordnance Corps |
| RAPC | Royal Army Pay Corps |
| RASC | Royal Army Service Corps |
| RE | Royal Engineers |
| REC | Railway Executive Committee |
| RH&DR | Romney, Hythe & Dymchurch Railway |
| RMS | Royal mail steamship |
| RN | Royal Navy |
| RTC | Railway Training Company (REs) |
| RTO | Railway Traffic Officer |
| SER | South Eastern Railway |
| SECR | South Eastern & Chatham Railway |
| SM | Station master |
| SR | Southern Railway |
| STN | Special traffic notice |
| TANS | Territorial Army Nursing Service |
| Toc H | Talbot House |
| UK | United Kingdom |
| VAD | Voluntary Aid Detachment (of British Red Cross and St John Ambulance Brigade) |
| VC | Victoria Cross |
| WI | Women's Institute |
| WRNS | Women's Royal Naval Service |
| WVS | Women's Voluntary Service |
| YMCA | Young Men's Christian Association |

# Troop Trains through Redhill

## Operation Dynamo - Details of Trains Passing through Redhill
### In the order they passed through

| Train No. | From | To | From dep. point | At Redhill arr. | dep. | Route & remarks |
|---|---|---|---|---|---|---|
| **Monday 27th May** | | | | | | |
| V1 | Dover | Fleet | 7.00am | 9.52am | 10.03am | |
| V2 | Dover | Aldershot | 7.24am | 10.54am | 11.03am | |
| V3 | Dover | Aldershot | 12.50pm | 3.50pm | 3.57pm | |
| V4 | Dover | Fleet | 1.35pm | 4.38pm | 4.45pm | |
| V5 | Dover | North Camp | 2.40pm | 5.34pm | 5.41pm | SR loco, LMS & GWR stock |
| V6 | Dover | Blackwater | 3.25pm | 5.51pm | 5.57pm | SR loco & stock |
| V7 | Dover | Fleet | 5.05pm | 7.43pm | 7.48pm | SR loco & stock |
| | | | | | | 4 sets of GWR men booked off at Redhill |
| **Tuesday 28th May** | | | | | | |
| V8 | Dover | North Camp | 1.40am | 4.17am | 4.24am | SR loco & stock |
| V9 | Dover | North Camp | 2.05am | 4.50am | 4.57am | SR loco & stock |
| V10 | Dover | North Camp | 4.20am | 6.46pm | 6.52am | SR loco & stock |
| W1 | Folkestone | Salisbury SR | 5.57am | 8.37pm | 8.43am | |
| V11 | Dover | Winchester SR | 7.20am | 9.40am | 9.48am | |
| V12 | Dover | Dorchester SR | 9.00am | 11.54am | 12.04pm | |
| V13 | Dover | Blandford | 9.30am | 12.09pm | 12.23pm | |
| V14 | Dover | Exeter SR | 9.55am | 12.47pm | 12.53pm | |
| V15 | Dover | Portland | 10.28am | 1.00pm | 1.07pm | GWR stock |
| V16 | Dover | Blackwater | 10.45am | 1.14pm | 1.23pm | |
| V17 | Dover | Aldershot | 11.15am | 2.28pm | 2.36pm | |
| V18 | Dover | Blackwater | 12.20pm | 2.43pm | 2.52pm | |
| V19 | Dover | Salisbury | 1.15pm | 3.38pm | 3.43pm | |
| V20 | Dover | Aldershot | 3.00pm | 5.25pm | 5.32pm | |
| V21 | Dover | Salisbury | 3.10pm | 5.39pm | 5.45pm | |
| V22 | Dover | North Camp | 3.38pm | 6.32pm | 6.38pm | |
| V23 | Dover | Porton | 4.10pm | 6.42pm | 6.47pm | |
| V24 | Dover | Aldershot | 6.54pm | 9.16pm | 9.21pm | |
| V25 | Dover | Wool | 7.20pm | 9.50pm | 9.55pm | |
| R1 | Ramsgate | ? | 3.32pm | - | - | Via Kensington |
| M1 | Margate | ? | 3.54pm | - | - | Via Kensington |
| R2 | Ramsgate | ? | 4.30pm | - | - | Via Kensington |
| S1 | Sheerness | ? | 4.35pm | - | - | Via Kensington |
| R3 | Ramsgate | ? | 4.50pm | - | - | Via Kensington |
| S2 | Sheerness | ? | 5.05pm | - | - | Via Kensington |
| V26 | Dover | North Camp | 7.40pm | 10.26pm | 10.33pm | |
| V27 | Dover | Wool | 8.15pm | 10.51pm | 10.56pm | |
| V28 | Dover | Aldershot | 8.53pm | 11.01pm | 11.10pm | |
| **Wednesday 29th May** | | | | | | |
| V29 | Dover | Christchurch | 10.05pm | 12.36am | 12.42am | |
| V30 | Dover | North Camp | 10.55pm | 1.48am | 2.00am | |
| V31 | Dover | Amesbury | 11.20pm | 2.06am | 2.18am | |
| V32 | Dover | Aldershot | 11.42pm | 2.45am | 2.54am | |
| V33 | Dover | Bulford | 12.07am | 3.04am | 3.10am | |
| V34 | Dover | North Camp | 12.55am | 4.13am | 4.26am | |

| Train No. | From | To | Times From dep. point | At Redhill arr. | dep. | Route & remarks |
|---|---|---|---|---|---|---|
| V35 | Dover | Blandford | 1.25am | 4.55am | 5.05am | |
| V36 | Dover | Aldershot | 1.53am | 4.30am | 4.42am | |
| V37 | Dover | Wool | 2.22am | 5.09am | 5.29am | |
| V38 | Dover | North Camp | 2.48am | 5.55am | 6.09am | GWR stock |
| V39 | Dover | Ludgershall | 3.15am | 6.12am | 6.28am | Via Andover Jn |
| V40 | Dover | Aldershot | 3.52am | 6.35am | 6.44am | GWR stock |
| V41 | Dover | Yeovil Town SR | 5.08am | 7.40am | 7.47am | |
| V42 | Dover | North Camp | 5.32am | 7.50am | 8.05am | |
| V43 | Dover | Winchester SR | 6.00am | 8.23am | 8.27am | |
| V44 | Dover | Aldershot | 7.15am | 9.28am | 9.36am | |
| V45 | Dover | Salisbury | 8.50am | 11.02am | 11.09am | |
| V46 | Dover | North Camp | 10.45am | 1.19pm | 1.24pm | |
| V47 | Dover | Amesbury | 11.00am | 1.30pm | 1.36pm | |
| V48 | Dover | Aldershot | 11.34am | 1.40pm | 1.45pm | |
| V49 | Dover | Salisbury | 11.40am | 1.59pm | 2.03pm | |
| V50 | Dover | Aldershot | 11.50am | 2.21pm | 2.24pm | |
| V51 | Dover | Salisbury | 12.05pm | 2.48pm | 2.53pm | GWR stock |
| V52 | Dover | Bordon | 12.25pm | 3.01pm | 3.07pm | |
| V53 | Dover | Warminster | 12.55pm | 3.40pm | 3.47pm | |
| V54 | Dover | North Camp | 1.05pm | 3.52pm | 3.57pm | |
| V56 | Dover | Aldershot | 1.49pm | 4.16pm | 4.20pm | |
| V55 | Dover | Salisbury | 1.30pm | 4.26pm | 4.36pm | Overtaken en route? |
| V57 | Dover | Tidworth | 2.18pm | 4.48pm | 4.53pm | |
| V58 | Dover | Exeter | 2.40pm | 5.18pm | 5.25pm | GWR stock |
| W2 | Folkestone | Bordon | 2.30pm | 5.43pm | 6.01pm | |
| V59 | Dover | North Camp | 3.03pm | 6.08pm | 6.20pm | |
| W3 | Folkestone | North Camp | 3.00pm | 6.25pm | 6.33pm | |
| V60 | Dover | Aldershot | 3.31pm | 6.43pm | 6.52pm | |
| V61 | Dover | Salisbury | 3.45pm | 6.58pm | 7.03pm | |
| V62 | Dover | Salisbury | 4.10pm | 7.10pm | 7.17pm | GWR stock |
| W4 | Folkestone | Bordon | 3.45pm | 7.24pm | 7.30pm | |
| V63 | Dover | North Camp | 4.30pm | 7.41pm | 7.47pm | |
| V64 | Dover | Blandford | 4.40pm | 7.56pm | 8.20pm | |
| V65 | Dover | Bordon | 5.10pm | 8.29pm | 8.35pm | |
| W5 | Folkestone | Aldershot | 4.53pm | 9.03pm | 9.13pm | |
| V67 | Dover | North Camp | 6.00pm | 9.17pm | 9.54pm | Overtaken by V66 at Redhill |
| V66 | Dover | Winchester SR | 5.40pm | 9.30pm | 9.38pm | |
| W7 | Folkestone | Wool | 5.58pm | 10.21pm | 10.40pm | |
| W6 | Folkestone | Bulford | 5.10pm | 10.45pm | 10.54pm | Overtaken! |
| V68 | Dover | Exeter SR | 6.10pm | 11.00pm | 11.06pm | |
| V69 | Dover | Aldershot | 6.30pm | 11.16pm | 11.33pm | |
| R3-8 | Ramsgate | ? | | | | Via Kensington |
| M2-5 | Margate | ? | | | | Via Kensington |

**Thursday 30th May**

| | | | | | | |
|---|---|---|---|---|---|---|
| V70 | Dover | Tidworth | 7.00pm | 11.38pm | 12.26am | Via Andover Jn |
| W8 | Folkestone | Bordon | 6.32pm | 12.32am | 12.55am | |
| V71 | Dover | Blackwater | 7.15pm | 1.02am | 1.09am | |
| W9 | Folkestone | Wool | 7.20pm | 1.15am | 1.22am | |
| V72 | Dover | Aldershot | 7.50pm | 1.32am | 1.41am | |
| W10 | Folkestone | Bordon | 7.55pm | 1.45am | 1.54am | |
| V73 | Dover | Portland | 8.47pm | 1.58am | 2.24am | |
| W11 | Folkestone | Yeovil Town | 8.42pm | 2.28am | 2.36am | |
| V74 | Dover | Bulford | 9.35pm | 2.48am | 3.03am | |
| V75 | Dover | Tidworth | 10.31pm | 3.15am | 3.20am | Via Andover Jn |
| V76 | Dover | North Camp | 11.10pm | 3.19am | 3.35am | |
| V77 | Dover | Ludgershall | 11.32pm | 3.38am | 3.49am | Via Andover Jn |
| V78 | Dover | Blandford | 12.13am | 4.16am | 4.25am | |

| Train No. | From | To | Times | | | Route & remarks |
|---|---|---|---|---|---|---|
| | | | From dep. point | At Redhill arr. | dep. | |
| V79 | Dover | Tidworth | 12.45am | 4.29am | 4.38am | Via Andover Jn |
| V80 | Dover | Blackwater | 1.00am | 4.46am | 4.57am | |
| V81 | Dover | Porton | 1.42am | 5.02am | 5.21am | |
| V82 | Dover | Ludgershall | 2.20am | 5.25am | 5.32am | Via Andover Jn |
| V83 | Dover | Blandford | 2.46am | - | - | Via Clapham Jn |
| V84 | Dover | Blackwater | 3.14am | 6.07am | 6.16am | |
| V85 | Dover | Tidworth | 3.25am | - | - | Via Clapham Jn |
| V86 | Dover | Exeter SR | 4.05am | - | - | |
| V87 | Dover | Bulford | 5.36am | - | - | Via Clapham Jn |
| R9 | Ramsgate | ? | 6.38am | - | - | Via Kensington |
| V88 | Dover | Salisbury | 8.05am | 10.30am | 10.40am | |
| V89 | Dover | Salisbury area | 9.05am | - | - | Via Clapham Jn |
| V90 | Dover | Salisbury | 9.15am | 12.00nn | 12.06pm | |
| V91 | Dover | Devizes | 9.40am | 12.13pm | 12.25pm | Via Reading, 12 coaches, 357 tons |
| V92 | Dover | Salisbury area | 10.10am | 12.35pm | 12.48pm | |
| V93 | Dover | Salisbury area | 10.35am | 12.58pm | 1.06pm | GWR stock |
| V94 | Dover | Northampton | 11.00am | 1.16pm | 1.24pm | Via Reading, 12 coaches 362 tons |
| R14 | Ramsgate | Salisbury | 10.48am | 1.44pm | 1.50pm | |
| V95 | Dover | Salisbury | 11.22am | 2.01pm | 2.06pm | |
| V96 | Dover | Salisbury area | 11.36am | - | - | Via Clapham Jn |
| V97 | Dover | Salisbury area | 11.55am | 2.32pm | 3.06pm | Waiting for engine |
| V98 | Dover | Salisbury area | 12.10pm | 3.11pm | 3.33pm | Waiting for engine |
| V99 | Dover | Worcester | 12.30pm | 3.37pm | 3.42pm | Via Reading, 10 coaches 308 tons |
| V100 | Dover | Salisbury area | 12.35pm | 3.50pm | 4.02pm | |
| V101 | Dover | Salisbury area | 1.07pm | 4.00pm | 4.06pm | GWR stock |
| V102 | Dover | Salisbury area | 1.30pm | 4.11pm | 4.15pm | |
| R18 | Ramsgate | Salisbury area | 1.22pm | 4.21pm | 4.30pm | |
| V103 | Dover | Shrivenham | 1.50pm | 4.34pm | 4.44pm | Via Reading, 11 coaches, 308 tons |
| R19 | Ramsgate | Salisbury | 1.42pm | 4.43pm | 4.57pm | |
| V104 | Dover | Salisbury area | 2.30pm | 5.29pm | 5.34pm | |
| V105 | Dover | Warwick | 2.47pm | 5.43pm | 5.47pm | Via Reading, 11 coaches, 308 tons |
| V106 | Dover | Salisbury area | 2.57pm | 5.49pm | 5.55pm | |
| V107 | Dover | Salisbury area | 3.10pm | 6.02pm | 6.09pm | |
| V108 | Dover | Salisbury area | 3.25pm | 6.13pm | 6.23pm | |
| V109 | Dover | Salisbury area | 3.40pm | 6.28pm | 6.34pm | |
| V110 | Dover | Reading SR | 4.00pm | 6.40pm | 6.48pm | |
| V111 | Dover | Yeovil SR | 4.15pm | 6.56pm | 7.03pm | |
| V112 | Dover | Salisbury area | 4.25pm | 7.08pm | 7.12pm | |
| V113 | Dover | Salisbury area | 4.40pm | 7.33pm | 7.37pm | |
| V114 | Dover | Warwick | 4.52pm | 7.45pm | 7.55pm | Via Reading, 11 coaches |
| V115 | Dover | Salisbury area | 5.05pm | 8.05pm | 8.09pm | |
| V116 | Dover | Salisbury area | 5.35pm | 8.52pm | 8.58pm | |
| V117 | Dover | Salisbury area | 5.50pm | 9.05pm | 9.09pm | |
| V118 | Dover | Salisbury area | 6.20pm | 9.18pm | 9.23pm | |
| V119 | Dover | Blandford | 7.20pm | - | - | Via Clapham Jn |
| W12 | Folkestone | Devizes* | 7.20pm | 9.40pm | 9.42pm | Via Reading, overtaken! |
| V120 | Dover | Northampton* | 7.40pm | 10.08pm | 10.16pm | Via Reading & Oxford |
| W13 | Folkestone | Exeter SR* | 7.35pm | 10.23pm | 10.28pm | |
| V121 | Dover | Southampton | 8.00pm | - | - | Via Clapham Jn |
| V122 | Dover | ? | 8.30pm | - | - | Via Clapham Jn |
| V123 | Dover | Chiseldon GWR | 8.20pm | 10.33pm | 10.40pm | Via Reading |
| V124 | Dover | Southampton | 8.45pm | ? | 11.59pm | |
| V125 | Dover | Dorchester SR | 9.00pm | - | - | Via Clapham Jn |

* Later diverted to Southampton

| Train No. | From | To | Times From dep. point | At Redhill arr. | dep. | Route & remarks |
|---|---|---|---|---|---|---|
| **Friday 31st May** | | | | | | |
| V126 | Dover | Newbury | 9.15pm | 12.26am | 12.40am | Via Reading |
| V 127 | Dover | Chipping Sodbury | 10.10pm | 1.03am | 1.08am | Via Reading |
| W14 | Folkestone | Yeovil Town | 9.40pm | - | - | Via Clapham Jn |
| W15 | Folkestone | Southampton | 10.20pm | - | - | Via Clapham Jn |
| V128 | Dover | Tidworth | 10.20pm | 1.18am | 1.27am | |
| V129 | Dover | Ludgershall | 11.15pm | 2.40am | 2.51am | Via Andover Jn |
| W16 | Folkestone | Porton | 11.15pm | - | - | Via Clapham Jn |
| W17 | Folkestone | Southampton | 11.43pm | 3.00am | 3.08am | |
| V130 | Dover | Swindon | 11.43pm | - | - | Via Clapham Jn & Reading |
| V131 | Dover | Tidworth | 11.55pm | - | - | Via Clapham Jn & Andover |
| V132 | Dover | Ludgershall | 12.12am | 3.38am | 3.43pm | Via Andover Jn |
| V133 | Dover | Blandford | 12.37am | - | - | Via Clapham Jn |
| V134 | Dover | Tidworth | 12.45am | 3.57am | 4.14am | Via Andover Jn |
| V135 | Dover | Stapleton Road | 1.10am | - | - | Via Clapham Jn & Reading |
| V136 | Dover | Blandford | 1.30am | 4.39am | 4.44am | |
| V137 | Dover | Bulford | 1.40am | 4.45am | 4.52am | |
| V138 | Dover | Devizes | 1.55am | 4.57am | 5.04am | Via Reading |
| V139 | Dover | Exeter SR | 2.20am | 5.18am | 5.30am | |
| V140 | Dover | Reading SR | 2.43am | 5.32am | 5.40am | |
| V141 | Dover | Winchester SR | 2.55am | 5.43am | 5.54am | |
| V142 | Dover | Exeter SR | 3.15am | 6.26am | 6.32am | |
| V143 | Dover | Bulford | 3.35am | 6.46am | 6.51am | |
| V144 | Dover | Worcester | 3.45am | 6.55am | 7.05am | Via Reading, GWR loco |
| V145 | Dover | Yeovil Town SR | 3.55am | 7.05am | 7.11am | |
| V146 | Dover | Dorchester SR | 4.10am | 7.20am | 7.25am | |
| V147 | Dover | Warwick | 4.25am | 7.37am | 7.45am | Via Reading, GWR loco |
| V148 | Dover | Southampton | 5.35am | ? | ? | |
| V149 | Dover | Salisbury | 6.25am | 8.50am | 8.56am | |
| V150 | Dover | Salisbury | 6.48am | 8.58am | 9.08am | |
| V151 | Dover | Devizes | 7.05am | 9.20am | 9.35am | Via Reading |
| W18 | Folkestone | Bulford | 7.15am | 9.48am | 9.55am | |
| W19 | Folkestone | Southampton | 8.45am | ? | ? | |
| V152 | Dover | Chiseldon | 7.30am | 10.25am | 10.32am | Via Reading, GWR stock |
| V153 | Dover | Devizes | 8.07am | 10.36am | 10.43am | Via Reading, GWR stock |
| V154 | Dover | Warwick | 8.15am | 10.44am | 10.50am | Via Reading |
| V155 | Dover | Reading GWR | 8.25am | - | - | Via Kensington |
| V156 | Dover | Northampton | 8.47am | 11.37am | 11.45am | Via Reading & Oxford |
| V157 | Dover | Blandford | 8.55am | - | - | Via Clapham Jn |
| V158 | Dover | Reading SR | 9.08am | 11.55am | 12.03pm | |
| V159 | Dover | Reading GWR | 9.25am | - | - | Via Kensington |
| W20 | Folkestone | Salisbury | 8.45am | 12.16pm | 12.26pm | |
| V160 | Dover | Stratford-on-Avon GWR | 9.35am | 12.30pm | 12.36pm | |
| V161 | Dover | Blandford | 10.00am | - | - | Via Clapham Jn |
| V162 | Dover | Dursley | 10.15am | 12.53pm | 1.01pm | Via Reading & Yate |
| V163 | Dover | Warwick | 10.20am | 1.21pm | 1.28pm | Via Reading |
| V164 | Dover | Reading GWR | 10.30am | - | - | Via Kensington |
| M31 | Margate | Ludgershall | 10.54am | 2.22pm | 2.27pm | Via Andover Jn |
| V165 | Dover | Worcester | 10.38am | 2.50pm | 3.00pm | Via Reading, GWR loco 6318 |
| V166 | Dover | Reading SR | 11.20am | 3.05pm | 3.09pm | |
| V168 | Dover | Worcester | 11.52am | 3.21pm | 3.27pm | |
| V167 | Dover | Shrivenham | 11.34am | 3.34pm | 3.43pm | Via Reading, overtaken! |
| V169 | Dover | Stapleton Road | 12.03pm | 4.13pm | 4.18pm | Via Reading |
| M33 | Margate | Ludgershall | 11.15am | 4.38pm | 4.45pm | Via Andover Jn |
| V170 | Dover | Shrivenham | 12.13pm | 4.43pm | 4.50pm | Via Reading |
| V171 | Dover | Bulford | 1.25pm | 4.54pm | 5.01pm | |
| W22 | Folkestone | Hereford | 2.22pm | 5.22pm | 5.28pm | Via Reading & Worcester |
| W23 | Folkestone | Barry | 2.50pm | 5.30pm | 5.40pm | Via Reading |

| Train No. | From | To | Times From dep. point | At Redhill arr. | dep. | Route & remarks |
|------|------|-----|------|------|------|------|
| V172 | Dover | Chepstow | 3.20pm | 5.43pm | 5.56pm | Via Reading & Gloucester |
| V173 | Dover | Newport | 3.45pm | 6.10pm | 6.18pm | Via Reading |
| V174 | Dover | Plymouth North Rd | 3.50pm | 6.22pm | 6.30pm | Via Reading |
| V175 | Dover | Tenby | 4.00pm | 6.39pm | 6.58pm | Via Reading |
| W24 | Folkestone | Hereford | 4.20pm | 7.00pm | 7.08pm | Via Reading & Worcester |
| V177 | Dover | Devonport SR | 5.10pm | 7.28pm | 7.33pm | |
| W25 | Folkestone | Tidworth | 5.25pm | 7.52pm | 7.59pm | Via Andover Jn |
| V176 | Dover | Blandford | 4.50pm | 8.06pm | 8.12pm | Overtaken! |
| V178 | Dover | Ludgershall | 5.25pm | 8.30pm | 8.36pm | Via Andover Jn |
| V179 | Dover | Blandford | 5.50pm | 9.04pm | 9.16pm | |
| V180 | Dover | Cardiff | 6.05pm | 9.13pm | 9.27pm | Via Reading |
| V181 | Dover | Plymouth North Rd | 6.15pm | 9.33pm | 9.47pm | Via Reading |
| W26 | Folkestone | Warminster | 6.00pm | 8.41pm | 9.11pm | Via Salisbury, GWR loco 6355 |
| W27 | Folkestone | Devonport SR | 6.50pm | 9.51pm | 9.57pm | |
| V182 | Dover | Pembroke Dock | 7.18pm | 10.16pm | 10.24pm | Via Reading |
| V183 | Dover | Blandford | 7.20pm | 10.27pm | 10.33pm | |
| V185 | Dover | Bournemouth | 7.30pm | 10.49pm | 11.01pm | |
| M40 | Margate | Marsh Mills GWR | 7.46pm | 11.05pm | 11.12pm | Via Reading, GWR loco 6391 |
| W28 | Folkestone | Bournemouth | 8.28pm | 11.21pm | 11.29pm | |
| V186 | Dover | Bournemouth | 8.20pm | 11.36pm | 11.42pm | |
| V184 | Dover | Warminster | 9.05pm | 12.09pm | 12.35am | Via Salisbury |

### Saturday 1st June

| Train No. | From | To | Times From dep. point | At Redhill arr. | dep. | Route & remarks |
|------|------|-----|------|------|------|------|
| V189 | Dover | Plymouth North Rd | 9.10pm | 12.47am | 1.00am | Via Reading |
| V188 | Dover | Lichfield LMS | 9.25pm | - | - | Via Kensington & Leamington |
| V187 | Dover | Warminster | 9.50pm | 1.20am | 1.36am | Via Reading? formerly for Hereford, overtaken! |
| V190 | Dover | Bournemouth | 10.20pm | 1.51am | 2.00am | 11 LMS coaches |
| V191 | Dover | Plymouth Friary | 10.30pm | 2.01am | 2.18am | |
| V192 | Dover | Lichfield LMS | 10.55pm | - | - | Via Kensington & Leamington |
| V193 | Dover | Cardiff | 11.10pm | 2.29am | 2.38am | Via Reading, GWR loco 6399 |
| V194 | Dover | Bournemouth | 11.20pm | 2.42am | 2.50am | 9 SR Coaches Set 900 |
| V195 | Dover | Bournemouth | 11.40pm | 2.54am | 3.09am | 8 LNER articulated coaches |
| V196 | Dover | Plymouth Mill Bay | 11.55pm | 3.45am | 3.52am | Via Reading |
| W29 | Folkestone | Hereford | 11.50pm | - | - | Via Kensington, dep. 5.15am |
| W30 | Folkestone | Warminster | 12.20am | 4.03am | 4.15am | Via Reading |
| V197 | Dover | Bournemouth | 12.46am | 4.20am | 4.25am | 9 SR Continental coaches |
| V198 | Dover | Bournemouth | 1.20am | 4.33am | 4.45am | 12 GWR coaches |
| V199 | Dover | Devonport SR | 1.35am | 4.53am | 5.01am | |
| V200 | Dover | Banbury | 2.02am | - | - | Via Kensington |
| V201 | Dover | Ludlow | 2.37am | 5.07am | 5.23am | Via Reading & Gloucester |
| V202 | Dover | Bournemouth | 2.43am | 5.29am | 5.53am | |
| V203 | Dover | Bournemouth | 3.04am | 5.58am | 6.08am | |
| V204 | Dover | Plymouth North Rd | 3.23am | 6.16am | 6.22am | Via Reading, GWR loco 6354 |
| V205 | Dover | Bournemouth | 3.46am | 6.35am | 6.41am | |
| V206 | Dover | Pembroke Dock | 4.25am | 7.35am | 7.40am | Via Reading, GWR loco 7811 |
| V207 | Dover | Bournemouth | 4.53am | 7.47am | 7.52am | |
| V208 | Dover | Plymouth Friary | 5.05am | 8.00am | 8.10am | |
| V209 | Dover | Banbury | 5.33am | 8.07am | 8.50am | Via Reading, waiting for loco |
| W31 | Folkestone | Cardiff | 5.25am | 8.14am | 8.26am | Via Reading, GWR loco 5355 |
| V210 | Dover | Bournemouth | 5.50am | 9.00am | 9.05am | |
| R37 | Ramsgate | Banbury | 5.52am | 9.09am | 9.15am | Via Reading |
| V211 | Dover | Bournemouth | 6.08am | 9.19am | 9.27am | |
| V212 | Dover | Devonport SR | 6.15am | 9.40am | 9.57am | |
| V213 | Dover | Penally | 6.35am | 10.00am | 10.06am | Via Reading |
| V214 | Dover | Leominster | 6.55am | 10.12am | 10.23am | Via Reading |
| V215 | Dover | Bournemouth | 7.38am | 10.35am | 10.41am | |
| V216 | Dover | Brecon | 8.00am | 11.10am | 11.18am | Via Reading |
| R39 | Ramsgate | Plymouth | 7.57am | 11.37am | 11.48am | Via Reading |
| V217 | Dover | Usk | 8.28am | 11.43am | 12.20pm | Via Reading |
| V218 | Dover | Bournemouth | 8.38am | 12.05pm | 12.32pm | Waiting for loco |
| M47 | Margate | Plymouth | 8.08am | 12.23pm | 12.33pm | Via Reading |

| Train No. | From | To | Times From dep. point | At Redhill arr. | dep. | Route & remarks |
|---|---|---|---|---|---|---|
| V219 | Dover | Pembroke Dock | 9.00am | 12.35pm | 12.46pm | Via Reading |
| V220 | Dover | Porthcawl | 9.18am | 12.51pm | 12.56pm | Via Reading |
| V221 | Dover | Abergavenny GWR | 9.35am | 12.59pm | 1.20pm | Via Reading, waiting for loco |
| W32 | Folkestone | Pembroke | 9.30am | 1.16pm | 1.40pm | Via Reading, waiting for loco |
| V222 | Dover | Llantwit Major | 9.45am | 1.37pm | 1.55pm | Via Reading |
| V223 | Dover | Brecon | 10.08am | 2.14pm | 2.18pm | Via Reading |
| V224 | Dover | Marsh Mills GWR | 10.13am | 2.24pm | 2.30pm | Via Reading |
| W33 | Folkestone | Bournemouth | 10.20am | 2.30pm | 2.36pm | |
| M49 | Margate | Bournemouth | 11.10am | 2.45pm | 3.04pm | Waiting for loco |
| R42 | Ramsgate | Bournemouth | 10.24am | - | - | |
| V225 | Dover | Manorbier | 10.32am | 3.06pm | 3.21pm | Via Reading |
| W34 | Folkestone | Bournemouth | 10.34am | 3.22pm | 3.55pm | Waiting for loco |
| V226 | Dover | Porthcawl | 10.45am | 3.36pm | 3.45pm | Via Reading |
| V227 | Dover | Reading GWR | 11.00am | 3.48pm | 4.35pm | Waiting for loco |
| V228 | Dover | Cardiff | 11.15am | 4.38pm | 4.55pm | Via Reading |
| V229 | Dover | Porthcawl | 11.29am | 4.28pm | 4.40pm | Via Reading |
| V231 | Dover | Tenby | 11.52am | 5.00pm | 5.06pm | Via Reading |
| W35 | Folkestone | Weymouth | 12.00nn | 5.00pm | 5.15pm | Via Reading, arrival concurrent with V231! |
| V230 | Dover | Plymouth | 12.00nn | 5.20pm | 5.30pm | Via Reading, out of sequence! |
| R45 | Ramsgate | Plymouth | 12.20pm | 5.32pm | 5.36pm | Via Reading |
| V232 | Dover | Porthcawl | 12.16pm | 5.48pm | 5.54pm | Via Reading |
| V233 | Dover | Brecon | 12.30pm | 6.07pm | 6.13pm | Via Reading |
| V234 | Dover | Aldershot | 1.03pm | 6.17pm | 6.23pm | |
| W36 | Folkestone | Weymouth GWR | 1.25pm | 6.28pm | 6.33pm | Via Reading |
| V235 | Dover | Plymouth | 1.30pm | 6.40pm | 6.47pm | Via Reading |
| W37 | Folkestone | Plymouth | 2.00pm | 6.52pm | 6.58pm | Via Reading |
| V236 | Dover | Weymouth SR | 2.29pm | 7.33pm | 7.37pm | |
| V237 | Dover | Plymouth | 2.35pm | 7.27pm | 7.45pm | Via Reading |
| W38 | Folkestone | Weymouth GWR | 2.35pm | 7.43pm | 8.24pm | Via Reading, waiting for loco |
| M53 | Margate | Plymouth | 2.46pm | 7.50pm | 8.09pm | Via Reading |
| V238 | Dover | Weymouth SR | 2.55pm | 8.16pm | 8.25pm | |
| V239 | Dover | Aldershot | 3.00pm | 8.27pm | 8.55pm | Waiting for loco |
| V240 | Dover | Aldershot | 3.20pm | 8.46pm | 9.05pm | |
| V241 | Dover | Plymouth | 3.28pm | 8.59pm | 9.46pm | Via Reading, waiting for loco |
| V242 | Dover | Aldershot | 3.40pm | 9.13pm | 9.55pm | Formerly for Blackwater, waiting for loco |
| R47 | Ramsgate | Weymouth SR | 4.16pm | 9.54pm | 10.34pm | Waiting for loco |
| V243 | Dover | Plymouth | 4.28pm | 10.38pm | 10.51pm | Via Reading |
| W39 | Folkestone | Weymouth SR | 5.12pm | 11.00pm | 11.29pm | |
| V244 | Dover | Blackwater | 5.43pm | 11.48pm | 12.03am | |

### Sunday 2nd June

| Train No. | From | To | Times From dep. point | At Redhill arr. | dep. | Route & remarks |
|---|---|---|---|---|---|---|
| S14 | Sheerness | ? | 1.18pm | | | 403 fit Allies |
| W40 | Folkestone | Plymouth SR | 6.20pm | 12.11am | 12.23am | Formerly Plymouth via Reading |
| M56 | Margate | Weymouth SR | 6.22pm | 12.29am | 12.50am | |
| V245 | Dover | Plymouth GWR | 6.40pm | 12.55am | 1.02am | Via Reading |
| R49 | Ramsgate | Plymouth GWR | 6.45pm | 1.08am | 1.20am | Via Reading |
| V246 | Dover | Weymouth SR | 7.10pm | 1.29am | 1.55am | |
| W41 | Folkestone | Bordon | 7.00pm | 1.58am | 2.12am | |
| M57 | Margate | Weymouth SR | 7.01pm | 2.16am | 2.22am | |
| R50 | Ramsgate | Southampton | 7.40pm | 2.28am | 2.37am | 9 SR coaches set 695 |
| W42 | Folkestone | Tidworth | 7.35pm | 2.41am | 2.48am | Via Andover Jn |
| M58 | Margate | Plymouth GWR | 7.22pm | 2.52am | 3.08am | Via Reading |
| W44 | Folkestone | Aldershot | 8.35pm | 3.14am | 3.38am | |
| R52 | Ramsgate | Weymouth SR | 8.17pm | 3.43am | 4.15am | 8 SR coaches set 520 |
| R53 | Ramsgate | Salisbury | 9.25pm | 4.05am | 4.27am | 11 SR coaches sets 519 & 666 |
| V247 | Dover | Aldershot | 9.55pm | 4.21am | 4.39am | |
| W45 | Folkestone | Plymouth GWR | 10.55pm | - | - | Via Clapham Jn & Reading |
| R55 | Ramsgate | Plymouth GWR | 11.27pm | - | - | Via Clapham Jn & Reading |
| V248 | Dover | Salisbury SR | 11.35pm | 4.46am | 4.55am | |
| M59 | Margate | Plymouth GWR | 10.52pm | - | - | Via Clapham Jn & Reading |

| Train No. | From | To | Times From dep. point | At Redhill arr. | dep. | Route & remarks |
|-----------|------|-----|----------------------|-----------------|------|-----------------|
| S13 | Sheerness | Plymouth GWR | 9.24pm | - | - | Via Clapham Jn & Reading |
| V249 | Dover | North Camp | 3.37am | 6.33am | 6.40am | |
| V251 | Dover | North Camp | 4.08am | 7.10am | 7.19am | |
| V252 | Dover | Blackwater | 4.25am | 7.26am | 7.34am | |
| V253 | Dover | North Camp | 4.33am | 7.37am | 7.45am | |
| V254 | Dover | Southampton | 4.55am | 7.46am | 8.00am | 11 LMS coaches |
| V255 | Dover | Bordon | 5. 07am | 8.03am | 8.12am | |
| V256 | Dover | Aldershot | 5.15am | 8.15am | 8.25am | |
| V257 | Dover | Aldershot | 5.51am | 8.39am | 8.45am | |
| V258 | Dover | Aldershot | 6.05am | 9.18am | 9.23am | |
| V259 | Dover | Aldershot | 6.20am | 9.26am | 9.32am | |
| V261 | Dover | Southampton | 6.58am | 9.36am | 9.41am | |
| V260 | Dover | Plymouth GWR | 6.30am | 9.46am | 9.55am | Via Reading, 12 coaches |
| V262 | Dover | Plymouth GWR | 8.35am | 11.20am | 11.26am | 11 coaches |
| V263 | Dover | Aldershot | 8.45am | 11.38am | 11.45am | |
| V264 | Dover | Aldershot | 9.00am | 12.04pm | 12.10pm | |
| V265 | Dover | Plymouth SR | 9.30am | 12.23pm | 12.30pm | |
| V266 | Dover | Southampton | 9.55am | 12.39pm | 12.44pm | |
| V267 | Dover | Aldershot | 11. 5am | 1.42pm | 2.00pm | |
| V268 | Dover | Tidworth | 11.33am | 2.17pm | 2.35pm | Via Andover Jn |
| V269 | Dover | ? | 11.35am | - | - | Via London |
| V270 | Dover | Bournemouth | 12.15pm | 3.09pm | 3.15pm | |
| V271 | Dover | Bournemouth | 12.30pm | 3.18pm | 3.30pm | |
| V272 | Dover | ? | 12.40pm | - | - | Via London |
| V273 | Dover | Bournemouth | 1.10pm | 3.57pm | 4.06pm | |
| V274 | Dover | Salisbury SR | 3.05pm | 5.45pm | 5.50pm | |
| | | | | | | |
| **Monday 3rd June** | | | | | | |
| V275 | Dover | Aldershot | 2.04am | 4.40am | 4.45am | |
| V276 | Dover | Aldershot | 2.20am | 5.05am | 5.10am | |
| V277 | Dover | North Camp | 2.40am | 5.27am | 5.32am | |
| V278 | Dover | Aldershot | 2.59am | - | - | Via Clapham Jn |
| V279 | Dover | North Camp | 3.15am | 5.57am | 6.04am | |
| V280 | Dover | Aldershot | 3.20am | 6.23am | 6.30am | |
| M66 | Margate | Plymouth SR | 3.05am | - | - | Via Clapham Jn |
| V281 | Dover | Aldershot | 4.20am | 7.12am | 7.19am | |
| V282 | Dover | Plymouth GWR | 4.40am | - | - | Via Clapham Jn & Reading |
| V283 | Dover | Aldershot | 4.50am | 7.24am | 7.30am | |
| W46 | Folkestone | Bournemouth | 5.10am | 7.49am | 7.56am | |
| W47 | Folkestone | North Camp | 5.30am | 8.14am | 8.20am | |
| W48 | Folkestone | Aldershot | 6.10am | - | - | Via Clapham Jn |
| W49 | Folkestone | Salisbury SR | 6.59am | - | - | |
| V284 | Dover | Plymouth SR | 6.53am | 9.33am | 9.39am | |
| W50 | Dover | Plymouth GWR | 7.15am | 9.44am | 9.50am | Via Reading, 12 coaches |
| V285 | Dover | Plymouth SR | 7.25am | - | - | Via Clapham Jn |
| V286 | Dover | Southern Command Area | 7.43am | - | - | Via Clapham Jn |
| W51 | Folkestone | Southern Command Area | 7.50am | - | - | Via Clapham Jn |
| V287 | Dover | Plymouth GWR | 8.05am | - | - | Via Clapham Jn & Reading |
| V288 | Dover | Plymouth SR | 8.05am | 10.04am | 10.10am | |
| V289 | Dover | Plymouth SR | 8.23am | 11.20am | 11.30am | |
| W52 | Folkestone | Bournemouth | 8.32am | 11.30am | 11.40am | |
| V290 | Dover | Bournemouth | 8.50am | 11.37am | 11.45am | |
| V291 | Dover | Plymouth GWR | 8.55am | 11.51am | 11.56am | Via Reading, 12 LNER coaches |
| V292 | Dover | Tidworth | 9.20am | - | - | Via Clapham Jn & Andover Jn |
| V293 | Dover | Plymouth GWR | 9.30am | - | - | Via Clapham Jn & Reading |
| V294 | Dover | Bournemouth | ? | - | - | |
| W54 | Folkestone | Aldershot | 9.41am | 12.42pm | 12.49pm | |
| W55 | Folkestone | Aldershot | 10.25am | 1.10pm | 1.14pm | |
| R70 | Ramsgate | Salisbury SR | 10.25am | - | - | Via Clapham Jn |
| M71 | Margate | Salisbury SR | 10.03am | - | - | Via Clapham Jn |

| Train No. | From | To | From dep. point | At Redhill arr. | dep. | Route & remarks |
|---|---|---|---|---|---|---|
| S15 | Sheerness | Plymouth GWR | 11.37am | - | - | Via Kensington, 447 French |
| R72 | Ramsgate | Plymouth GWR | 12.07pm | - | - | Via Kensington |
| V295 | Dover | ? | 1.36pm | - | - | Via Clapham Jn |
| R73 | Ramsgate | Salisbury SR | 3.39pm | - | - | Via Clapham Jn |
| R74 | Ramsgate | Salisbury SR | 4.35pm | - | - | Via Clapham Jn |
| V296 | Dover | Salisbury SR | 4.45pm | 7.21pm | 7.26pm | |
| V297 | Dover | Salisbury SR | 5.00pm | 7.40pm | 7.44pm | |
| V298 | Dover | Salisbury SR | 5.30pm | 8.23pm | 8.28pm | |
| V299 | Dover | ? | 6.09pm | - | - | Via Clapham Jn |
| S16 | Sheerness | ? | | | | 520 fit Allies |

### Tuesday 4th June

| Train No. | From | To | From dep. point | At Redhill arr. | dep. | Route & remarks |
|---|---|---|---|---|---|---|
| V300 | Dover | Tidworth | 5.20am | 7.53am | 7.57am | Via Andover Jn |
| V301 | Dover | Bournemouth | 5.30am | 8.05am | 8.11am | |
| V302 | Dover | Bournemouth | 6.57am | 9.33am | 9.37am | |
| V303 | Dover | Plymouth SR | 7.16am | - | - | Via Clapham Jn |
| V304 | Dover | Plymouth GWR | 7.24am | 9.52am | 9.57am | Via Reading, 11 coaches |
| V305 | Dover | Salisbury SR | 7.40am | 10.15am | 10.19am | |
| V306 | Dover | Salisbury SR | 7.46am | 10.29am | 10.34am | |
| R76 | Ramsgate | ? | 8.00am | - | - | Via Clapham Jn |
| V307 | Dover | ? | 8.00am | - | - | Via Clapham Jn |
| V308 | Dover | Plymouth GWR | 8.00am | - | - | Via Reading, 9 (8wh) + 2 (6wh) coaches |
| W56 | Folkestone | Plymouth GWR | 7.57am | 11.08am | 11.12am | Via Reading, 10 coaches |
| M72 | Margate | Plymouth SR | 8.17am | - | - | Via Clapham Jn |
| V309 | Dover | Plymouth SR | 8.17am | 11.34am | 11.38am | |
| V310 | Dover | Plymouth GWR | 8.32am | 11.42am | 11.50am | Via Reading, 10 coaches |
| W57 | Folkestone | Plymouth SR | 8.45am | - | - | Via Clapham Jn |
| V311 | Dover | Plymouth SR | 8.45am | 12.01pm | 12.06am | |
| W58 | Folkestone | Southern Command Area | ? | 12.20pm | 12.25pm | |
| V312 | Dover | Plymouth GWR | 9.00am | - | - | Via Kensington |
| V313 | Dover | Plymouth GWR | 9.30am | 12.30pm | 12.35pm | Via Reading |
| V314 | Dover | Southern Command Area | 9.50am | 12.56pm | 1.01pm | |
| V315 | Dover | Plymouth SR | 9.55am | - | - | Via Clapham Jn |
| V316 | Dover | Southern Command Area | 10.07am | 1.06am | 1.10pm | |
| V317 | Dover | Southern Command Area | 10.20am | 1.19pm | 1.23pm | |
| W60 | Folkestone | Plymouth GWR | 10.23am | - | - | Via Kensington |
| V318 | Dover | Plymouth GWR | 10.28am | 1.28pm | 1.33pm | Via Reading, 10 coaches |
| V319 | Dover | Southern Command Area | 10.45am | 1.45am | 1.50pm | |
| V320 | Dover | Plymouth SR | 10.53am | 1.58pm | 2.03pm | |
| W61 | Folkestone | Plymouth SR | 11.00am | - | - | Via Clapham Jn |
| V321 | Dover | Southern Command Area | 11.10am | - | - | Via Clapham Jn |
| R81 | Ramsgate | Plymouth SR | 11.33am | - | - | Via Clapham Jn |
| V322 | Dover | Plymouth GWR | 11.35am | 2.38pm | 2.42pm | Via Reading, 12 coaches |
| W62 | Folkestone | Salisbury GWR | 11.45am | 2.42pm | 2.47pm | Via Reading |
| M75 | Margate | Tidworth | 12.00nn | - | - | Via Kensington |
| R82 | Ramsgate | Salisbury | 12.00nn | - | - | Via Clapham Jn |
| W63 | Folkestone | Salisbury | 12.38pm | - | - | Via Clapham Jn |
| V323 | Dover | Tidworth | 12.45pm | 3.32pm | 3.36pm | Via Andover Jn |
| V325 | Dover | Salisbury SR | 12.53pm | 3.52pm | 3.56pm | |
| V324 | Dover | Salisbury SR | 1.08pm | 4.15pm | 4.18pm | |
| M76 | Margate | Plymouth SR | 1.15pm | - | - | Via Clapham Jn |
| W64 | Folkestone | Tidworth | 1.30pm | 4.25pm | 4.34pm | Via Andover Jn |

# SOUTHERN RAILWAY

4th. June, 1940.

From the General Manager.

To all Southern Railway Staff.

Now that the task of conveying the B.E.F. on its homeward journey is over I want to express to you all my unbounded admiration for the way in which this work has been planned and carried out.

The long hours and devoted service of thousands of Railwaymen and Women have enabled this most difficult operation to be brought to a successful conclusion and I feel sure that everyone of you who has taken part in it will always remember it with pride and thankfulness as I do.

THANK YOU

*[signature]*

A letter from Eustace J. Missenden General Manager of the staff of the Southern Railway.
*Author's Collection*

# Appendix Three

## Letters of appreciation from members of the Government and others

*From Anthony Eden, Secretary of State for War:*

I should be very glad if you would convey the thanks of the Army Council to the management and staff of those railway companies which played such an important part in the evacuation of our troops from Flanders. We fully realise the magnitude of the task which was due to the excellent organisation and willing cooperation of all grades of the railway companies concerned.

We are all most grateful.

(signed) Anthony Eden


*From Sir John Reith, Minister of Transport to Sir Ralph Wedgwood, Chairman of the Railway Executive Committee:*

I am writing to congratulate the railways on their masterly handling of the train movements of British and allied troops evacuated from France. To organise and carry through without a hitch an operation of this magnitude is an achievement of which anybody and everybody might be proud, especially at a time when the railways were heavily engaged otherwise on the haulage of Government traffic and on long and considerable movements of evacuated children.

I should be glad if you would convey to the managements and all ranks of railway employees the Government's high appreciation of the splendid way in which they are playing their part in the national war effort. Whatever calls it may be necessary to make on the efficiency and endurance of railwaymen, they will surely be found ready and willing.

(signed) J.W.C. Reith


*From Major-General Gilbert S. Szlumper, Director-General of Transportation & Movements, War Office and General Manager of the SR until 1939, to Eustace J. Missenden General Manager of the Southern Railway:*

My Dear Missenden

In due course you will doubtless receive an official letter from the War Office, for the very great services the Southern Railway has rendered in connection with the return of the BEF from Northern France. But apart from whatever sentiments may be expressed in that letter, I must send a personal line to tell you of the pride and admiration I feel at the magnificent effort you and the whole of the SR team have exerted and the astounding share they have taken in successfully bringing back the men from Flanders to their stations in this country.

Knowing the SR as I do, I had no doubt what their answer would be when the War Office asked them to perform the impossible – but they have achieved even more than I expected. I doubt if any other railway in the World has a staff so able, so cool and possessing the necessary initiative to deal with so formidable a task.

I am envious of you being their leader, but nevertheless, I send to you and through you, to every member of the staff, my heart-felt admiration and congratulations. Bravo the Southern – go on thus to victory!

*From General A. Lelong, Chief of the French Mission in London to Lt General Sir Walter Venning, the Quartermaster-General to the Forces:*

14th June, 1940
Dear Sir Walter

At the moment when most of the French troops landed in this country from Flanders have already found their way back to France, the time has come to thank the British Army and, in particular, your Department, for the help that has been given unhesitatingly to the full, and sympathetically.

The achievement of this masterpiece of improvised organisation is a success that all Services concerned can look upon with pride.

Please convey to all officers who have contributed to it my sincerest thanks in the name of the French Army.

Yours sincerely

(signed) A. Lelong


*From Lieut-General W.K. Venning, Quartermaster-General to the Forces to Alderman P.W.T. Hayward, Mayor of Bournemouth:*

The War Office
Whitehall
London, SW1

Dear Mr Mayor,

The recent evacuation of the British Expeditionary Force from Flanders involved a sudden call on yourself and your staff for assistance in accommodating large numbers of soldiers of our Allies who came over to our shores in company with the British Army.

This call was met not only with alacrity but with enthusiasm and I should be most grateful, Mr Mayor, if you would convey the thanks of the Army Council to members of your staff and to all those others who so readily came to their assistance.

I can assure you that this action will be deeply appreciated by our Allies and that it will give additional proof of our unity in the great cause in which we are engaged.

Very truly yours

(signed) W.K. Venning


A similar letter was also received by the Mayor from Lieut-General B.D. Fisher, Commander-in-Chief, Southern Command, while the French Ambassador officially acknowledged his thanks to Lord Halifax on 14th June.

# Acknowledgements

A work of this nature is largely dependent on the availability of official and unofficial written records in the custody of national and more local public and private bodies. In this case resource has been made to those held by: Army Catering Corps Association; *Bournemouth Echo*; British Broadcasting Corporation; British Pathe News; Imperial War Museum, Lambeth, London; Kent Archives Service, Maidstone; Lymington Public Library; National Archives, Kew, London; Subterranea Britannica; and Surrey History Centre, Woking. Private individuals have also kindly delved in their memories and private archives to my benefit. These include: David Austin; Richard Beckett, Michael Blakemore, Peter Borrough, Leslie Daniels, John Davenport, Margaret R. Elston; Bernard Holden MBE; Gerald Jacobs; Rhiannon Looseley; Alix MacAndrews; Yo McKinnon; David Rose, *Surrey Advertiser*; Chris Scott; Leslie Singleton; David Solley; Ian Stockley; Brian Weeden, Alan Williams, British Red Cross; and Sam Woods. Work of this nature is supported by a number of specialist societies and in this case I have made useful contacts through: the Headcorn Local History Society, Historical Model Railway Society; M&D and East Kent Bus Club; Railway & Canal Historical Society; and World War Two Railway Study Group.

For the source of some of the photographs I am indebted to: Jim Bartle; Blencowe Collection; Kidderminster Railway Museum; Colin G. Maggs MBE; Milepost 92½; North-Eastern Locomotive Preservation Group; Rail Archive Stephenson; and Transport Treasury.

Winston Churchill took over from Neville Chamberlain as Prime Minister on 10th May, 1940, the very day the Germans invaded the Netherlands, Belgium and Luxembourg. He made great efforts to raise the nation's morale and motivate the armed forces and civilian population to resist the Axis forces. Churchill is seen here on a tour in the north-east of England among munitions workers. *Author's Collection*

# Bibliography and References

*Publications*

Acutt, D.G.F., *Brigade in action*, Sherren, Weymouth, [1946].

Atkin, N., *The forgotten French, exiles in the British Isles, 1940-44*, Manchester University Press, 2003.

Bell, R., *History of the British railways during the war 1939-45*, The Railway Gazette, 1946.

Brook, A., *Operations of BEF, France from 12 June to 19 June 1940*, Supplement to the *London Gazette*, 21st May, 1946, HMSO, pp.2433-2439.

Brown, A., *Dunkirk and the Great Western*, Great Western Railway, 1945.

Cambray, P.G. & Briggs, G.G.B., *Red Cross & St John – The official record of the humanitarian services of the War Organisation of the British Red Cross Society & the Order of St John of Jerusalem 1939-1947*, 1949.

*Caring on the home front – The work of the Joint War Organisation of the British Red Cross & the Order of St John in World War Two*, St John Ambulance and British Red Cross, 2005.

Carter, E.F., *Railways in wartime*, Muller, 1964, pp.151-154.

Casserley, H.C., *Railways since 1939*, David & Charles, 1972.

Chadderton, E.K., *The epic of Dunkirk*, Hurst & Blackett, 1940.

*Chronicle of the Second World War*, JL International Publishing, 1990

Collyer, G. & Rose, D., *Guildford – The war years 1939-45*, Breedon Books, 1999.

Churchill, W.S., *The Second World War*, Vols 1 – *The gathering storm* & 2 – *Their finest hour*, Cassell, 1948 & 1949.

Crump, N., *By rail to victory*, London & North Eastern Railway, 1947.

Daniell, D.S., *History of the East Surrey Regiment, Volume 4, 1920-1952*, Ernest Benn, 1957.

Darwin, R., *War on the line*, Southern Railway, 1946.

Earnshaw, A., *Britain's railways at war*, Atlantic Transport Publishers, 1995.

Ellis, L.F., *History of the Second World War, The war in France and Flanders 1939-1940*, HMSO,1953.

Fairman, J.R., *Netley Hospital & its railway*, Kingfisher, 1984.

Gallico, P., *The snow goose*, Mitchell Joseph, 1941.

Gort, *1st & 2nd dispatches*, Supplement to the *London Gazette*, 10th October, 1941, HMSO, pp 5899-5934.

Graves, C., *Women in green (The story of the WVS)*, Heinemann, 1948.

Gun Buster, *Return via Dunkirk*, Hodder & Stoughton, 1940.

Holden, B., *Let smoke make steam*, Off the Rails, 2004.

*Home from Dunkirk – A photographic record in aid of the British Red Cross and St John*, John Murray, 1940.

Jackson, R, *Dunkirk the British evacuation, 1940*, Cassell, 2002.

John, E., *Time table for victory*, British Railways, nd.

Knox, C., *The unbeaten track*, Cassell, 1944.

Looseley, R., *Paradise after Hell*, History today, Vol. 56, No. 6, (June 2006), pp.32-38.

Lord, W., *The miracle of Dunkirk*, Wordsworth, 1998.

Magnississ, C.H., *Back to Blighty*, British Army Review, (1998?)

Masefield, J., *The nine days wonder*, W. Heinemann, 1941.

*Memories of war, Members of the Naval and Military Club recall World War II; fifty interviews,* Naval and Military Club, Melbourne, Australia, 2004.

Munns, R.T., *Milk churns to Merry-Go-Round, a century of train operation,* David & Charles, 1986.

Nash, C., *The LMS at war,* London Midland & Scottish Railway, 1946.

Nock, O.S., *Britain's railways at war 1939-1945,* Ian Allan, 1971.

Ogley, R., *Kent at war, the unconquered county 1939-1945,* Froglet, 1994, pp 36-43.

Panter-Downes, M., *London war notes,* Longman, 1972.

Plumridge, J.H., *Hospital ships & ambulance trains,* Seeley, Service & Co., 1975, pp.138-155.

*Railway Magazine,* Vol. 86, July 1940, p 419.

Ransome-Wallis, P., *Train ferries of Western Europe,* Ian Allan, 1968.

Ramsey, B.H., *The evacuation of allied armies from Dunkirk and neighbouring beaches,* Supplement to the *London Gazette,* 15th July, 1947, HMSO, pp 3295-3318.

Savage, C.I., *A history of the Second World War, United Kingdom Civil Series, Inland transport,* HMSO, 1957.

Shaw, F. & J., *We remember Dunkirk over 100 personal accounts,* authors, 1990.

*The war that went on wheels, - The war record of the Tilling Group of companies 1939-1949,* nd.

Thompson, Julian, *Dunkirk, retreat to victory,* Sidgwick & Jackson, 2008.

Wadge, D.C., *Women in Uniform,* Marston, 1946.

Winkworth, D.W., *Southern special traffic,* Irwell Press, 2000.

Winser, J. de, *BEF ships before, at and after Dunkirk,* World Ship Society, 1999.

Woodward, J.G., *Dunkirk Evacuation Traffic,* Southern Notebook, spring 1990.

### References

Baker, Mrs D., *Memories of a WREN,* IWM, 91/4/1.

Balfour, E. & Cullen, M.F., edts, *The story of the Hampshire County branch of the British Red Cross 1909-1991,* 1994.

Billett, J., *Notes of interview with Capt Hester Hopkins* on 28th October, 1999, Oral History Project, Naval and Military Club, Melbourne, Australia.

Boyd, D, *British equipment losses at Dunkirk and situation post Dunkirk,* http://www.wwiiequipment.com

British Broadcasting Corporation history website: www.bbc.co.uk/history.worldwars/wwtwo/dunkirk

British Pathe News website: www.britishpathe.com

*Channel ports; evacuation from Dunkirk area,* NA, WO 106/1613.

Dutton, D., *Letters to Jenny, the wartime letters of a Cheshire soldier in India,* edt Bate H.J., IWM 01/32/1.

*Dynamo Movement Instructions Nos. 1 & 2,* War Office, NA ref WO197/88.

*The evacuation from Dunkirk of the British Expeditionary Force and French troops, Operation Dynamo, 26th May-4th June 1940,* BR 1736 (32), Battle Summary No. 41, NA ADM 234/360.

*Evacuation of British Expeditionary Forces from Dunkirk,* May June 1940 (Dynamo Plan), Partridge, G.H., and Clinker, C.R., Clinker Collection War Box, Brunel University.

Fisher, A.R., Surgeon Capt RN, *Organisation for the reception of casualties at Dover*, IWM 76/30/1.

Higham, J.B. & Knighton, E.A., *Movements*, War Office, 1955, pp.85-88 & 103-105, NA, WO277/17.

Hitchcock, A.W.E., *A Dunkirk Diary*, Surrey History Centre, 7502/BB/19/2.

Holborow, R.W., Lt, *My war years 1939-1946, Recollections of Richard W Holborow*, IWM, 07/23/1.

*Garaging of military ambulance trains, (Home)*, Instruction Books for Movement Control 1939.

Lane, A., *Evacuation of British Expeditionary Force from Dunkirk – May to June 1940*, World War Two Railway Study Group Bulletin, Vol. 18, No. 6 (Nov/Dec 2008), pp 18.147-160.

Liddel, M., *BEF trains*, Surrey History Centre, 1532/4/46.

Lloyd, H., *This deliverance, how the BEF passed through Guildford station*, Surrey History Centre, 1532/4/53.

Looseley, R., *Le Paradis après l'Enfer*: the French Soldiers Evacuated from Dunkirk in 1940. Unpublished University of Reading MA dissertation, 2005.

Magazines and journals: *Great Western Railway Magazine; The London Gazette; Railway Gazette; Railway Observer; Stephenson Locomotive Society Journal; and Southern Railway Magazine.*

Newspapers: *Bournemouth Daily Echo; Bournemouth Times; Church Times; Daily Mirror; Daily Sketch; Kent Messenger; and Times.*

Nicholson, T.V., *A humble man's notes on World War II*, www.movcon.org.uk/History/Documents/DID/D-MCHS%200160.htm

Palmer, B.H., Report on the medical organisation at Ramsgate Naval Base during the evacuation of the BEF from the French coast, NA, ADM 199/788A.

*Reception and distribution of troops evacuated from France*, The history of railways during the war - September 1939 to 15th August, 1945 (VJ Day), Paper 2a, Part 5, Section 6. Railway Clearing House, January 1946, NA RAIL 1085/122.

*A short account of the evacuation from France and quartering of the BEF after Dunkirk, May/June 1940*, War Office, August 1941, NA WO197/134.

Subterranea Britannia website: www.subbrit.org.uk.

Tatlow, A., *Dunkerque 1st June 1940*, Surrey Historical Centre, 7502/BB/20/42.

*Working of ambulance trains*, Special Notice AMB No. 1, Southern Railway.

*1/6th East Surrey Battalion Messages - France 1940*, Surrey History Centre, 7502/BB/20/16.

# Index